EXPLORATIONS INTO
THE SELF

THE LIBRARY OF ANALYTICAL PSYCHOLOGY
VOLUME VII

EXPLORATIONS INTO THE SELF

BY

Michael Fordham

Routledge
Taylor & Francis Group
LONDON AND NEW YORK

First published 1985 by
ACADEMIC PRESS INC. (London) Ltd.
United States Edition published by ACADEMIC PRESS, INC. ORLANDO

This edition 2002 published by
Karnac Books Ltd.

Published 2019 by Routledge
2 Park Square, Milton Park, Abingdon, Oxon OX14 4RN
52 Vanderbilt Avenue, New York, NY 10017

First issued in hardback 2019

Routledge is an imprint of the Taylor & Francis Group, an informa business

British Library Cataloguing in Publication Data
1. Self I. Title II. Series
155.2 BF697
A C.I.P. for this book is available from the British Library

ISBN 13: 978-0-367-10741-3 (hbk)
ISBN 13: 978-1-85575-971-8 (pbk)

Contents

Foreword

It is consonant with the contemporary increase of interest in the concept of the self among analysts of many schools that The Library of Analytical Psychology should, in 1985, be publishing two volumes on precisely that subject – dealing with it, however, from somewhat different angles. In fact, the event has arisen hardly at all out of editorial contrivance and simply represents a response to a spontaneous literary emergence out of the creative interests of the two authors involved. The present volume by Michael Fordham (the other is by Joseph Redfearn) is the product of many years of sustained observation of and reflection about phenomena arising out of three broad topics in the field of analytical psychology. In the first place, Michael Fordham, as is widely known, has over a number of years contributed much to studies of emergence and development of self in early infancy and childhood. Secondly, Fordham has been concerned with the task of clarifying some of the confusions that have arisen out of the various senses in which Jung uses the concept of the self – and not only that, for he has made contributions towards extending its content as well. In Chapter 1 he describes how he card-indexed all of Jung's references to the self and then sorted out the themes that recurred very often from those that appeared as isolated references – as passing thoughts or off-the-cuff remarks. Out of the first cluster of references there emerged two main themes; the self is seen as a totality and the self is regarded as a dynamic ordering entity within which compensatory processes, the differentiation of the opposites and their integration by means of the transcendent function, progressions and regressions, and transformations of primitive libido can all be discerned to be taking place. Moreover, Fordham has proposed his innovative and original view of the self in a way that further extends our understanding of its dynamics. In the present volume he expounds his theory of the original undifferentiated self as a totality comprised of archetypal and ego potential. Very early indeed, perhaps in prenatal life and certainly in neonatal life, and in accordance with both activation from within and stimulus from outside, deintegrative processes take place. The archetypes unpack and emerge to tangle with their object-correlates in the real world or with well-known symbolic content in the cultural environment. As this takes place, then reintegration of the deintegrates takes place through internationalization. Further deintegrations and reintegrations take place resulting in the progressive enrichment of the self through the experience of time and space, and flesh and blood.

A third area of experience, in Part 3 of his book, that has long interested Michael Fordham, centres round the well-known fact that feelings connected with the self seem similar to those found among religious people. Indeed some of the dream and visionary symbolism of the self seems highly suggestive of symbols that arise in religion. Of course, the matter could be expressed in a reversed form; religious symbolism is really symbolism of the self but expressed in primitive imagery, projected onto the cosmos and accompanied by numinous feeling. Perhaps this is a too easy solution, and, indeed, Michael Fordham does not seem to favour it. Rather, in making use of Bion's notion of the vertex, he emphasizes the need for the individual to examine consciously his or her vertex and its influence upon his or her attitude towards either religion or psychology. Thus, whether he is considering the vertex of Harry Williams in his chapter entitled "Is God supernatural?" or the vertex of Saint John of the Cross and distinguishing both from his own, Fordham agrees to the validity for many people of religion understood as an activity standing in its own right. It might be added that the capacity for a religious attitude could be regarded as an element of the self. Religious people, indeed, from their vertex would be inclined to believe that the self is made in the image of an immanent God who is, nevertheless, understood utterly to transcend man's fullest notion of integration, let alone of the godhead.

Readers who work hard at Fordham's chapter on St John of the Cross, as well as at his chapter on Alchemy, are likely to be rewarded – to say nothing of being impressed by the masterly way in which he handles those topics and discerns the presence of the self behind or within both the religious and the alchemical experience.

Readers of the present volume as a whole will also find amplifications of Fordham's well-known work on infant and child development. Thus he indicates a more recently acquired growth of interest on his part in the observation of mother–infant interaction. This new development of the group study of the reports about actual mother–infant interaction brought in by individual members to the group and then discussed by all the members in interaction has been recognized by Fordham as an essential adjunct to the observation of psychodynamic processes in babies. He can see that the results of it may modify or correct most of the common notions that have been grown up and are now suspected of being based on too slight a basis of observation. On the positive side, evidence has accumulated to indicate a considerable capacity on the part of many babies to be effective in creating a sufficiently good maternal environment for themselves either by sparing their mothers, who may be depressed, uncertain of their capacities in various ways, or depleted, or by showing them how to make better responses to their infants' needs, or by making signals of need that the mothers can understand. In this way, rather inhibited, clumsy and depressed mothers may be helped by their babies to become more skilful at mothering in the ways indicated by, for instance, Winnicott and felt to be so necessary for the growth of the infant's personality and relationships all through his or her whole life span.

Finally – and this is likely to be of special interest to Jungians – Michael Fordham acknowledges his debt to Melanie Klein, not only for her innovative work in its own right but also for its striking complementariness to the work of Jung on the archetypes and the self. Of course some Jungians will emphasize the seeming disparateness of language and of focus in Klein and Jung – Klein concentrating on the forms of the spontaneous and unconscious fantasy life of early infancy, Jung more and more, as the years rolled on from his seventieth birthday onwards, focussing upon the cultural and historical expressions of the great archetypal themes of humanity. Fordham, however, is a pioneer in establishing some sense of the complementariness as well as the differences between those two great innovative thinkers, and gratitude to him is due for enabling us to benefit from that complementariness.

As in the five previous volumes of The Library of Analytical Psychology, all the references to Jung's writings are taken from the Collected Works, abbreviated as *Coll. Wks* followed by the volume number. The dates refer to the first publication in whatever language and not to the English translation.

The Editors wish to add their thanks to those of Dr Fordham for the very extensive work of editing carried out in the first instance by Dr Agnes Wilkinson.

Kenneth Lambert

Preface

This book contains essays on the self which I have written over the years. Most of them were published in journals published in England, the United States and as far afield as Pakistan. They have not previously been collected together nor brought up to date.

Most of the essays were written on request. Two of them have previously been published in a book entitled *The Objective Psyche*, now long out of print. They have all been subjected to revision and, whilst there is only one new publication, extensive changes have been made so that several of the chapters are virtually new essays.

Much has been written about the self from varying viewpoints, but it was Jung who brought its deeper nature into relation with empirical experience: he placed the philosophical and religious concepts on the base of psychic reality. That was a discovery made by himself first and, later, by more or less mature persons in the second half of life who took experiences of their inner life with great seriousness. Thus they were led to find a principle which they could call the self which had guided their lives all along without their knowing it.

It has been my contention that the same self can be recognized in childhood and that its actions underlie infantile experience from birth onwards. Thus self realization may now be conceived as a lifetime process in which actions of the self are converted into increasingly conscious reflection.

It must be understood that I do not aim to construct a system or theory but have rather collected a number of facts and reflections in the hope of shedding light upon a difficult and obscure subject. I hope that the collection will be of interest to practising analytical psychologists and to the larger public who have been moved by the studies made of unconscious processes and their derivatives.

Michael Fordham

Acknowledgements

I wish to express my gratitude to the many people who have helped me in the production of this book which, somewhat to my surprise, has grown to its present size.

First of all there is my wife Frieda who has listened interminably, helped me to acquire whatever skill in writing I now possess and whose perceptive comments have again and again helped what I write to take shape.

I am also indebted to Agnes Wilkinson for reading through the whole book. She helped me to clarify passages which were obscure, encouraged me and in fact did so much purely editorial work that I am pleased to say the final editing by Kenneth Lambert was comparatively light.

Finally, Gianna Henry introduced me to the importance of observing mothers and their babies, about which I had developed a skeletal theory, that could only grow when observations were collected and perceptively reflected upon. It is with her help that speculation has begun to be replaced with knowledge.

All but two of the chapters (Chapters 2 and 16) have previously been published before in journals and books, but much revision has taken place, so that there is more new material than would appear at first sight. Notes are appended indicating how much alteration has taken place. I am grateful to the various editors for permission to republish, namely the Editors of *The Journal of Analytical Psychology*, *The British Journal of Medical Psychology*, *The Revue Suisse de Psychologie et de Psychologie appliqué*, *The Journal of Psychology (Lahore)*, *Contemporary Psychoanalysis*, *Theology* and *Spring* for permission to use material already published by them.

Michael Fordham

Introduction

When I thought it might be worth while publishing a collection of my papers on the self I did not realize quite what I was in for. I did not grasp just how much of my studies had changed their direction since I first wrote about them.

Originally my work was orientated mainly towards expounding Jung's views to an English audience and my editorship of his *Collected Works* gave me a familiarity with them which fitted me for that task. That first endeavour brought me to study religion in, I soon realized, a rather amateurish way. Then I became interested in mysticism, theology and alchemy, only later to occupy myself with matters with which I was more qualified to deal: analytic technique and the structure of analytic interviews.

These investigations ran concurrently with the other field of study that I had set myself inspired by the belief that the findings of analytical psychologists, based as they usually are on the theory of archetypes, could never be soundly based unless the roots of the data were related to childhood and adolescence. These periods in life were almost entirely ignored by analytical psychologists and that led them to an intensive comparative study of myths with the aim of creating a geography of the psyche. In so doing, however, their studies tended to become horizontal rather than vertical.

I have divided this volume into three parts. The first studies Jung's data and views on the self and individuation and then introduces my own theory of the self as a dynamic system. The second part develops further my views especially in relation to psychoanalysis. The third returns to the psychology of religion and alchemy.

It is a volume that cannot be taken entirely alone. It partly replaces another one now long out of print (*The Objective Psyche*) and is complementary to two volumes on childhood (*Children as Individuals* and *The Self and Autism*).

The reader may be led to reflect, as I do myself, why the division? The reason is in part at least personal. My interests were scientific in the first place. I studied biology and physiology at Cambridge and went up to hospital with a burning interest in scientific medicine and neurology. At that time I found the psychology of Freud the more sympathetic but I did not study his work in detail nor undergo a psychoanalysis. Before I could do so a number of more or less fortuitous events ordained that I should start an analysis with H. G. Baynes. He introduced me to Jung's idea of irrational facts which did not fit in with theoretical preconceptions. As such facts are an essential component of scientific research, I could begin to accept Jung's position.

Later on, however, I became very aware of the tendency of analytical psychology to become a quasi-religious cult, not at all Jung's idea as I understood him both from his writings and personally. I therefore embarked on a number of publications seeking to underline Jung's scientific status – they were collected together in *The Objective Psyche*. Some are republished in the present volume though mostly greatly revised and their vertex altered.

Since a major element in my writings has been the idea that Jung's work wanted relating to individual development I pursued that interest and became convinced that the aim was possible to achieve. The theoretical endeavour was supported by my finding that Jungian analysis without that dimension was often lacking in depth. It was here that I came across the writings of Melanie Klein who had uncovered "unconscious fantasy" life in small children. Here was a psychoanalyst following a parallel path to Jung. Her work became central to my study of the early life of a child and infancy, and it was her work that provided me with the tools to analyse children. At that time there were no Jungian child analysts, and so for many years I was working alone.

I have therefore been influenced by the writings of two great innovators. Latterly it has seemed to me that Bion has also presented much matter which needs to be assimilated by analytical psychologists – I have attempted to begin that process which will be reflected in parts of this book.

Part One

Empirical foundation, hypotheses and theories

Chapter One

*The self in Jung's works**

This first chapter is lengthy and somewhat heavy going – not perhaps the one to start interesting a reader anxious to obtain a concise understanding of what Jung meant by the self. However, I consider it vital to go into his method, his use of observational data and his abstraction of them. As will be seen, his discovery of the self grew out of his opening-up of a new dimension of the psyche: an inner world of almost unlimited dimensions. It was from there that the self emerged.

At the time Jung was pioneering the field almost alone, but since then the self has come to occupy the interests of many others and especially psychoanalysts to whose publications I shall frequently refer. They differ from Jung's radical understanding and so special attention needs to be given not only to Jung's conceptions but also to the empirical foundations on which they rest.

Jung's writings are extensive and it is easy to overlook important contributions on any particular topic. Therefore in the original version of this chapter, published in 1963, here much revised,* I attempted to avoid errors by using the indices in the *Collected Works* to sample and extract passages on the self. These were recorded on cards and then indexed alphabetically under subject headings. Thus the tendency to select quotations and distort summaries to suit the writer's convenience, was, if not eradicated, at least kept in check. Furthermore, by using this sampling technique it was possible to decide what Jung said once and what he said repeatedly, to which statements he gave weight and which were intuitions thrown out in passing. The method was found to have another advantage; it became easier to notice when different

*Originally published as "Empirical foundations and theories of the self in Jung's works" in *The Journal of Analytical Psychology* vol. 8, no. 1, 1963. Republished in *Analytical Psychology: a Modern Science*, London, Heinemann, 1973. The present version is much revised and expanded.

In 1963 much of Jung's work on alchemy was not translated. Since then I have studied his books on that subject without finding need to amend my conclusions.

formulations were the result of a major or a minor change in his views.

It was claimed that what was recorded in that paper gave the main trends in Jung's developing concepts of the self. Two incompatible definitions emerged and I now believe that they derive partly from his method of investigation. That gives me an opportunity to start considering the place of abstraction in Jung's presentations, in the context of his method of procedure.

Jung's Method of Investigation

It is doubtful whether Jung ever developed a theory of the self. For instance, in *The Undiscovered Self* (Jung, 1957) he states: "Since self-knowledge is a matter of getting to know the individual facts, theories are of very little help" (Jung, 1957, p. 249). This statement and others like it are curious in a number of respects. It may for instance be questioned whether a theory that does not illumine "individual facts" is performing its proper function. The statement is surprising also since he consistently held that his theoretical position depended upon clinical data. The following passage, though written in 1917, is characteristic of his scientific method and he refers to it again and again:

> My habit in my daily practical work is to confine myself for some time to studying my human material. I then abstract as general a formula as possible from the data collected, obtaining from it a point of view and applying it in my practical work until it has either been confirmed, modified, or else abandoned. If it has been confirmed, I publish it as a general view-point without giving the empirical material. I introduce the material amassed in the course of my practice only in the form of example or illustration (Jung, 1917, p. 294).

Alongside the abstracting process of scientific deduction he employed amplification. He collected parallels from myths, legends and other ethnological material at his disposal. That material he first used to elucidate clinical matter but, as time went on, myth, legend and the subject of religion increasingly became the main focus of his study. The theory of types grew out of clinical observations, that of the collective unconscious from his studies in mythology. In the latter he could not possibly fail to notice the ubiquity of the mythological motifs in different cultures and also in their history.

Once he had formulated his basic conceptions he could then use them as a frame of reference; his concept of the collective unconscious especially enabled him to give meaning to the imagery he had collected from innumerable sources and as a result he could amplify his clinical material to make sense out of irrational data – apparent chaos. Thus he could illuminate numerous aspects of human behaviour whether individual or collective. There can be no doubt that, however individual the self may be ultimately, it is also a general phenomenon and Jung actually shows it to be so. So wherein lie his doubts about the use of theory?

In 1912 Jung published the *Psychology of the Unconscious*. There, in the chapter "Concerning two kinds of thinking", he distinguishes between directed thinking which leads to coherent logical patterns and undirected thinking which is controlled, as later became apparent, by the archetypal forms in the unconscious: it is thinking in metaphorical imagery which is loosely called symbolic. It may at first appear chaotic because the images amplify and overlap each other thus confusing organized thought processes which may then become defensive and so are of "very little help". Since Jung contends that this "undirected" activity of the psyche, not controlled by the ego, is important and objective, he approaches attempts at replacing it with abstract conceptual statements with caution. Therefore he can say (Jung, 1951a, p. 33): "It is not the concept that matters; the concept is only a word, a counter, and it has meaning and use only because it stands for a certain sum of experience". Here and in other places he shows his distrust of abstraction: "Once metaphysical ideas have lost their capacity to recall and evoke the original experience they have not only become useless but prove to be the actual impediments on the road to wider development" (ibid., p. 34). The same applies in metapsychological theorizing. It would appear that Jung refers to theories and classifications that become defensive or masquerade as "science" to hide their autonomous sterility.

In the question just cited, Jung refers to "the original experience" and that needs further attention. An important feature in Jung's exposition is his contention that theories are the equivalent of myth-like elements. To demonstrate this he gives a list of primitive equivalents of his thesis "On psychic energy" (Jung, 1928a, p. 67), and elsewhere amongst other examples he reminds us of Robert Meyer's discovery of the theory of the conservation of energy which took place more by inspiration than by logic (Jung, 1943, p. 67). The same might be said of Kekule's visions which by abstraction made the discovery of the benzene ring possible. Examples could be multiplied but to no further purpose.

The interlacing of theory and primitive image, first presented in "Two kinds of thinking", became a feature of Jung's exposition: he uses myth to keep the imaginal experience alive and models or other forms of abstraction to contain, translate or explain them. Thus he struggles to ensure that the abstract propositions do not become divorced from their relation to metaphorically expressed structures of the mind.

It may be useful to consider an example of Jung's way of interlacing myth and model. In the chapter on "Death" in "Psychology of the transference'' (Jung, 1946, p. 256ff), he expounds alchemical metaphors about a dropsical state of the king and queen. These he interprets, i.e. explains, as depicting the tendency for inflation to occur when assimilating unconscious contents. Then continuing with the alchemist's statement he says that the process can lead to death. However, ''The alchemists assert that death is at once the conception of the *filius philosophorum* a peculiar variation of the Anthropos . . .''. This *filius philosophorum* Jung then amplifies by drawing a parallel with the Gnostic Christ and continues: ''This 'son' is the new man, the product of the union of the king and the queen though here he is not born of the queen; but king and queen are themselves transformed into the new birth.''

Translated into the language of psychology the mythologem runs: ''. . . the union of the conscious mind or ego-personality [the king] with the unconscious personified as the anima [the queen] produces a new personality [the self] compounded of both'' (ibid., p. 264). Here he deploys his theory of two kinds of thinking thereby recognizing that his abstract concepts and myth are analogous.

It must be said, however, that theories have advantages over myths in scientific studies: they do jobs of the kind that the theory of the collective unconscious performed for Jung; furthermore, they can lead into areas where we are ignorant, can orientate those who think, can become a means of communication, can explain observations and are the stuff of good interpretations especially in their transformative capacities. Evidently theories modify, usefully, the primitive phenomena from which, at the same time, they are abstracted. I shall contend that the two conceptions of the self found in Jung's works, stem from the interlacing of primitive experience and the abstractions from them.

Since Jung has apparently two ways of conceiving the self, it may be enquired whether there is an inherent objection in his writings to that state of affairs. It would seem that he sometimes thought not, but in 1913 he developed his theory of types to account for the different positions of Freud, Adler and himself; each theory seemed then to cover adequately the same observations. He developed his position later at great length in *Psychological Types* (Jung, 1921). He did indeed seem to support the idea that contending theories are, at one level, desirable. Yet all the same, it may be reflected, by introducing into the often acrimonious discussion between Freud and Adler a theory of types, Jung clearly tried to resolve the supposed incompatibility that was so apparent in the early conflicts amongst psychoanalysts. That will also be my aim in this chapter when considering Jung's two formulations on the nature of the self.

I am persuaded that Jung's method of presentation stems from his attempt to find ways of expressing the wholeness of the self. In doing so he ran up against the lack of adequate language for so doing. Scientific discourse relies too heavily on abstract theorizing about well-defined data and seeks to exclude the symbolic metaphors through which the unconscious finds expression. So in his later exposition he relied more and more on paradox especially using those found in alchemy.

His attitude would also seem to have stemmed from the notion of the psyche being at once the subject and the object of cognition. That is a proposition which derives from the possibility of making the abstraction from primitive thought a subject for investigation as Jung himself demonstrated in his "The theological disputes of the ancient church" to be found in *Psychological Types*.

So it is eventually a question of what matter is chosen for investigation and it follows that the very abstractions Jung made can themselves be a matter for study. This argument looks circular but I would rather consider it as an attempt to envisage the spiral resulting from the interacting relation between the conscious mind, the unconscious and differing layers of consciousness.

I will add a further comment on Jung's periodic warning about the danger of theories. It was not only the emptiness of metaphysical proposition that has already been noted but also his accusation that Freud made a dogma out of his sexual theory of the libido. For such reasons as well as the frequent confusion in the literature, I will consider what aids we have to orientate ourselves amongst the more abstract forms of mental activity.

Having selected a subject matter for study, such as dreams or active imaginings and having decided that it is the less personal or even impersonal contents of these to which we wish to pay attention, we may then wish to organize them or draw conclusions about them.

If we are very uncertain about how to pursue these objectives, we can construct a proposition for instance that such data are not to be considered as the result of personal developmental processes. We can further seek to explain them by considering them as the expression of inherited tendencies. Both propositions can act as stimulants to further investigation but they lack support and can not be proved under prevailing conditions of knowledge – when that is so, they are to be classed as hypotheses.

But if evidence accumulates so that enough support is gained and if no other proposition carries equal weight, then the proposition at first assessed as an hypothesis becomes up graded and gains the status of a theory. I am not putting forward more criteria for deciding whether a proposition is to be considered as one or the other, all I want to establish is that there are ideas which may help in orientating ourselves. Nor am I considering the proposition that it is more important to show that the theory or hypothesis cannot be disproved.

Another way of proceeding to organize the data of experience is to construct models. These are less abstract and more pictorial than either hypotheses or theories. They are nearer to metaphors but are more complex in their structure than that which most metaphors express. They are abstract and generalized pictures of mental or other elements in the psyche and as such may be more helpful than their abstract equivalents.

The last instrument to consider is definition, especially since Jung paid much attention to the need for it and devoted a section of *Psychological Types* to formulating ones that he thought significant – there are fifty-seven of them. Their positive function is to make a proposition sufficiently definite for it to be used or manipulated. Their negative valence is that they exclude from the field of investigation everything that is not in the definition and so they can become excluding and defensive. However, the proper objective of definition is to exclude irrelevant data and so further the process of clarification – their defensiveness has that advantage.

It may be asked, and it is asked: why do you want to abstract? why not be content with describing? There are a number of considerations relevant to that question:

(1) If description were to be complete, it would be extremely cumbersome and, however detailed, would be incomplete.
(2) There is therefore a need to organize and generalize and explain the data by containing or penetrating them so as to gain greater understanding how the elements in the data of experience operate and come into being.
(3) There is a need to evaluate what is described.
(4) By abstracting and so getting a distance from the data, it is possible to define a way to make new experimental discoveries.

All these "rules" for considering the abstracting process are instruments of the conscious mind and in as much as directed thinking is in operation they orientate, but they can also be used against the expressions of undirected thinking which manifests the "unconscious". In revenge, the "unconscious" can penetrate any of the instruments by making them into undesirable and unintended dogma.

Other methods for handling abstractions have been devised by psychoanalysis in their metapsychology and other abstruse techniques have been devised by Bion. It is not necessary to do more than note that they exist since they would unduly complicate my argument.

There is a tendency amongst analysts to try and make our science conform to the less penetrating natural sciences, but that will not serve my purpose. There is a psychology of facts just as there is a psychology of theories, hypotheses and models. Jung took up the subject of facts when he considered the sensation type which relied on the perception of facts, but because he linked it up with typology the conception was still-born.

The tendency of scientists to assume that their psychology does not enter into their labours is on the wane, and that gives space for analysts to put forward what they know without minding when told that what they do is not "scientific". Science depends upon imaginative leaps just as much as on detailed observation and experiment. Basically it is a discipline that endeavours to increase knowledge, knowing that ultimate knowledge is beyond its reach – a statement that will be qualified later on. That, however, is the significance of that philosophy of science which asserts that a scientific hypothesis will be taken as provisionally valid if it can not be disproved.

Clinical Experiences

Many years ago, in his first publication (1902), Jung recorded his study of a hysterical medium. Towards the end of his investigations, the young woman developed visions of world forces which became a mystical system. To express her experiences she used concentric circles divided by two diameters into four parts. Although today the diagram is unmistakably a mandala, its significance as a symbol of the self was not appreciated by Jung. Indeed it was not until 1921 when he published *Psychological Types* that we hear much if anything about the self.

Between 1902 and that time a great deal had happened to Jung: he had discovered psychoanalysis and had been one of those who investigated religion and mysticism with its newly developed instruments. It was this work which contributed to his differences with Freud and his separation from psychoanalysis proper. Soon afterwards he plunged into an inner turmoil which lasted several years and during that time there was very little that he could publish. Only one small essay ("The transcendent function") written in 1916, but not published till 1958c, was significant to his development.

From the start Jung showed interest in religious data; that interest had personal determinants: he came from a family in which religion was important and the fact that he lived in a country where traditional customs and superstition were not only indigenous but more stable than elsewhere must have contributed as well. *The Psychology of the Unconscious* (Jung, 1943) shows very well the comprehensiveness of his study. But he was not satisfied with his work for when he had finished it he writes: "So I suspected that myth had a meaning which I was sure to miss if I lived outside it in the haze of my own speculations. . . . So, in the most natural way, I took it upon myself to get to know 'my' myth, and regarded this as the task of tasks . . ." (Jung, 1952a, pp. xxiv–v). That was the starting point for his "confrontation with the unconscious" and his discovery of the self as an immediate experience. Since I shall be referring to mandalas especially, it is interesting to know how Jung discovered them: He tells us:

> In 1918–19 I was in Chateau d'Oex as Commandant de la Région Anglaise des Internes de Guerre. While I was there I sketched every morning in a note book a small circular drawing, a mandala, which seemed to correspond to my inner situation at the time. With the help of these drawings I could observe my psychic transformations from day to day . . .
>
> Only gradually did I discover what the mandala really is: "Formations, Transformations, Eternal Mind's eternal recreation" . . .
>
> Mandalas were cryptograms concerning the state of the self which were presented to me anew every day. In them I saw the self – that is my whole being – actively at work. To be sure, at first I could only dimly understand them; but they seemed to me highly significant, and I guarded them like precious pearls (Jung, 1963, p. 187).

The importance of these experiences can scarcely be over-estimated. Of them he says: ". . . I had attained what was for me the ultimate" and "this insight gave me stability and gradually my inner peace returned" (ibid., p. 188). But it left him isolated and it was not until he painted a picture with Chinese characteristics and shortly afterwards received a letter from Richard Wilhelm "enclosing the manuscript of a Taoist-alchemical treatise entitled *The secret of the golden flower* . . ." that it was breached. "That was the first event which broke through my isolation; I could establish ties with something and someone' (ibid., p. 189).

Though he found a comparable symbol, i.e. forms appearing in his patients, he was loath to say anything about them publicly lest they be copied and so not be genuine experiences of the patient's self. It was not until 1929 that he published with Wilhelm *The Secret of the Golden Flower* (Wilhelm and Jung, 1929). It was only then that he felt he had enough objective evidence from his patients to confirm that the mandala represented the end of a genuine goal seeking development.

In the dream series of his patients and in the introverted method of active imagination, Jung found the same development as he had found in himself. The images, amongst them mandala forms, were often impressive, sublime and cosmic.

In *Psychology and Alchemy* (Jung, 1944a) he published the first dream series in which the symbolism of the self was demonstrated at length. It will now be briefly considered in order to bring out some of the salient features.

The patient, a young man of "excellent scientific education", recorded four hundred dreams, which for the sake of convenience Jung divided up into eight groups of fifty. There seems to have been a sort of spurt of mandalas in the first twenty-two dreams of group one, all of them relatively simple, one might even say childlike, though Jung does not say that. They are listed by Jung as follows:

(1) The snake that described a circle round the dreamer.
(2) The blue flower.
(3) The man with the gold coins in his hand, and the enclosed space for a variety performance.
(4) The red ball.
(5) The globe (Jung, 1944a, p. 99).

Following this the frequency of mandalas is less till the fourth group. Thereafter they become progressively more frequent; moreover they also become more complex and various combinations of forms occur to make up a basically consistent pattern; the circle and centre become closely bound up with the number four expressed either in structures such as a cross or a squared circle, or as four persons etc. Eventually he arrived at the final impressive figure – the Great Vision – called "the World Clock" having a manifestly cosmic character. It was recorded as follows:

> There is a vertical and a horizontal circle, having a common centre. This is the world clock. It is supported by the black bird. The vertical circle is a blue disc with a white border divided into 4 × 8 = 32 partitions. A pointer rotates upon it. The horizontal circle consists of four colours. On it stand four little men with pendulums, and round about it is laid the ring that was once dark and is now golden (formerly carried by the children). The 'clock' has three rhythms or pulses:
> 1. The small pulse: the pointer on the blue vertical disc advances by 1/32.
> 2. The middle pulse: one complete revolution of the pointer. At the same time the horizontal circle advances by 1/32.
> 3. The great pulse: 32 middle pulses are equal to one revolution of the golden ring (ibid., p. 194).

In his commentary Jung begins by saying: "This remarkable vision made a deep and lasting impression on the dreamer, an impression of 'the most sublime harmony' as he himself put it" (ibid., p. 194). That kind of experience is important, indeed it is central in his thesis. It came to be called "numinus".

The development from simple to complex imagery shown in this sequence was, it appears, frequently found by Jung, for in *Aion* (1951a) he writes:

> To the conscious mind the mandala appears at first as an unimpressive point or dot, and a great deal of hard and painstaking work as well as the integration of many projections are generally required before the full range of the symbol can be anything like completely understood (Jung, 1951a, p. 32).

Other examples of mandala imagery are to be found in "A study in the process of individuation" (Jung, 1950a). Here the mandala pictures are more stable and persistent than in the dreams of the young scientist and what is inside and outside the circle is depicted. The pictures were painted by a woman, a psychologist who

> had studied [the subject] for nine years. She had read all the more recent literature in this field. In 1928 at the age of fifty-five, she came to Europe in order to continue her studies under my guidance. As the daughter of an exceptional father she had varied interests, was extremely cultured and possessed a lively turn of mind (ibid., p. 291).

She was thus, as the young scientist probably was also an unusual person. I mention this because there is reason to believe that Jung's patients tended to be exceptional.

The third significant paper is "Concerning mandala symbolism" (Jung, 1950b). In it there are fifty-four pictures made by approximately twenty-two patients, excluding those taken from other sources. They were predominantly female, there being in all approximately twenty females and two males – Jung's reporting is incomplete in respect of sex. Thirteen of the pictures were painted by twelve women and one man; all of this group were aged 35 years or more; most were relatively healthy, but one woman was "schizoid". The rest of the pictures were painted by two children (one male aged 7 years, and one female aged 11 years) and seven younger women, two of whom were neurotic and one "schizoid". It is thus clear that, contrary to first impressions, mandalas can occur both in younger persons (of seven years or more) and also in abnormal persons. These observations have been confirmed more extensively for children by Fordham (1944, 1957c) and by Perry (1953, 1957) for schizophrenia.

In only three of Jung's cases is there any comment on what the patients thought or felt.* Jung would not conceive of that as important because the images are experienced as impersonal.

The main impression one gets from this series is the great variety of content in a basically similar structural form. Since that structural form has a world wide distribution, it conforms with that characteristic of an archetype and indeed in his commentary it appears that Jung here thinks of it as such. There is no reference to any patient having an experience of the intensity of Jung's own: only in his amplifications are there references to many that are comparable. One is more impressed by the mandala as representing a stage in the individuation process, a sort of summary as to where the patient has got and not yet representing anything like "the ultimate".

*Investigation of circular figures in childhood leads to some interesting results:

(1) They can be related to ego formation.
(2) They can be related to separation.
(3) They can seem to preserve a good object against dangerous invasive emotionally charged elements.
(4) They can represent efforts to control a bad object.
(5) The circle can contain inner structures in a way that without doubt indicates the action of the self.

Critical Reflections

So far I have considered the clinical experiences that formed the basis for his theoretical formulations. That material has a number of features which require further consideration.

(1) Can Jung's data be generalized? His case material often appears to be treated as if it were a random sample implying that anybody could have the experience from the world population (Jung, 1957). It is perhaps the term collective unconscious and the objective way he treats the self that fosters such daring. However, a dream or a vision, is not the only way through which the self can be known – as I shall show later (pp. 57–63) – though his presentations only refer to persons with a well-developed inner life. That applies to other studies (Wickes, 1938; Adler, 1961) and supports the commonly held view that Jung's patients had already achieved a great deal of inner development or if they had not done so were capable of it under treatment. Furthermore, he gives indications that they belonged to a specific class which he had difficulty in defining. A few were schizoid (cf. also Baynes's case studies) or frankly schizophrenic, but the majority seem to have been mildly depressed (Jung, 1916, p. 82ff). From many of his warnings of the danger of inflation, disintegration or schizophrenia etc. it seems likely that a schizoid element was often found combined with the depression. And then there were the supposedly normal persons whose achievements had been considerable but for whom life had lost its meaning. We may note in passing that recently such persons are being interestingly investigated by psychoanalysts under the heading of "narcissistic personality disorders" (Kernberg, 1975). These patients may need analyses in the "first half of life" if their success in life provides inadequate narcissistic supplies for their basically weak self organization. Kernberg justifies his often lengthy analyses on the grounds that in later life success is no longer a useful support because it has been achieved: such personalities then suffer from severe mental distress and crippling disorders of the kind that Jung seems to have dealt with. If that is so, then it would make sense of the case reports by Jung's followers as well as by himself which indicate that the need to construct (or discover) the self is widespread and need not be confined to the second half of life.

That Jung's case material could only be generalized with caution is suggested by some other factors: his patients were often attracted to him by reading his books; there would be a chain reaction resulting from the successful treatment of patients and the effect of unresolved transferences. These factors influencing his practice are the fate of any well-known analyst and Jung was no exception.

(2) Jung's material refers almost exclusively to introverted symbolism, the images coming into consciousness during sleep or states of meditation unrelated to the external world, i.e. in solitude.

In the states of introversion described it would seem that the ego structures designed to adapt the organism to the external world are not being constellated. Furthermore, the empirical experiences collected under the heading "self" stem from the unconscious. Do the "inner" experiences contain evidence of ego structures and functions? If so, they must result from the ego turning inwards, as occurs in active imagination; therefore we may look for the inner aspect of the ego reflected in the symbols. It is in line with this conclusion when patients associate colours with the four functions (Jung, 1950a, p. 335). Yet though Jung himself has gone into the question of ego functions in the self at length in *Psychology and Alchemy* (1944, *vide* index), the reader will search in vain for much reference to the ego in external objects. The answer sometimes given is that the patient's relation to external objects and people has been dealt with or is relatively unimportant. The primary need is for introversion so that the transpersonal character of the self may be realized. Personal relations must not, however, be neglected when considering the nature of the self even though Jung can assert: "As for the self it is completely outside the personal sphere" (Jung, 1951a, p. 30).

(3) What has happened to introjected objects, parents, friends, wives, husbands, not to mention children, recording past object relationships; are these represented or even referred to in the images; They are not. Yet there is increasing evidence that through the analysis of these introjected records of interpersonal relationships and images reprojected into the transference something very like wholeness can be achieved. Further, there is reason to suspect that, because the interrelation between the internal and the external is taken more clearly into account, the result is more enduring than if emphasis is laid on imagination and experience in transpersonal solitude. However, I believe that it was only sometimes that Jung considered his patient's personal thinking or feeling unimportant. If that is so, we still have to account for the omission. One reason for it is that Jung objected to including personal materials: in *Psychology and Alchemy* he states that the omission is ". . . because the dreams touch to some extent on the intimacies of personal life and must therefore remain unpublished. So I had to confine myself to the impersonal material" (Jung, 1944a, p. 207). Thus it would not seem that he overlooked personal relationships in his analytic work. How much of it is there which was not published?

In the case in *Psychology and Alchemy*, only parts of fifty-nine dreams out of three hundred and ninety-nine are discussed, and it must be assumed that what he does not publish was saturated with the "intimacies of personal life". This means that considerably less than one-sixth of his material is presented, the rest being omitted for "personal" reasons, a reflection which brings the case much closer to everyday experience in analytic work where personal relationships predominate. Yet it is only in a footnote that the following remark is to be found: "wholeness is the result of an intra-psychic process which depends essentially on the relationship of one individual to another" (Jung, 1946, p. 244, n.15). He does not, however, expand this, but only goes on to say, "Such a relationship paves the way for individuation and makes it possible . . .'. The relationship must mean the transference relationship on which Jung wrote a long essay using parallels from an alchemical text, the *Rosarium Philosophorum*.

(4) The omission of personal material from Jung's presentations is not, however, only a matter of tact and discretion, for in his analytic work he emphasized the objectivity of archetypal material with parallels and he recommended his patients to enhance that aspect of their dreams and fantasies by writing them down, painting the images and working on them as if they were objective material. This objectivity applies to the self and we find Jung emphasizing that over and over again.

Cosmic mandalas are the extreme form of "objective" mandala in that they depict world forces and imply the subject's relation to them. They give expression to man's need to know the world he lives in and his relation to it. Historically this knowledge has been provided by religion, which answered the need with stories, myths and the products of contemplation. It is only comparatively lately that science has developed the need to know in a very different and often incompatible way. It seeks for explanations and in biology it investigates history, phylogenetic and ontogenetic. Yet, because of Jung's ongoing interests and his comparative method, there is a signal lack of attempt at genetic study or explanation. Nowhere – except in Jung's own "autobiography" – is much of the "mature" material related to childhood let alone infancy. There is however a reference in the vision to "the ring (previously carried by the children)". That event is interesting because of my attempt to relate the self to childhood and infancy. There are several dreams in which the child or childhood are mentioned (dreams 11, 44 and 56). Jung's interpretations indicate a double attitude: first, the danger of remaining a child too long especially in that it fosters idealizing aspirations, and secondly that to keep contact with childhood is to be in touch with the formative roots of the personality. He amplifies the motif with reference to the myths of cabiri and the dwarfs, and that was taken up later in "The psychology of the child archetype" (Jung, 1950c) in which he relates the child to the archetype of the self. It is evident that in the dream series under consideration the children initiate the dreamer into the mandala motif.

There is an element in the mandala symbolism on which I wish to comment here. I shall take it up later in Part 2, Chapter 11. It appears that there is an acknowledged defensive content of the symbol which Jung alludes to when he reminds us of the magic circle which cannot be penetrated and cannot be broken from within. In calling this defensive, I do not wish to allude to ego defences but to an absolute protection of the symbol at the centre of the figure which combines and transcends opposites – at least that is how I understand Jung's meaning.

Comparative Material

The other sources of Jung's study are derived from comparative religion, folklore and alchemy, with the aid of which he succeeded in generalizing, illuminating and amplifying his clinical observations. Originally, particularly in *Psychological Types*, he paid attention to Buddhism, Hinduism and Taoism in each of which the ideas of the self is a central feature, as Brahman, Atman and Tao.

Though there was much to interest him in the Eastern mystics and though he studied other texts than those mentioned in *Psychological Types* ("The Tibetan book of the dead" (see Jung, 1953) and the "Secret of the golden flower" (see Jung, 1929)), by far the greater interest was given to developments in the Christian religion, in Gnosticism, Alchemy and Christian heretical cults which he thought of as compensating the onesidedness of Christianity. Amongst Christian mystics he was interested in Meister Eckhart and Angelus Silesius because they expressed the interdependence of God and the soul of man, the one being dependent on the other. This theme was developed forcefully in "Answer to Job" (Jung, 1952b) in which he daringly identifies God's wish to become man as the source of the birth of Christ. Jung's work on the Christian tradition culminates in *Aion* (1951a) and there he gives a list of self symbols. Amongst them are images that he has selected for special studies elsewhere such as the child, the philosophical tree and alchemical expressions of it such as Mercurius, but he adds theriomorphic forms like the bull, tortoise, etc. Such a plethora of symbols requires some criteria for their selection. It is that any symbol that carries the experience of or which is postulated as having a greater totality than man himself can be a symbol of the self.

Most of the ethnological material Jung studied – the Assumption of Mary the mother of Christ being an exception – is historical. History is important he maintained, since, without the information it provides, patients can become divorced from the cultural roots in which they are embedded. The archetypal roots of the psyche are indeed essentially historical and the self is no exception; so what, in Jung's view, is its history? It has previously been projected and has only recently emerged as a psychological entity; that he believed is coming into man's consciousness anyway and analytical psychology has provided a method with which to manage transpersonal affects previously integrated into religious or metaphysical dogma or theology. So the method and the concepts of ''self'' and individuation have grown out of an urgent need. Most, if not all, of the historical material cited by Jung comes from a time when science was either quiescent or in such a rudimentary state that one man could get a good grasp of all its branches. That has some important implications. If, for instance, a man of that time was a visionary he could adapt his vision to the established knowledge of the period, and construct a feasible system of philosophy. If he could not do so, that could not be attributed to the impossibility of doing so, and he would create one and form a cult. In the *Hermetic Corpus* to which the alchemists frequently refer, it is recounted that Hermes Trismegistos had a vision in which the spirit Poimandres appeared. Poimandres revealed to Hermes the nature of the universe and directed him to go and teach mankind the truth which had been revealed to him. This Hermes did to a number of initiates in a large number of discourses of a philosophic kind. The reader of these accounts is transported into a way of thinking about the world entirely different from the modern one. A great deal that is said about matter is couched in terms of essences, spirits and abstract elements, while many of the ideas are manifestly part of current scholarship, some of it Platonic, to which the revelation is being adapted under our eyes. In this case the different idiom becomes obvious and it shows how much the form of visions must be determined by the state of conscious knowledge and the general view of the world current at any given time. If this is so, the question arises: How relevant is it to apply the experiences steeped in other cultural milieux to modern states of consciousness and so to the dreams and fantasies of our patients? There is a serious danger that essential elements in their contemporary and personal experiences get overlooked. And surely it must influence us today that knowledge has become so extensive and changes so rapidly that it cannot be grasped as a whole. Further, it must evidently have an effect that there is a concept of individuation. In short, modern consciousness leads to historical metaphysical experience being expressed in a more and more individualized way and so, in spite of Jung's apparent denial, more and more in terms of human relationships. This may be why the transference becomes so important (*vide* Fordham, 1957e).

These reflections point to Jung's idea that his psychological views and discoveries need to be related to his own psychology and to those like it. Inasmuch as he is a type, others will see the psyche as he does and have comparable experiences. This sort of psychology, if valid, would have a history and be represented in an introverted tradition which his material presents and whose history he narrates.

Theories of the Self

The Totality Definition

Jung himself says that he derived his concept of the self from Eastern mysticism, though it is possible that William James also contributed.

Many Oriental formulations refer to a totality, as the following citation shows; it comes from *Psychological Types:* "When by the disposition/of his heart/he becomes indifferent to all objects, he obtains eternal happiness both in this world and after death. He who has in this manner gradually given up all attachment and is free from all pairs of opposites reposes in Brahman alone" (cited from *The Laws of Manu* (Jung, 1921, p. 195)). This frame of reference makes the self the wholeness of the personality outside time space and desire. This comes into being and is expressed in symbolic experience which is transpersonal and transcends opposites. It is of the kind already cited ("The vision of the World Clock"), (p. 13 *supra*).

The concept of the self, however, also seems to have grown out of Jung's idea of the *transcendent function* mooted in 1916. He says: "The shuttling to and fro of arguments and affects represents the transcendent function of opposites. The confrontation of the two positions generates a tension charged with energy and creates a living third thing . . . a movement out of the suspension between opposites, a living birth that leads to a new level of being, a new situation" (Jung, 1916, p. 90). Later, in *Psychological Types* (1921, p. 115, 1) is the following somewhat different definition: "This function of mediating between opposites I have termed the *transcendent function*, by which I mean . . . a combined function of conscious and unconscious elements." The function is clearly related to the theory of the symbol which, by uniting opposites in a "living third", is little if at all different from the self (*vide* Fordham, 1957a, pp. 60ff.).

In *Psychological Types* there is an early, probably the first, definition of the self. It is placed in the definition of the "Ego". There Jung discriminates between the ego and the self and states that the self is ". . . the subject of my total psyche which also includes the unconscious. In this sense the self would be an ideal entity which embraces the ego." This definition is amplified in the special definition, now distinct, from the ego that he wrote for the *Collected Works* in 1971.

Since Jung had observed the importance of distinguishing the empirical ego, i.e. the ego as experienced, from the spontaneous images of imagination (non-ego), he had clearly defined the ego as a part system, i.e. one system among others of a different kind. So he needed another term for the total psyche. It is a short step to expand this definition into the formula, self = ego + archetypes, which easily equates with the more usual formula: union or combination of the conscious with the unconscious. There are some implications of this which are sufficiently important to discuss further.

If the self is the whole psyche, then it cannot be observed intrapsychically since the ego is contained in it as a part and cannot function as an observer. It is only when some part of the ego stands separate from or only participates up to a point in the rest of the whole that data about the self can be collected. The data are called "symbols of the self". These considerations give a basis for the frequent statement that the self is "unknowable" and does not exist as such. It is outside space and time – it is timeless. Jung explicitly takes this position on a number of occasions; a passage in "The holy men of India" shows it:

> India is "prepsychological": when it speaks of the "self", it posits such a thing as existing. Psychology does not do this. . . . Though very well acquainted with the self's peculiar and paradoxical phenomenology, we remain conscious of the fact that we are discerning . . . something essentially unknown and expressing it in terms of psychic structures . . . (Jung, 1944b, p. 580).

It may well be reflected that, by summating inferences derived from data about each incomplete symbol, a complete image of the self could be constructed; it would be a theoretical construct which could not be tested directly. The summation would differ in more or less important respects from any primordial experience and be outside and beyond it. The self as a whole is not therefore unknowable so much as inexperienceable. Jung omits discussion of this deduction, partly because he deliberately combines logical with "prelogical" thinking, but also because of his dislike of relying on theoretical constructs already noted above (pp. 7f.). At the end of the passage quoted, he refers to "the nature of what is to be known", and it here seems that he is hypostatizing a scientific thought, i.e. he treats a scientific inference as if it were a known empirical fact as he says the Indian mystics do. Elsewhere he specifically justifies hypostatization (1954a, p. 262, no. 18) which is indeed implied in the phrase "realization of the self" in individuation; the reason for it has already been discussed above and leads to his frequent assertion that the self is a "psychic reality" or "a fact". These phrases, used by him in various contexts, mean that inner experiences are to be given equal status with the facts of the external world; however, when he uses the phrases with reference to the self, he tends to add such statements as: "[It is] no mere concept or logical postulate" (1948a, p. 157), a negative assertion which sounds defensive, though the antagonist is not identified. The assertion, however, also implies that the self is a special case in that a concept of the totality is particularly difficult to construct. Indeed it is impossible.

The images, Jung often makes clear, cannot be *the actual self*; at best they are representatives of it. They are approximations representing states of relative wholeness which alone are possible, while bits of ego are split off and function as observers. Therefore, when the images are referred to as *the* self, this is not a theoretical but a metaphorical statement – or hypostatized thinking. They would seem to be a basis for assertions that the self is a thing which exists and not a theory or postulate. It is also why some English translators want to spell the term with a capital "S", not only to differentiate it from the self as ego, but also to emphasize its special position in analytical psychology.

It must be now apparent that the self is not only manifested in mysticism, the concept is mystical. As I have a high regard for mystics and mysticism, that statement does not carry for me the frequent derogatory undertones it often carries for others. Later chapters will study the topic through the writings of St John of the Cross, (Part 3 *infra*).

It is part of my thesis that Jung's abstract ideas have their origins in experience. So what are the experiences that can be related to the definition under discussion? It seems quite natural to think of the period in which he was making pictures of mandalas: "In them I saw the self – that is my whole being actively at work. I had attained the ultimate." It was an insight that "gave me stability and gradually my peace of mind returned". The difficulties in taking the primordial experience to represent the totality of the psyche are many, but the greatest so far considered is that experiences in solitude, however important in themselves, leave out the organism's adaptation to external objects whether personal or otherwise. A number of statements made by analysts and by Jung himself bring out other difficulties:

(1) The ego is stated to be an entity separate from the self conceived as the totality of the psyche (Jung, 1939a, p. 542; 1944b, pp. 579ff.). So long as it is clearly kept in mind that the ego is part of the self, it is justifiable to distinguish the two; but it can be confusing to refer to the ego *and* the self as though they were or could be separate entities.

(2) Arising out of (1) the two (ego and self) are treated as if they could be in conflict each with the other, or as if there could be a self–ego axis (e.g. Neumann, 1955), or that the self could inflate the ego by becoming identical with it, producing "dissociation of the personality" (Jung, 1940a, p. 95).

(3) It is stated that in infancy mother (or father) is the carrier of the self while the infant is the ego (e.g. Neumann, 1959). What this means is not at all evident, but the statement clearly involves treating ego and self as two different entities.

(4) It is stated that the self can be projected (Jung, 1946, p. 244, n.15; 1954a, pp. 260 and 262; 1958a, p. 79); introjected (Jung, 1940a, p. 95); that it is in or a function of the soul (Jung, 1921, pp. 315 ff.; 1948a, p. 156); that it can assimilate the ego or the unconscious (Jung, 1946, p. 263, n. 13; 1951a, p. 24.)

(5) It is stated that the self can be integrated (Jung, 1946, p. 264; 1954a, pp. 260 and 263).

All these statements, and it would be possible to collect more, mean that the self is not the whole psyche-soma since the ego is no part of it.

Self as Archetype

Now that we have considered one attempt to translate observations into theory and pointed out difficulties, we can go on to the other definition which contradicts the totality thesis and has already been mentioned as being apparently incompatible with it. There can be no difficulty in finding experience that underlie the definition of the self as an archetype; they are those archetypal images which have cosmic or other holistic references. So it is no surprise to find that Jung repeatedly refers to the self as an archetype. In *Aion* he goes so far as to say that the self is "the real organizing principle of the unconscious, the quaternity, or squared circle of the self" (Jung, 1951a, p. 204), and in various other places he defines or implies that the self is the archetype of order (1944a, 1954a, p. 284; 1958a, pp. 328 and 424.)

The definition of the self as an archetype does not contradict the self as unknowable for the symbolic imagery can only refer to it and, furthermore, the archetype itself is an unconscious function. Yet data indicating actions of the self cannot also be the totality since, in Jung's general theory of the psyche, a part of it, the ego, is specifically differentiated from the archetypes and is the only means for generating consciousness.

Many otherwise puzzling sayings by Jung are cognizant with the definition of the self as an archetype. The most striking is his tendency to identify God with the unconscious, for instance, in "Answer to Job"; indeed, it is apparent that the ideas centring round God's need of man through whom to become conscious require the concept of God as an archetype rather than the totality. If this definition is nearer the phenomena described, it follows that the experience of wholeness is not a reliable basis upon which to construct a definition of the self as the total psyche.

In considering the importance of any contradiction, there are several conditions to be fulfilled: it is necessary to look at the context in which

Jung is writing and also to see whether the statements were made intuitively or thrown out as suggestions which are not repeated. The two definitions occur in varying contexts and are repeated again and again. Another possibility is that one definition is earlier than the other and has been discarded in favour of the later one. This is not so, for, in *Aion*, he refers to the self as an archetype more than once, and also says: "I have suggested calling the total personality which, though present, cannot be fully known, the self. The ego is, by definition, subordinate to the self and is related to it like a part to the whole" (Jung, 1951a, p. 5). Though the word "like" seems to imply that he wants a loophole he can use if he is pressed, it is sufficiently explicit, and it is strikingly close to the early definition in *Psychological Types* (1921) (*vide supra* p. 20). However, there is no doubt that the concept of the self as an archetype began after the idea of it as the totality of the psyche, for the first form of the theory of archetypes was published in 1919, two years before the appearance of *Psychological Types*.

There have been several attempts to deal with problems posed by the data which each definition attempts to cover. Perhaps the most interesting is that proposed by Perry (1957). In studying schizophrenia Perry recorded self images which were related neither to integration nor to individuation in its classical sense (cf. *infra* pp. 42 ff.). He defines the self as an archetype, however, without considering the contradiction in Jung's writings, but he sees one problem which, in her essay on individuation, I suspect Jacobi (1967) was trying to solve; the ubiquity of self images. It is this which had made difficult the exclusive alliance of the self with individuation. Self images appear not only in individuation but in schizophrenia and in childhood as well, though not in the "first dreams of early infancy" as Jung (1954b) has stated (cf. my essay on children's dreams in *Children as Individuals* (Fordham, 1969)). These observations make it necessary either to detach the concept of the self from that of individuation or to expand the concept as Jacobi has done.

With reference to schizophrenia, Perry suggested that another name be given to the archetype lying behind the images. He used the term "central archetype". Jung seems to have considered it also, for he refers to "a central archetype", and often to the archetype of the self.

Perry observed that self images occur in states of chaos. This was also recorded by Jung (1951a, pp. 31–2 and 194–5, etc.; 1952b, pp. 456–7). The images began to arise when the relation between the ego and archetypal images gets difficult and the free play of fantasy gets out of hand. Since, in these circumstances, mandala forms occur as one among many images, they cannot represent the whole every time, but at best could represent only the possibility of wholeness in a disorganized, even fragmented, psyche. This may very well be the case in relatively healthy personalities, and this would account for the varying contents of mandala forms, which thus reflect the varying psychic contents integrated.

Other Formulations

The two formulations so far discussed (i.e. the definitions of the self as the total psyche and as an archetype) are not the only ones that Jung has made. However, they stand out in relation to his general theory.

It would go too far to discuss all the others, but to illustrate some we can list ideas put forward in *Two Essays on Analytical Psychology* (1926) over and above the main definitions. There Jung refers to the "individual self" (1926, p. 159) as containing the past and "the fertile soil from which all future life will spring" (ibid., p. 192); again it "could be characterized as a kind of compensation for the conflict between inside and outside" (ibid., p. 239). In this book he also links it with individuation which consists in "coming to selfhood", or it is "nothing less than to divest the self of its false wrappings of the persona on the one hand and the suggestive power of the primordial images on the other" (ibid. p. 174). And finally he says that the self is beyond proof, beyond science (ibid., p. 238). It will be recognized that some of these are ideas which recur, others are tentative and intuitive, reaching out after further understanding.

It may also be mentioned that there are a number of passages in which Jung combines the idea of totality with that of the archetype. Though these are often graphic word-pictures they are theoretically confusing, and perhaps he means them to be so. A passage in *Aion* is characteristic. Definable psychic products emerging from the unconscious manifestly indicate

> the psychic totality of the individual. They indicate the presence of an archetype of like nature, one of whose derivatives would seem to be the quaternity of functions that orient consciousness to an indefinite and indeterminable extent, it invariably includes the unconscious in its orbit and hence the totality of all archetypes. But the archetypes are complementary equivalents of the "outside world" and therefore possess a "cosmic" character (Jung, 1951a, p. 196).

Earlier on I referred to the fact that Jung kept his abstract formulations related to empirical affective experiences. I have written with that idea in mind. There is another aspect of this principle which I will now consider, for if one follows Jung's "analytic" work and relates this to the abstract propositions, further light can be shed on them.

First it should be remembered that Jung's patients were persons who had either lost contact with the self or in whom it had never attained sufficient representation; which was the case cannot be ascertained from his presentation, but invariably a complex structure had developed, part of which needed to be analysed before the synthetic processes directed by the self could come into operation. Then the procedure of recording and treating significant images synthetically in dreams or active imagination could take place. Certain of these images would be experienced as numinous and greater and more powerful than the ego. The forms may appear to symbolize a powerful integrative influence. As the development proceeds, a centralizing process may be discerned which draws together the numinous images in the mandala form. That may be a summary of where integration has led the subject and ultimately it can include the cosmos and, as with Jung, "the ultimate". It is now possible to understand Jung's shifting, when he abstracts his experience between defining the self as the totality of the psyche (the ultimate) which gives partial expression to itself in numinous images (the archetypes).

This view that the self gives partial expression to itself in the archetypal forms presupposes a division in the self. Considered developmentally against the background of history, the divisions in the primary Godhead were delineated by Jung, not only in the creation myths, or Eastern mysticism, but also in his studies of Western religion. It is shown impressively in "Answer to Job" that there are parts of God; both Satan (his doubting thoughts) and Sophia (his Eros) derive from him whilst we also learn that Yahweh can "forget" or become separated from his justice and his wisdom. To the process of development which leads to these parts of God* (inasmuch as he represents the self) I have given the term deintegration.

I shall now consider formulations about the self as envisaged in two other disciplines: psychoanalysis and general psychology. Psychoanalysis needs further consideration than the brief account detailed here but I introduce an overview leaving the more extensive discussion in Part 2.

Sprott's account is extracted from the large literature on the self evolved by general (or academic) psychologists. Academic psychologists are able to achieve great clarity because they are not encumbered with the often difficult clinical experience with which analysis are confronted and which they try to describe and assimilate into their abstractions. I conceive that the clarity is valuable though inaccurate with relation to the analytic experience.

It must be born in mind that the vertex, in terms of which the psychoanalytic work is undertaken, is often significantly different from that of analytical psychology. I mention this because their findings need to be digested before they can be used.

*Rosemary Gordon wrote interestingly about these "parts of god" in her paper "Gods and deintegrates" (Gordon, 1963).

The Self in Other Disciplines

Psychoanalysis

Psychoanalysis have introduced self theory mostly in the United States. These investigations have evoked considerable interest amongst analytical psychologists: Schwartz-Salant has considered their work in his detailed book *Narcissism and Character Formation* and Jacoby has considered Kohut's formulations carefully (Jacoby, 1981).

It was Hartmann, probably deriving his ideas from Federn, who introduced the self as a theoretical entity arguing that the opposite of object cathexis was not ego but self cathexis. As such the self was the totality of mental operations. His distinction was taken up by numerous psychoanalysts, amongst them Jacobson, who defined a primary psychosomatic self, containing neutral energy, from which infant development starts. These psychoanalysts exhibited a tendency to confuse the self with its representations in very much the same way as Jungian analysts confuse the self with its archetypal symbolic representations.

There is also much discussion about the relation between the self and the ego; sometimes the self is conceived of as a sub-system in the ego and sometimes it is treated as a separate entity having status of its own, whose strength or weakness depends on the amount of narcissistic libido with which it is cathected. Whichever view is taken, to these writers the self is a system which develops as psychic structures grow. Kohut alone has given transcendence to the self and claims to have introduced a revolution into psychoanalysis thereby doing away with libido and drive theory.

Turning to the English school, the term has been used rather loosely by Melanie Klein and occasionally to include the whole psyche: ego, id and superego. However, the self is implicit in all that she writes about infancy and childhood. That, to my mind, is not surprising for it was she who investigated the origins of the infant's inner world deriving from the activity of the "epistemophilic instinct". It was that which promoted the infant's intense interest in his own and his mother's body and their respective contents.

Three analysts influenced by Klein made interesting developments: Winnicott, Scott and Bion. Scott developed his concept of the body scheme which is cosmic and in that sense is close to Jung (*vide infra* pp. 97f). Winnicott conceptualized a true and false self which are like Jung's self and persona, but there the similarity ends. He conceived, wrongly as infant observations strongly suggest, that an infant is unintegrated at the start and so the self – meaning the sense of self, a self representation – is a product of ego growth. Finally Bion, though he does not use very much the term self, conceived its equivalent in "0": a creative absence.

All these developments have arisen because psychoanalysts have extended their investigations outside the traditional field of operation (the psychoneuroses) and have studied border-line states, the psychoses, character disorders and the recently defined narcissitic neuroses. Much of their work is strangely familiar though set in a different frame of reference deriving from a different vertex (*vide infra* pp. 94f). That is frustrating to those who want a standard terminology. Nevertheless these formulations of psychoanalysts cover a field to which Jung previously paid a great deal of attention and if one translates narcissim by introversion and internal object relations, it is quite possible to see the same concepts and practices at work: the idealizing transference, grandiose self and mirror transference are no strangers to analytical psychologists. Furthermore, some modifications in technique advocated by such writers as Searles, Margaret Little (*vide infra* p. 108) and Racker are very much along the lines that Jung advocated.

General Psychology

Since the study of the psyche in bits, as factors, as perception etc., has been better suited to the experimental method, the term "self" tends to be left out of writings by contemporary psychologists. However, there is a chapter on the subject in Sprott's (1947) *General Psychology* which I have selected from others of its kind because of the clarity and conciseness of the author's exposition. The fact that in it he records the work of William James and Calcins in the U.S.A. and of Aveling in Britain is of special interest because it is probable that Jung was influenced by William James, whose writings contain a long discussion of the self.

In his textbook, Sprott divides up the subject in the following way: first he considers the empirical self which refers to the experience of being an "I" to which objects are referable; this covers the sense of being aware of "myself" as a discrete person, separate from all others. He goes on to consider the idea of the self in which not only the subject's experience but also observations and statements of others are included: this leads to more complex theoretical constructs. Finally he considers theories of what the self could be. He then discusses what mind might be, and does so in terms of a number of related happenings among which is to be found the idea of the self persisting in time. It is interesting that he includes the views of Lewin, and also Koffka's theory of the ego, under the heading of organismic theories of the self; these are the nearest equivalent of Jung's concept.

According to the organismic theory, the organism acts as a whole, is an "end seeking totality" (Stern), and is more than the sum of its parts. Behaviour is conceived to be an expression of the total organism, an idea which Gestalt psychologists have used to some effect. The distinction between total self and environment means that the two act in a reciprocal manner. From this arises the theory that it is the change in the distribution of boundaries that determines whether a perceived object is felt as part of myself, is related to myself, or is a thing in itself (not in Kant's sense). Without pursuing this theory it can be pointed out that once the dichotomy self-environment is accepted, then perception of the whole self could best be arrived at by an introversion that excluded external objects. Jung does not discuss this point, and there are reasons for supposing that he omits it advisedly; first, the self is frequently referred to as cosmic and, second, his theory of synchronicity infers a boundaryless state between the archetype and material objects.

Sprott brings out important distinctions: the differences between the empirical self, ideas of the self, and theories about it. Jung's idea of the ego is very much like what Sprott terms "the empirical self" and also ideas about it; however, Jung's concept of the self seems to correspond to the theoretical heading. In Sprott's thesis, what Jung may well claim to have done is to obtain empirical evidence to support the organismic theory. It is interesting that Aveling also holds that it is possible to apprehend the self as a "basic totality acting in some way".

It is evident that there is a place for thinking of the ego and the self as separate though interrelated entities, and it is clear that if the self is an archetype, there is no difficulty in doing so. The dichotomy is clarifying, for instance, in relation to active imagination and religious matters. To translate God as self and man as ego makes it easier to study their interrelation. If the theory of the self is confused in the respects already considered, a number of questions present themselves. Is it enough to run two incompatible theories side by side, to say that the self is the totality of the psyche and then treat it as if it were an archetype among others or even an organizer of the archetypes? Is it enough to say that it is effective, prelogical experience that counts and then play down theory?

The sources of Jung's theoretical concept of the self as a totality are in oriental texts like the ones cited earlier. From them the theory of the self as the totality of the psyche and as an entity solving the conflict of opposites evidently arose. Jung also found data of the oriental kind in his patients, and these have been confirmed by other analysts. The theoretical quandary thus arises through the translation of this experience into a general theory. Bearing in mind the probable affective archetypal root of theories, the following are possible steps in the translation of the affective experience into theory.

(1) First of all, there is the experience of the self which could run as follows: "I experience the presence of God, feel loved, cared for

by him. I feel redeemed, free from excessively painful conflicts, whole and united in love with the world.''

(2) Then this ''real'' experience becomes a memory and can be translated into a vivid metaphor.

(3) When reflected upon, it becomes an ''as if'' experience, i.e. it was ''as if'' that really happened.

(4) It then becomes possible to build up tentative hypotheses and test them against clinical observation within or as part of the transference. Through reading books, it can be found that this type of experience, though varying in detail, is basically general among religious people. Indeed its geographical distribution may be universal.

(5) Then it is justifiable to develop the following theory: The experience was due to the psyche functioning as a whole with the opposites united; the tension between the unconscious and the conscious has become transcended.

(6) We can test this idea further and find that, though the implications are difficult, it is still useful and others can use it as well.

(7) Testing this theory against more extensive data shows that it is necessary to develop other hypotheses which make the first formulation untenable and it therefore needs revision. Either it is to be regarded as a metaphor only or it has a different application from the one at first supposed.

If we now again review the writings on the self, a good deal can be cleared up. It can be understood how it happens that Jung sometimes uses the abstract statement as a metaphor or mixes the two in one context. He slides from one level of expression to another. This easily makes for a confusion sometimes found in analytical psychology so that when, in the face of new data, revisions in theory have been made, metaphor gets used so as to blur theoretical contradictions. I consider that this confusion led Edinger (1960) to conclude that there is an essential paradox in the very nature of the relation between the ego and the self and that is not true.

It is commonly held that theoretical contradiction is no disadvantage when formulating ideas about the self, and that, if we want abstract concepts of it to reflect the affective experience, it is necessary to include the opposites in them. This is supposed to leave room for paradox – a false issue since the whole is not an opposite of its parts in any important sense. The point is as follows: since the self contains opposites, formulations about its contents can be stated paradoxically. The position is quite different when applied to theory in the present sense, for neither the totality theory nor the archetype concept refers to the contents of the self but to its place in the theoretical model of the psyche.

The Nature of the Self

Can a hypothesis be formulated closer to the experiences accumulated and capable of being tested by or used to organize them?

In discussing Jung's two definitions, I have related them to his experiences of "the absolute" and relative knowledge of the self as expressed in symbolic archetypal forms. These may be taken as symbols of the self when their characteristics suggest wholeness. It is arbitrary what number of characteristics must be there for an archetypal image to be called a symbol of the self and this can lead to confusion if a concise notation is required. There can be no doubt that Jung's work has been taken to mean that the self is essentially integrative – it draws the various functions of the personality together; that will be especially well illustrated when we consider individuation. That the archetypal self can paradoxically be destructive is suggested, for instance, in Jung's "Answer to Job" or in the Biblical metaphor: "it is a terrible thing to fall into the hands of God", but these considerations do not feature prominently: Integration is the main function of the self (the archetype of order).

In 1947 I put forward the idea that the self functioned not only integratively but that it could deintegrate, as a contribution to understanding the development of infants. I knew that I was introducing a revolutionary idea, but I had not thought that the conception might prove useful in elucidating the two ideas about the self considered here. In my thesis I postulated a primary state of integration expressed in the infant's individuality, continuity of being and adaptive capacity. The self integrate had no means through which it could come into relation with its environment so a process of deintegration was needed. The primary self had not developed the characteristics of consciousness nor was there anything that could be called unconscious for those characteristics do not arise until sufficient structure has developed.

A deintegrate of the self was assumed to carry with it characteristics of the original wholeness. How many depends on the variety of mental activities, the degree to which the dichotomy conscious–unconscious has developed the kind of ego structures that have come into being and the degree of differentiation between archetypal deintegrates in the unconscious that has taken place, i.e. how much there is differentiation between the shadow, animus–anima, old wise man etc.

The deintegrates develop symbolic and other forms by reason of their interaction with the environment which provides perceptual images. These images make a pool and some of them are used in the organism's adaptation to the external world, (ego activities) others to form inner symbolic images (the archetypal forms).

States of integration and deintegration can be observed objectively in behaviour or subjectively as feelings of good and bad, love and hate in object relations. Jung has paid particular attention to states of integration and has documented them sufficiently. Deintegration takes on many forms from which I will select the development of a dream, active imagination, instinctual behaviour, in children's play and in myths. The deintegration postulate is thus useful because it provides a bridge between wholeness and its expression in relatively formed archetypes referring to it. They can be observed as inner images and behaviour patterns.*

That formulation does not give an adequate account of the ego which, we are told in Jung's definition, is "embraced" and "included" in the self. It may be assumed that, like the archetypes, the ego is potential within the self. It is evident from observations of adult persons that each archetypal image of the self has ego content, otherwise it could not become conscious. This has happened because the archetypal functions have been disintegrated out of the self and structurals have been built up in the psyche. Looking at this developmentally: when some ego has formed it will be as a number of small nuclei the result of deintegration, which soon become linked together so that one can speak of a centre of consciousness as in Jung's writings. In that process the integrating function of the self plays an essential part. The main body of the ego, sometimes called the central ego, has a special relation to the archetype of the self. That central archetype can then be thought of an an organizer of the unconscious: it contributes significantly to the formation of the central ego in which it finds expression especially in conscious experiences of selfhood. In progressing from unknowing to knowing, it can be understood that the self has a powerful creative influence in the formation of mental structures whilst still remaining unknown and unknowable.

*Since writing this chapter I have had the opportunity of reading Redfearn's book *My Self, My Many Selves* (1985). In it he appears to study states of deintegration but considers that the notion of the total personality is hypothetical, a view contrasting with that of Jung, who took the step of removing the study of the self from speculative fields into that of experience. As a deintegrate is conceived to maintain its relation to the "total self", the comparison is not truly valid.

A feature of Redfearn's thesis is that he introduces a new terminology of "sub-personalities". This appears to aid the purpose of description. The process of active imagination was designed to objectify the non-ego parts of the self - also found in dreams - which expressed themselves in varying guises. Jung, however, wisely hesitated to call these elements of the self "personalities" on account of their mostly fragmentary nature (Jung, 1939b).

The most valuable part of Redfearn's essay is its descriptive content. He has published much clinical material from his patients, many of whom express psychotic characteristics or who have developed, presumably under his guidance, a number of "sub-personalities". Of special interest is his study of mandalas in relation to states of mind in his patients. The importance of so doing had not been fully developed by Jung and what Redfearn says is in line with my own observations in children. However, he does not consider the mandala as representing a container for bad objects (Fordham, 1957c, p. 136). There are also interesting speculations on the relation between states of consciousness and brain functioning.

It is beyond the scope of this book to enter into a critical estimation of Refearn's thesis, but I can not refrain from saying that he appears to be working in the area of the psychoses and dissociated schizoid personalities and that therefore the discovery of the self in individuation receives little consideration.

It is a matter of experience that all the archetypal images can express something of the wholeness of the organism; but the central archetype, with its clear relation to the central ego, expresses it best in that is transcends and unites opposites.

In this formulation, the central archetype, being a part system in the total self, can be introjected, projected, can assimilate other unconscious elements, identify with the ego, be the source of religious experience, the source of the central ego, and function mostly in the unconscious in a compensatory manner until it gets realized, i.e. largely integrated into the ego in individuation; indeed it would appear that there is not a characteristic or mechanism that Jung has not mentioned and which cannot be attributed to it without contradiction. At the same time, room is left for the personal life of the individual and his relation to the external world as a whole, within the self conceived of as the superordinate totality.

I conclude with a reflection on "the ultimate". I take it to represent a state in which there is no past and no future, though it is present like a point which has position by no magnitude. It has no desires, no memory, no thoughts, no images but out of it by transformation all of these can deintegrate. There is no consciousness and so no unconscious – it is a pregnant absence. I shall use this idea in later chapters especially that on countertransference, and must record my debt to Bion in this formulation, which no doubt is not what he would have meant precisely.

Chapter Two

*Individuation and ego development**

The Classical Concept

The concept of individuation has played a significant part in the history of dynamic psychology: it provided a basis for a psychology of maturity at a time when psychonanalysts were investigating its infantile components. As a sophisticated development the concept opened the way for the analysis of older people and defined a psychology of ongoing processes. In past decades analytical psychologists have been virtually alone pioneering in this field.

A root of Jung's concept is to be found in a letter to Dr Loy written in 1913. There he says: "The discovery of the value of human personality is reserved for a riper age" (1914a, p. 287). In *Psychological Types* (1921) he discusses and defines the meaning and symbolism of individuation alongside the problem of types, but it was first compactly defined when he wrote "The relations between the ego and the unconscious" (Jung, 1928b), which is still the best introduction to the subject. Later discussions of it will be found in *Psychology and Alchemy* (1944a), *Mysterium Coniunctionis* (1955–6), the "Psychology of the transference" (1946) and *Aion* (1951a). Several essays published between the major works give specific indications of the development in his thoughts on that subject.

By 1940 Jung had come to consider the process as a natural phenomenon: "If the process of individuation is an *empirical fact* [my italics], rather than a theory, one must expect the problem to have its history" (1940b, p. 282). In *The Integration of the Personality* he published two case studies, one of which, together with "The idea of redemption in alchemy" (1937a), formed the prototype of *Psychology and Alchemy* in which his historical study is started. The establishment of the process as an

*Originally published in *The Journal of Analytical Psychology* vol. 3, no. 2, 1958. It has been revised and expanded.

"empirical fact"* is important because it modifies the conception of it as an ideal which Jung has occasionally taken it to be and in no uncertain terms.

> . . . individuation is indispensable for certain people, not only as a therapeutic necessity, but as a high ideal, an idea of the best we can do. Nor should I omit to remark that it is at the same time the primitive Christian ideal of the Kingdom of Heaven which "is within you". The idea at the bottom of this ideal is that right action comes from right thinking, and that there is no cure and no improving of the world that does not begin with the individual himself. (1944a, pp. 225f).

Certainly images of the self appear in idealized form and it is probable that the collapse of the idealized self image is at the root of the depression and tendency to dissociation which Jung describes as characteristic of his patients for whom individuation is a "therapeutic necessity" and in whom this difficult spiritual development can be observed to occur.

The grounds for the conception began with clinical studies. Jung found that after the "personal unconscious" has been investigated, and also the ego defences, a change begins to occur. It becomes increasingly realized that the personality is not controllable by the conscious mind, which is only part and not even the centre of an inner psychic reality. At first this fact is only vaguely appreciated by the ego, which yet, slowly, gives up its illusions of dominance. As that happens the archetypal images, laden with effect, come more and more into the field of consciousness; if the ego relates to these adequately, a development begins and progresses in a fairly regular way, which can be described in terms of a sequence culminating in the emergence of self symbols, considered in Chapter 1.

The process is "circumambulation". That means that the images do not represent the self directly and all at once, rather they do so gradually by showing different aspects of it: they move round it in spiral fashion as Jung showed in some detail when discussing the image of the "World Clock" (*vide* p. 13). However, to consider individuation in terms of an inner sequence of images, as is sometimes done, is to look at only one aspect of the process, and indeed creates a false impression: it takes the ego insufficiently into account and it appears to exclude individual differences.

The subject of the ego will be considered more extensively later, but I wish to comment here that Jung's cases seemed to suffer from ego omnipotence which he, with some justification, identifies with a cultural style at the present time. Whether it is quite as widespread as he contends may be doubted but it would follow, according to his view, from the

*I have not been able to trace this statement in the revised version of Jung's article but the sense of it remains (cf. Jung, 1939b).

relative collapse of religious practices which do so much to contain unconscious archetypal processes. Once belief is lost, there is no place for their containment; they then threaten ego consciousness which defensively comes to assume omnipotence. Jung frequently attacks the unwarranted assumption that the ego has or should have complete control over the whole psyche, indeed, for individuation to start, it is necessary for the ego to become disabused of its illusion and submit to the action of the previously unconscious inner world.

The intense concentration on inner imagery and the focussing on the unconscious fantasies as they emerge can lead to the belief that the individual becomes isolated from the society in which he lives. That was not Jung's view when he says:

> As the individual is not just a single separate being but, by his very existence, presupposes a collective relationship, it follows that the process of individuation must lead to more intense and broader collective relationship, not to *isolation*. (1921, p. 448).

Nonetheless, when describing his own experience in *Memories, Dreams, Reflections*, Jung (1963) tells us that his inner experiences did lead him to a feeling of isolation which only began to break down when he made a relationship with Richard Wilhelm and began to study the *Secret of the Golden Flower*. It is therefore significant that in the "Psychology of the transference"* he laid such emphasis on the transference, for in it another person – an analytic therapist – can participate in the individuation process. Then the archetypal images can be experienced in relation to another person and amplified or interpreted as occasion arises. Thus, hopefully, a persistent sense of isolation never need arise and the rather excessive emphasis on the transpersonal and objective nature of the process may be modified. The personal reference of many if not all archetypal processes is important for the full understanding of the personality but it seems to be played down by Jung. It may be reflected that Jung, being a pioneer, had no analyst to share his experience and presumably wanted to spare his patients that painful state.

A further quotation from Jung's writings clarifies his position:

> . . . individuation is the process by which individual beings are formed and differentiated. In particular, it is the development of the psychological *individual* (q.v.) as being distinct from the general, collective psychology. Individuation, therefore is a process of *differentiation* (q.v.) having for its goal the development of the individual personality. (Jung, 1921, p. 448).

*Jung's emphasis on the importance of transference varied considerably in the course of time (see Fordham, 1974a).

It will be apparent by now that introversion only depicts an aspect of a process which, in reality, involves the whole personality. Therefore the ego must find more place than would seem to be indicated by a phrase like giving up its central role.

In an inner sense the significance of the ego may be indicated by the importance given to it in active imagination: it is the activity of the ego which decides whether the imagination is active or passive. It may initiate the process and then go along with the unconscious activity helping to shape the images by painting, sculpting or play. It was by the latter method that Jung initiated his "confrontation with the unconscious". He took stones and made a whole village and a church with a special red stone for an altar. When that was in place he felt particularly satisfied: he had found it by chance and it reminded him of an impressive dream from his childhood depicting an underground phallus. These play activities continued for a considerable time: they gave rise to a flow of fantasy which he carefully wrote down. Later he painted or sculpted some of them.

In all these activities his ego was actively involved; that, he thought, was the essential component of active imagination. The subject or ego could let the fantasies go on and remain passive, doing nothing about the imaginary events. That was not active imagination: in it the ego must take steps i.e. become active in any way that seemed possible, treating the images as though they were a special kind of reality.

The process of relaxing control is not easy and is evidently only relative as the following passage shows:

> Conscious and unconscious do not make a whole when one of them is suppressed or injured by the other. If they must contend, let it at least be a fair fight with equal right on both sides. Both are aspects of life. Consciousness should defend its reason and protect itself and the chaotic life of the unconscious should be given the chance of having its own way too – as much of it as we can stand. This means open conflict and open collaboration . . . It is the old game of hammer and anvil: between them the patient iron is forged into an unbreakable whole, an "individual".
>
> This roughly is what I mean by the individuation process (Jung, 1939b, p. 288).

Jung here describes a development in persons with a well-established ego. Indeed he has underlined the importance of it on numerous occasions where individuation is conceived of as an introverted development in mature people in the second half of life. Although examples of the imagery have been observed in younger people, it is only after a considerable consciousness and experience of life has been achieved that, in the classical view, the development can take place.

It might be held that time and libido are not available for intensive introversion in the first half of life when, at least in our society, the main interest is directed to practical considerations, but the more cogent argument is that the process in significant respects has a personal and historical aspect.

There is a natural tendency for older people to become increasingly philosophic and less affected by the problems and anxieties that beset the young – they become wise. Some of them develop a philosophy of life founded in a well-organized and differentiated attitude towards the inner and outer worlds. For such a dynamic structure to be differentiated and stable, a considerable experience of life is a necessity, otherwise a closed system is liable to develop which cannot assimilate and modify or even dissolve and rebuild itself in the face of new experience. A philosophy of life, in this plastic sense, is impersonal and is amongst the manifestations of individuation. It is said to come about because there lie centuries of historical development behind it: So individuation is not to be conceived of as only the culmination of the individual's personal history.

This conclusion was arrived at because of the sometimes overt, sometimes scarcely concealed primitiveness of the material produced both by Jung himself and his patients. To understand that primitiveness Jung found it valuable, if not essential, to study the history of symbolism in detail. With the aid of that knowledge he could become orientated in the mass of material that seemed to arise from another century rather than the patients' personal relationships. Because of these observations the imagery was said to be objective and transpersonal.

Amongst these studies alchemy became of special importance to Jung – it fascinated him and the results of his researches filled the major part of his later writings. It is clear that he came to regard its extraordinary products as a precursor of individuation. I shall give an example of how an alchemist worked and the "practical" and visionary nature of alchemy in Part 2 chapter 3, so in the present chapter I will only sketch some of its more general features as Jung organized them in so far as I have understood what he says: he is not always consistent whilst the complexity of the symbolism and the odd terminology used by the alchemists makes for other difficulties in comprehension.

Jung's idea is as follows: the alchemists projected their unconscious processes into their chemical experiments and this resulted in a peculiar mixture of chemistry and symbolic imagery. It is probable that its "incomprehensibility" is partly due to this confusion but also to the individual nature of its products; though there was an extensive alchemical literature, alchemists tended to work on their own and try to express their own unique findings.

There were two kinds of alchemist – those who believed that the aim of their work was chemical, i.e. they held that the philosophers stone – gold – could really be produced by laboratory work, and others who were more philosophically minded. Amongst the "philosophers" Jung thought that Dorn, a pupil of Paracelsus, came nearest to understanding the psychological nature of what he was doing.

The "philosophic" alchemists thought that the soul is related on one hand to the body which it fills with desirousness, evil in nature, and on the other to the spirit. When it is bound to the body, it fills it with cravings and forms the *unus mundus* which corresponds to the state of primary identity in which there was a unity of man with his environmental cosmos. The first part of the alchemical work was to extract the soul from the body (the alchemists equated the human body with chemical substances - one source of confusion). This process would correspond with the analysis of the shadow.

The second part of the work led to the union of the soul with the spirit, leading to the *unio mentalis* in which the soul ascends to the *coelum* (analogous to heaven), which had long been divided from the earth in the creation. This meant death of the now purified body (equated with ashes in the alchemical vessel). For some reason Jung, in the *Mysterium Coniunctionis* (1955–6), relates this to individuation. It is an idea that I find surprising and is not followed by him in other places (e.g. "Psychology of the transference" (1946)). It cannot be correct because it involves a split between body and spirit. However, it might be part of the individuation process in that during the work two aspects of man become conscious, his libidinal nature on one hand and his ethical moral and spiritual nature on the other.

The third part of the alchemical work consists in reuniting and vivifying the ashes of the dead body, and for this purpose a complex mixture has to be prepared composed of a large number of substances having, according to Jung, symbolic significance. One such mixture is as follows: "honey, Cheldonia of the Rosemary flowers, Mercurialis of the red lily and human blood" etc. (Jung, 1955–6, pp. 479f).

The result of combining the *coelum* and the ashes or earth and so the spirit with the soul and the body was expressed symbolically. An example of this symbol is given by Jung in "Psychology of the transference"; it is called the Rebis and is a monstrous figure combining spiritual and cthonic forms. It is meant to achieve the wholeness which the alchemists sought to achieve (but never did so) within their frame of reference.

Jung relates this work with a historical argument about the Anthropos, the god in matter, who was left behind in the underworld, the earth, when the Christian development took place symbolized by Christ's ascent into heaven. The split in the psyche which that involved, between spirit and body, good and evil, was consolidated with the aim of achieving perfection. The alchemists were involved in attempting to heal the division by combining spirit and earth, good and evil, and so aiming at a paradoxical completeness - that is the aim of individuation.

To recapitulate: individuation is a development resulting in growing consciousness of the self; it begins in the second half of life and continues through it. A considerable degree of ego maturity is required for it to begin and, once started, it leads to a development in consciousness and the formation of an individual attitude to life giving increasing moral autonomy and a sustained transpersonal attitude to the inner and outer worlds based on the symbolic experience of the self.

The Extended Concept

The above view of the matter represents, with some minor modifications, what I conceive to be the main trends in Jung's argument. The case in *Psychology and Alchemy* (1944a) is that of a young scientist and must consequently be taken as an exception, for in "The stages of life" (1930–1), "The development of the personality" (1934), and, it may be added, in many of his essays on psychotherapy, he underlines the importance of the varying aims of life in different age groups.

At the end of his definition in *Psychological Types*, however, Jung includes the following paragraph:

> Individuation is practically the same as the development of consciousness out of the original *state of identity*. It is thus an extension of the sphere of consciousness, an enriching of the conscious psychological life (Jung, 1921, pp. 449–50).

Definition 25 on "Identity" states:

> It is characteristic of the primitive mentality, and is the real foundation of *participation mystique* which is nothing but a relic of the original non-differentiation of subject and object and hence of the primordial unconscious state. It is also a characteristic of early infancy and finally is characteristic of the unconscious of the civilised adult, which, in so far as it has not become a content of consciousness, remains in a permanent state of identity with objects (ibid., p. 441).

Although Jung has clearly established that individuation can be observed as the enriching of consciousness in the second half of life, yet the combination of these definitions might easily lead the reader to deduce that he believed it began in infancy. It would follow that the "exception" is no exception at all.

In spite of his insistence on the clear need for children to adapt themselves to the requirements of society, with which everybody agrees, even though the often implied sacrifice of the inner world to this end is dubious, there are many passages in Jung's works which could give rise to a wider interpretation of individuation. And when we read that it "leads to a more intensive collective relationship", this would make it seem as if there were no theoretical difficulties in taking individuation, i.e. realization of the self, as the aim of a whole life. The aim of the first half of life might then be thought of in a new sense as somehow contributing to the ultimate conscious appreciation of psychic totality.

Perry, though he seems recently to have withdrawn from his earlier position, asserts:

> This drive toward individuation is apparently a spontaneous urge, *not under the leadership of the ego, but of the archetypal movement in the unconscious* [my italics], the non-ego, toward the fulfilment of the specific basic pattern of the individual, striving toward wholeness, totality, and the differentiation of the specific potentialities that are innately destined to form the particular personality in question. The unconscious is the matrix out of which these various qualities arise step by step toward differentiation in consciousness, which they approach first in symbolic guise until the ego learns to understand and incorporate them. In this unconscious matrix, then, the pattern of the wholeness of the personality lies hidden awaiting the hand of experience to stir it into activity; it is not an ego ideal formed by upbringing, but a dynamic urge emanating from the core of one's being, laden with affect and presenting itself to consciousness in terms of the archetypal symbols (Perry, 1953, p. 45.)

It will be noticed that Perry here implies an innate teleological process, starting from the unconscious.

In *The Mythology of the Soul* Baynes (1955) also links individuation up with instinct psychology, and he has related it to the physical tendency in animals towards completeness, but elsewhere he follows Jung, saying that the process employs an introverted symbolism and leads to the surrender of the ego to the self.

The concept of the process as instinctive is also expressed by Esther Harding, who believes it to be "the instinct of self-preservation on a higher plane" (Harding, 1947).*

Criticism of the Extended Thesis

If current views of instinct be accepted, the notion that individuation is an instinct is antiquated. The loose use of the term instinct makes any criticism almost impossible because of the variety of different meanings given to the word.

The formulations, to which reference has been made above, may be compressed into the statement that individuation is an innate teleological tendency originating in the unconscious. The ego plays a subsidiary part in it by becoming aware of the processes as they emerge and by

*This usage has no advantage. Indeed, in cutting across trends in biological thinking, it gives an antiquated air to the thinking of analytical psychologists and tends to get their theories dismissed out of hand (cf. Fordham, 1974a).

integrating a number of ill-defined elements into its structure. It is here that lies the main difference from the classical concept in which the ego is conceived of as taking a major part in the whole development.

Baynes's parallel with the tendency of organisms to repair damage or even to replace lost organs must be taken not as a one to one correspondence with individuation, but in the nature of an analogy, and as such it refers to the synthetic function of the self; it is at variance with his acceptance of the place which the ego, defined as the centre of consciousness, takes in the whole procedure.

In introducing a teleological view it needs to be remembered that biologists had a hard struggle to get away from the sterilizing influence of this view in their own sphere. Jung, possibly realizing this, found it necessary to point out in a footnote that his final energic concept did not imply teleology, and he devoted a large part of one essay (1940b) to questioning the existence of anything like a personality in the unconscious, which is implied in the emphasis given to the innate concept of individuation. The extended conception would indeed appear to necessitate a regression to rather old-fashioned teleology. If the end is pre-ordained in the unconscious, it is difficult to see how either of these postulates could be established. They imply a prediction that cannot be tested.

Unconscious aims are recognized as an essential feature of instinctive life (cf. Fordham, 1957b) whose manifestations can be extended in range by various means, of which the interaction between the conscious and the instincts in the unconscious is one. When this happens the rigidity of the instinctual aim becomes modified and transformed in ways that diminish rather than increase the predictability of its manifestations. Indeed the range of possible solutions to any particular problem progressively increases. Thus any specific inherited pattern which is conceived to unfold is subject to unpredictable modification.*

A further serious difficulty in accepting the extended thesis in the terms presented by these authors is the clinical material instanced to support it. All analytical psychologists who have sought to extend the concept, Baynes and Perry† among them, rely upon adult case material, much

*In this connection it is germane to note the relevance of synchronicity, defined as meaningful coincidence even though a separate chapter will be devoted to that subject later in Part 2. The phenomena embraced under this heading are intimately related to the archetypes in the unconscious and so indicate the nature of unconscious processes. The attribute of meaning does not carry with it the concept of purpose; on the contrary, a meaningful coincidence is much more like a chance event, even though the idea of synchronicity involves a radical criticism of the ubiquity of the chance–cause pair of opposites. If this scientific conception is criticized, so also is the notion of an unconscious purposive drive to individuation.

†Baynes and Perry have both made a special study of psychotic processes. Like Jung (especially 1914) they both found that archetypal forms appeared in it. Perry evidently felt himself in a difficult theoretical position. Indeed in his essay "Acute catatonic schizophrenia" (Perry, 1957), he modified

of it pathological. But whether it may be relatively normal or highly pathological, it always shows evidence of a developed ego, a repressed personal unconscious, and all their patients show considerable ability in forming complex archetypal images, analogous to mythology. These organized forms do not exist at birth, or for several years after it. On the basis of this material they agree, following Jung, that in individuation the ego gives way to the self, which becomes a "new centre of the personality". But what of infants and children, who must inevitably be given some status on the thesis that the process is innate? In their case the ego is said to develop away from the self, for the wholeness of the self is, even *in utero*, dangerous to them for reasons which are the exact inverse of those found in adults (Fordham, 1957a). In all this, little or no recognition is given to modern researches into the early stages of ego development in infants, in whom sophisticated imagery cannot in any case be found: it is obvious that no infant could ever have painted the pictures so far published as manifesting the individuation process. This subject is further bedevilled by the tendency so often found in the writings of analytical psychologists about infancy to fit in with crude and often superseded theories. One of them is that the child (meaning infant) is undubitably part of the mother's psyche from birth onwards. This idea, which played a useful part in the history of child psychology, overlooks that the infant is primarily separate from his mother and has to go through a long process of getting to know her as she has to get to know him.

In this process mutual identity between mother and infant may help an understanding state of close intimacy between the couple. However, identity must be distinguished from identification, a more complex process which occurs later.

The extended thesis does have some justification in that it attempts to account for the manifestation of archetypal images, including those referring to the self, in a more simple form in children and young adults. These facts need to be met and have led to modification of the classical concept of individuation; the facts are agreed, their interpretation is questionable, and an alternative is to conceive of the images as integrative elements superordinate to the ego. They may operate in part consciously

his earlier view as follows: "In acute schizophrenia the central and most dynamic issue, I feel, concerns the self-image; this refers to two interrelated systems, the ego's severely damaged view of itself, and the ego's root archetype, the self, which tends to compensate this debasement with an exalted play of fantasy imagery full of its lost potential. Since I use the term self-image regularly in discussing the problem, I wish to avoid confusion of terms and call the former the *personal self-image* and the latter the *central archetype*; this archetype is here conceived as making its appearance at all phases of life and in all kinds of states of integration and disintegration, and thus is not always associated with the conscious experience of selfhood, in the sense of being an achievement requiring that long and arduous work of spiritual or psychological development specifically designated by Jung as the individuation process" (Perry, 1957, p. 137).

but can do so unconsciously, sometimes supporting, but also threatening, the integrative power of the ego.

Without doubt the observations complicate the whole problem, but they do not undermine the classical conception so long as we adhere to the crucial importance of the ego and keep clearly in mind that the study of non-ego integrative processes does not necessarily indicate individuation, and indeed can indicate the reverse for instance in the psychoses.

To solve the theoretical problem set by the discovery of archetypal images, including the self, in all stages of life, it has been necessary to discuss early ego development. This I have undertaken in an exploratory way in two books, *Children as Individuals* (1969) and *The Self and Autism* (1976). Following those essays I began to study mothers and infants in more detail.

In the original version of this chapter, I argued that because of the differences between the relation of the ego to the self in childhood and later life, individuation did not take place in childhood and that therefore one should adhere to the classical conception of it.

Since then I have changed my position because of developments in knowledge of infants and children. For instance, it has become established beyond question that an infant's perceptual capacities are far more developed than was previously thought possible and consequently he is not just an unconscious person. Indeed, at first the distinction between conscious and unconscious does not apply, so that it may be that there is no boundary between the two. That develops and then there can be the "open conflict and open collaboration", which Jung underlines, between the two. Largely as a result of this the child's individuality asserts itself, and ego growth can be observed.

On these grounds, and others as well, I stated in 1968:

> By the age of two . . . an infant can achieve every essential element in individuation in the sense that Jung would have accepted it. I say this advisedly, although he studied a different age group and therefore represented it very differently (Fordham, 1976, p. 40).

Individuation as a Special Case of Ego Development

Jung frequently stresses the importance of distinguishing the ego from the archetypal images, particularly when active imagination is employed. But this sharp distinction is not always relevant and indeed is only desirable under particular conditions which can be defined as follows:

(1) When a philosophical illusion dominates the scene stating that man's psyche is identical with his consciousness, i.e. when the ego is idealized.
(2) When any radical new development is indicated.

This second proposition is a corollary to the thesis that in infancy the archetypal forms are derived from the self through its deintegration; the deintegrates lead to the emergence of ego nuclei which are later drawn together through the integrative action of the self to form an ego centrum. It would seem that the rhythmic processes of integration and deintegration can be seen reflected in different age groups and in myths, and so repeat through life and have general significance. In my original paper (Fordham, 1955) analogies to the theory were drawn from Oriental religions and alchemy, both of which contained further material which it would not be in place to discuss here. I would, however, like to refer the reader to Taoism, in which the twin rhythm which I postulated seems to be part of the central formulations of that mystical philosophy.

If any development is initiated in the self, after the ego is established, its own deintegration is the first step. There is a danger here that the ego may be disintegrated catastrophically in the process of its boundaries with the deintegrates, the dynamic archetypal images, are not distinguished. However, if the boundaries of the ego are clearly defined, the opposition conscious–unconscious is set up, and the ego, in relating to the archetypal forms, is then in a position either to stabilize or to extend and modify its boundaries by incorporating previously unconscious contents.

When Jung (1954b, p. 202) states that he had "observed patients whose dreams pointed to a rich store of fantasy material without . . . their being able to tell me just where the inner pressure lay", he refers, on the present thesis, to the ego's becoming aware of the deintegrating self. Accordingly Jung sets the patient "the task of elaborating or developing his theme by giving free rein to his fantasy", and this leads to the "open conflict and open collaboration" defined earlier in this essay. Jung's technique assists the ego in defining its boundaries and puts it in a position to collaborate with the self in its "need" to become more conscious via the deintegrates – the archetypal forms.

Individuation and Ego Development

From these considerations it becomes possible that individuation in later life is a special case of ego development. But that is not usually stated so, probably because it involves a change in the established concept of the ego and its developmental capacity; further, it requires a distinction between the integrative activity of the self and individuation. It would follow that as the integration of unconscious contents proceeds, particularly that of the shadow, the ego must not only cease once and for all to be only the centre of consciousness, but it must also be as much an unconscious as a conscious function. It would appear, indeed, that the ego necessarily becomes more and more like the self in being a paradoxical entity; the concept of the self as the archetype of the ego, which is seeping into analytical psychology from various sources, is therefore particularly intriguing. Jung himself appears to arrive at such a conclusion in the *Mysterium Coniunctionis*. In discussing the symbolism of the king who is at the same time the sun ("King-Helios of post-classical syncretism"), he seems to exalt the ego which becomes "the most glorious and most divine of all the phenomena of creation" which he can call an archetype ("the one amongst the archetypes of the unconscious" (Jung, 1955–6, p. 357). Furthermore, he reflects on the paradox of the ego assimilating the unconscious for that is what the process of individuation implies and clearly indicates that the ego becomes more and more like the self. It is also relevant to my discussion that he tentatively concedes that "the unconscious complexes possess a kind of luminosity, a kind of consciousness" (ibid., p. 358), surely an heir to his earlier distinction between two kinds of thinking.

If consciousness becomes only an aspect of the ego, but not its totality, it would necessarily be conceived of as a surface phenomenon linked up and organized into a greater synthesis; further the ego and so consciousness could not be demarcated off from the unconscious as heretofore. The result is at once an extension and a limitation of consciousness, which can now rely on more ready access to the unconscious aspects of the ego. Further, the sharp distinction between the ego on one hand and the shadow and anima (or animus) on the other can no longer be maintained, even though the aspects of the totality represented by them remain essentially incapable of assimilation by the ego. All this depends upon realizing the ultimate nature of the self; it can only be experienced as the symbolic image of the indefinable archetypal totality. The whole can never be known because there is no subject to know it, nor any subject to perceive it.

Historical Considerations

Historical evidence can be used by analytical psychologists in two ways: first it can be scrutinized for archetypal manifestations, secondly it can be investigated to understand how consciousness develops. These two ways of using historical material can naturally be combined in varying degrees.

In *Aion* Jung (1951a) studied the manifestations of the self in early Christianity, gnosticism, astrology and alchemy, in the main with a view to shedding light on its structure and dynamics; he used history chiefly in the first way. In "Answer to Job" he laid more emphasis on the historical process as a development of consciousness, using as his starting point the conflict between Job and Yahweh, next considering how this could have led to the birth of Jesus, tracing the consequences through early Christianity, and leading up in modern times to the Assumption of the Virgin. He ends with the assertion that the main contemporary problem is the assimilation of evil into the image of the self, from which it had been removed during the development of Christianity: the dark side of God being split off and represented in the devil. The study of archetypal forms in history leads to the idea that as man becomes more conscious, at least as Western history seems to portray it, the idea and experience of God becomes progressively less metaphysical and more psychological. A progressive introjection of the archetypal forms occurs, so that what was only metaphysical becomes, in the course of time, increasingly psychic. Thus the need for the concepts of an objective psyche and of the self becomes apparent, and realization of the self becomes a contemporary issue to be manifested in the life of each individual person. The individual sometimes seems to become more interesting in his totality as a manifestation of a historical process which gives increasing importance to the self. From this essentially social point of view individuation as a concept can be used in an apparently broader sense than if each individual life is the focus of attention, and it is overlooked that history is based on a collection of records of adult activities alone; children are not considered.

Thus individuation is conceived of as a historical and evolutionary process. Biological research leads to the concept that all evolution within historical times is the consequence of nurture; heredity plays little direct part in it. Therefore, if the symbolic realization of the self in consciousness is the problem of our era, it would seem inevitable that it can only be grasped by mature persons who have acquired sufficient accumulated knowledge. The acquired conscious mind is then used to bring the self symbols into consciousness. The highly dynamic nature of this event depends upon the reaction of the unconscious to what is primarily an ego activity.

The view of individuation as an extension of the ego is the only possible one on evolutionary theory, which could not support the idea of individuation as an innate process, let alone an instinct. Here the question arises of how far children participate in or are influenced by this process. If children sense by empathy changes in the outlook of the times, they can only realize new ones when their conscious mind is sufficiently developed and educated. No innovation of general significance has ever been made by a child. Though he can be conscious of symbolic images of the self, he cannot realize their implications; though he may participate in the general trend towards its symbolic realization, he is still dependent upon his parents and his own maturation for giving him the instruments with which to give it an individual form of expression in his life.

The historical view, which we may reiterate is based on records of the activities of adult persons alone, can therefore only support Jung's original thesis from which we began: "The discovery of the value of human personality belongs to a riper age".

The Personal and Collective Unconscious

The concept of individuation that I am presenting requires me to reflect on Jung's distinction between the personal and the collective unconscious. We have seen that Jung plays down the importance of personal elements in both the self and the process of individuation, yet individuation in childhood leads to the progressive definition and more realistic appreciation of personal relationships. These changes are related to archetypal activity and its symbolization.

It was Jung who first opened up the "inner world" upon which Freud only touched. That "inner world" became enormously important to Jung both personally and scientifically and so he needed to demarcate his position from that of psychoanalysis. As part of that process he defined Freud's investigation as belonging to the personal sphere which covered all the person's life experience from childhood to maturity. Hence the term "personal" took on a special meaning and he designed it to contrast personal experience with that of the archetypal images whose nature was impersonal or transpersonal, ruthless and collective. It was both his experience and his theory that lead him to investigate them in their social and historical settings.

His was always a rough distinction, for not all life experiences in any age group are just personal or just collective and, furthermore, many personal experiences are related to the archetypal forms as Mary Williams (1963a) observed. It is now known that in childhood the archetypal images can be found from time to time and it is probable that they begin to form in the very earliest weeks or months of infancy. That might lead to the conclusion that an infant is impersonal and so incapable of appreciating his mother as a person.

It is indeed possible to conceive that an infant's experience is characterized by impersonal and ruthless part object relations, and that he progresses to appreciate his mother as a person (whole object) as his development proceeds. However, there is evidence that he adapts himself to his mother's physical and emotional life as a whole, i.e. he adapts himself to her as a person from the start. It appears for instance that babies can spare their mothers in the sense that they withhold their aggressive libidinal attacks on the breast when a mother is unable for various reasons to adapt herself to such attacks. Thus, almost from birth, they seem to create conditions for a good feeding experience. Some also to have a capacity, by giving remarkably precise signals, almost to show a hesitant mother how to establish a good feeding relationship by supporting and drawing out the capacities of a mother uncertain of her mothering functions. I regard such actions as actions of the self and not the ego adapting the infant to the conditions, physical and emotional, in which he finds himself. Is it going too far to state that a baby is, in the sense of self, acutely personal from the start and later on develops a non-personal relation to objects needed for ego development?

Such reasoning makes one more and more doubtful whether Jung's distinction, useful for opening up the inner world of man, is any longer helpful as a general proposition.

In *Children as Individuals* (Fordham, 1969), I discussed the relation of a child to the collective unconscious. Inasmuch as an infant self uses archetypal deintegrates in his adaptation to his mothering environment and develops the dichotomy conscious–unconscious, his ego may be said to come into relation with the collective unconscious expressed in pre-personal part objects. They may be located outside the infant self through reality perceptions or the action of projective identification and inside himself through introjective identification. But most of the dynamic images of the collective unconscious are far more complex structures than anything an infant can know. Furthermore, since Jung's frame of reference is historical and social, it does not seem that, in spite of the occasional visions of small children, the collective unconscious in its sophistic sense becomes a significant element in a child's life until his psychic structures have developed sufficiently for him to become related to the wider society outside his family.

Chapter Three

Integration–deintegration in infancy

Having postulated that individuation is a continuous process throughout life, the study of the self in infancy grows in importance: real infancy becomes a central focus of study.

I have developed that thesis in two books, *Children as Individuals* and *The Self and Autism*. I drew not on Jung's data but on abstraction from them and concluded that, although the manifestations in the two states of mind were vastly different, the basic process of individuation was the same. That position has had to be modified somewhat by the force of experience and especially the observations of mothers and infants. My propositions developed as follows:

(1) I started by finding symbols of the self in small children's play and fantasy. They appeared to be related to growth of the ego, i.e. individuation.
(2) Those observations lead to speculating about how early the self could be active. I postulated that it was primary, meaning thereby that an infant could be considered as starting from being integrated – a person distinct from his mother.
(3) It followed that, in order to come into relation with its environment, deintegration must occur. Deintegration could be witnessed during a feed and integration in sleep. Since that sequence repeated, sequences of deintegration–integration could be considered.
(4) According to current views, deintegration leads to primitive identity. Then, as growth proceeds and ego development takes place, an infant emerges out of the primitive state in the way that Jung held took place in the second half of life.

Application to Infancy

As part of the training in child analysis at the Society of Analytical Psychology, I initiated, with the help of Gianna Henry from the Tavistock

Clinic, mother–infant observation studies and seminars. The students made observations each week starting from as soon after birth as possible and continuing for two years. They reported their findings at weekly seminars which I attended and could listen to material presented. I am indebted both to the students and Mrs Henry for the material I shall use and I wish to express my gratitude to them. From their reports and discussions I discovered that my hypothesis facilitated observations. But more than that the postulate of the infant self changed to something like a description of the facts of an infant's life; what started as a speculative hypothesis acquired characteristics of a fact: the baby shows that he is a person whose nature is consistently recognizable (continuity of being), having an individuality of his own (no baby is the same as any other).

When applying the idea of deintegration to infancy it was primarily to conceive a process whereby the integrated infant, at first separate from his mother, could come into relation with her.

Observation

Here is an observation made when a baby was two weeks old. (I am indebted to Ann Brown for this account).

> Baby N was lying in his bassinet on his right side with his right arm tucked under his body and his left arm bent up so his hand was near his face. His head with its soft covering of jet black hair was touching the top of the bassinet and F [his mother] said he had wriggled his way right to the top of this [bassinet]. His eyes were open and he was moving the whole of his body slightly as if a little restless (he seemed neither awake nor asleep). F said he was probably hungry as it was near feeding time. N then suddenly quietened and for several minutes he lay absolutely still with his black eyes staring at the bassinet.

There follows a period when the observation of the baby was interrupted by F's account of the birth and how good it had been. N was her "Christmas baby". The observation continues:

> F picked up N and gave him to me [the observer]. N lay in my arms looking intently in my face and often opening his mouth and making noises. I [the observer] talked to him and he responded by fixedly looking in my face. Several times he looked as though he was trying to smile and finally he gave me a slight smile in response to my talking. Then he looked away as if exploring the room and when I spoke he turned his head back to me looking in the vicinity of my face but not able to immediately focus directly.
>
> I continued to hold N while F drank her coffee. She talked to N gently and lovingly, smiling a great deal at him and saying she couldn't believe he was really here. Then she took the baby and put him to her right breast to feed. It took a few attempts for N to get the nipple properly in his mouth but he then sucked loudly and greedily and hiccoughed. . . . [N] sucked vigorously occasionally stopping for a rest. At

first his eyes were wide open but after a couple of minutes they shut while he continued to suck. . . . F put him to her left breast and he sucked vigorously with lots of little grunts looking intently upwards. I thought he was trying to see her face but F said he was looking at her red jumper. He then fell asleep and stopped sucking.'

I have extracted this description from many of the interchanges between mother and baby, all of which are full of interest. In this one it is, I think, possible to get a glimpse into what intrauterine life may have been like (when he was in the bassinet) and the rather beautiful relation that had developed between this mother and her baby which is shown repeatedly in the early observations of breast feeding. Over all there is a development that starts from an inner stirring in the baby, facilitated by F and the observer which centres on the feed. When the baby has enjoyably fed enough he goes to sleep. It is just how I would have envisaged a deintegrative–integrative sequence.

I will illustrate the importance of self theory to behaviour of the baby I have described by comparing it with other views. There are those who would want to see how far the behaviour could be understood in terms of reflexes (Piaget), innate release mechanisms (Bowlby) or want to start looking for evidence of conditioned reflexes (numerous). It is more than doubtful whether any of these mechanisms, in their simple conceptual forms, operate in infancy at all because they are integrated into the whole nervous system. But let us acknowledge that these postulates are legitimate methods of study. All of them would be regarded from the point of view of self theory as identifying instruments of the self. It is just conceivable to think of the smiling response as a reflex but ordinary observation indicates that it is part of the baby's aim to endear himself to his mother. Similarly the baby's looking is active and is part of his exploration of his new environment.

By stretching the notion of innate release mechanism it could cover the activity that comes from within leading to N's waking up and feeding, but it is much easier to understand the restlessness as a signal to his mother that he is hungry as his mother divines.

I am in agreement with those (e.g. Bowlby, 1969) who want to bring our thinking into line with biological concepts. The one I choose is adaptation. That word remains a good one even though it has been debased into a sort of mechanical acquiescence with environmental realities. In its best sense it is much more than that and includes all that is involved in bringing influence to bear on reality and mastering it as part of the struggle for existence. In this sense a baby is born with capacities for adaptation from the start: the sequence that we have looked at is basic and can be built on and developed.

In the past my proposition had been prevented by the idea that a baby's perceptual apparatuses are very limited or vague, so one of the revolutionary advances in recent years has been the discovery that many of a baby's perceptual capacities are well developed: he can see accurately and hear discriminately. But there is more in that if we dare to trust our observations and make inferences from them. If mothers and babies are carefully observed, it seems that both have the capacity to know what the other is like as a whole. We know that infants are endowed with behaviours aiming at attaching themselves to their mothers. However, more recently it has become evident that they also behave so as to endear their mothers to them and have a large number of signals available for indicating their needs; amongst them are smiling, looking, crying, grumbling, nestling etc. A more astonishing capacity is that they appear to know about their mother's emotional capacities. In the mother–infant seminars, the observations of N compelled its members to think of him as a "sparing" baby: his mother had a very low tolerance for aggression and her inner resources were limited. Baby N seemed to know just that and how, at a very early stage, to get the best out of her by sparing her any aggressive attacks on the breast or undue screaming etc. Baby N was not unique and I would like to mention another baby whose mother was very uncertain as to her capacities as a mother. Her baby gave her such clear signs of what he needed that by following them she discovered what was in her and so she literally became a "good enough mother" under her baby's direction. It seemed that the baby had only to be near the breast for him to find his way to it and feed in a comfortable manner: if the mother followed his signals she got it right. Of course there are other babies that are not at all helpful and will only take the breast with difficulty or even reject it outright.

Why do I think the theory of deintegration gives meaning to such observations? The other theories do not include the responses of the whole organism. It is true that Freud introduced the very evocative notion of the amoeba which put out pseudopodia to indicate the action sometimes of the id, sometimes of the ego, but he did not think of the energy coming out of the self. That he did not do so is probably due to his analytic train of mind. The concept of the self is essentially pre- or post-analysis. It is the kind of concept which would have been anathematized in biology and physiology when I was at Cambridge as a student, for it stood in the way of the application of physics and chemistry in the development of those sciences. That we have discarded or rather relativized that kind of reasoning for psychology is I hope sufficiently evident, and the change has come about because experiences of the self are essential for analytical endeavours.

The interpolation does not answer my question: why do I think the theory make the observation of a baby easier. It is because it focuses attention on what a baby does as a person. It is true that what he does is mostly in relation to his mother but his actions remain his own even in unfavourable circumstances. It also makes possible the use of a language treating the baby as a whole person. That is like the language used by mothers about their babies, but that does not invalidate it. After all they have more experience of babies than anybody else is likely to have, so why should they not be right?

One of the further advantages of introducing the idea of deintegration into infancy was that it helps to recognize the infants' own capacities and to underline their individuality. The self had become so much associated with integration that it was difficult to look at a baby, who does not symbolize, as an individual person needing not more integration but something else that releases his capacities for adaptation without dissolving his personality. It is that which the idea of deintegration enlightens because a deintegrate is endowed with and is continuous with the self.

In the light of the above reflections it becomes likely that a baby is capable of quite a spectrum of experience. He does not just function in a continuous state of primitive identity in which subject and object can not be distinguished and where thought and action are one. He may show evidence of being in such a state of mind but not continuously. There is no longer one characteristic state of mind but many. There is no stage of primitive identity and it is for this reason that the view of individuation which I held previously needs modification. Being an individual from the start, individuation becomes realization of his condition through the development of self representations.

Nevertheless, primitive identity has played an important part in the thinking of analytical psychologists. As a hypothesis explaining *participation mystique* it opened up a field of study. But before Jung and most of his followers could exploit its psychodynamic possibilities, Melanie Klein did just that. She developed the concept of the paranoid–schizoid position. That position was associated, especially by Segal (1957), with non-differentiation between subject and object (symbolic equations) an event which Klein also developed in her paper on identification (1955). In that paper she differentiated a special type of identification and gave it the names of projective and introjective identification.

The other important concept was the depressive position. If the paranoid–schizoid position elucidates primitive identity, the result of deintegration, the depressive position elucidates integration and individuation.

Another consequence of my remarks is that we need to study the relation of an infant to his objects much more carefully.

Relation to Objects

It looks as if baby N was quite able to appreciate the reality of his mother and knew how to act in appropriate ways – the most obvious being that he knew how to take the nipple into his mouth. That, and many other features of his relating which we shall study, indicates the baby's capacity to adapt to his mother. Yet we want to believe that our all too familiar theories apply to small children: we want to have it that the baby relies on his archetypal capacities, that he progresses from unconsciousness to consciousness and to ego development, we want to find evidence of primary identity, growth etc. as characterizing the activity of unconscious mental processes.

When I began to study the characteristics of a real baby in relation to his mother, it was a shattering disappointment to find out that so many of the current theories and beliefs about them were, if not completely useless, at least something like that. There is no adequate theory of an infant's experience but the need for one seems to have led to premature generalization. However, if we can relinquish our wish for them, then much that has been imagined theoretically can be turned into instruments to facilitate observation. So I now think for instance that, besides the deintegrating–integrating sequences, the concept of archetypes is still fruitful since they refer to innate patterns of behaviour having mental concomitants. Their boundaries are not fixed but change about, thus facilitating the rapid cathectic shifts so characteristic of early infancy.

Another interesting feature of Jung's theorizing is that the archetypes have a psychoid pole which abuts very closely on bodily states if it is not identical with them (e.g. Jung, 1954b). With this idea in mind, I approached Bion's postulate of beta elements which have approximately if not actually the same significance. He, however, developed it in a useful way and brought them into relation with development through the action of alpha function. Alpha elements form the basis for the development of thoughts, dreams and myth. Beta elements may be correlated with the first deintegrates. They are as much psychic as physical, though their expression, as we can perceive it, seems to be physical.

This reflection can easily lead to hair-splitting about psyche and soma, but that realization makes it possible to say this: at the start such dichotomies as body–psyche, conscious–unconscious are unwelcome intruders. At the time I am talking about, we are studying the self which Jung taught us, combined and transcended opposites.

I am spending time on the nature of an infant's objects because so much has been said about their unreality and to say that they are unadapted to reality is profoundly untrue. It is true that alongside his subtle adaptive behaviour a baby endows his mother with unrealistic features and probably sees her in many ways that are almost impossible for us as adults to conceive, but that is not the impression that one gets from the majority of observations.

Let it be assumed that perception, whether in an adult or a baby, is an active event and also grant that any object perceived is composite. It is not only a record of what is "out there" but is also contributed to by a part of the self which is put into it to give the object meaning. When the object is mainly a record of reality, it may be called a reality object; when it is mainly constructed by the self and so records states of the self, made out of exteroceptive and introceptive sense data, then it may be called a self object. It used to be assumed among analytical psychologists (e.g. Neumann, 1973) that a baby's perception was predominantly through self objects and that he lived in a sort of mythological world, all the time only gradually building up a picture of reality. That is a very misleading account of infancy. If, however, a sliding scale is envisaged to cover the variable content of any particular perception (real object ⟷ self object) then one can study observations in that light. The scheme will accommodate projective identification when a self object can either gain information about the real object or eliminate it. It appears that self-objects increase in affectively charged states, whilst in quiet contemplative exploring activities real objects predominate. But such a tentative conclusion must not allow us to overlook states in which no clear image is defined, for instance when a baby's eyes do not immediately focus. Real objects can be perceived in other states: considering the observation of a feed recorded earlier on the propostion that real objects were being perceived throughout is the most appropriate. If we want to get evidence for the preponderance of self objects an infant's rage would do well or more simply the state of affairs when a hungry baby will not feed from the breast. Blissful states would occur when good self objects preponderate.

Good and Bad Objects

I have described a good object relation. However, it will not be long before, for one reason or another, distressful situations arise. A mother may be out of touch with her baby and he may not be able to make out what it is all about – under such conditions a bad object comes into being. Assuming that the bad object is a beta element, there are various ways in which it can be dealt with, but first it needs to be observed that an object can be bad in quite a transitory sense:

> Baby N was said to refuse the left breast but by the time the observer arrived he was feeding well from it: what is bad at one moment will be good at another without any noticeable change in the environment. If the distress is greater and painful it can be expressed along a number of pathways: crying, whimpering, screaming, vomiting, defaecating, urinating and so mother is compelled to do something about it.

Baby G was an active aggressive baby who could make his wishes known in no uncertain manner especially over nappy changes during which he made loud and noisy protests. One day a health visitor arrived during a breast feed and demanded information immediately. Mother interrupted the feed lying her baby down for a short period. He made protesting cries which "escalated into screaming and drowned all conversation; in addition he soaked and dirtied himself." At first he was not to be calmed down and mother became worried though in an appropriate way; she initiated and persisted in efforts to relieve her baby's distress. Finally she was successful so that the feed could be continued and was followed by sleep. Thus a potential disaster was well and adequately dealt with – integration took place. Such incidents are not at all unusual and they involve action.

But a mother does more than act: by holding her baby in her mind, by reflecting about him especially in a state of maternal revery, she relates directly to her baby's protomental life and helps in the transformation of beta into alpha elements. It is interactive experiences of this kind that form the basis for the affectively charged mental distinction between good and bad objects, between inside and outside. I would suggest that before bringing these distinctions about a baby has experiences that recur: deintegration brings about conditions of pleasure and displeasure and these result by integration and assimilation in a distinction, in a baby's mind, between what is good, what is bad, what is inside him and what outside. It is the start of making psychic structures based on opposites in the service of adaptation.

A special case of a bad object is the "no breast". It is bad since it is not there, either externally or internally, in states of hunger. The baby experiences that as a bad breast inside him, and he has to do something about the intolerable situation. He can do a number of things, for instance evacuate it by screams, bowel movements and the like. But we can infer that another pathway is open to him, he can transform it into thought which may take the form of an image and as such is a significant source of mental life – he seeks the breast in his mind. Later on I shall use this conception as an instrument with which to study mysticism but that discipline cannot be used in the description of a baby's state of mind.

Whole and Part Objects

The theory of the self that I am putting forward has relevance to the theory of whole and part objects. That theory included the assumption that an infant's early experience was defined by parts of his mother and himself. Later, as his perceptive experience expanded, he came to recognize people, especially his mother, as a whole. It may be remarked here that this formulation may be too much as an adult conceives it. The proposition may be modified by the recognition that a baby goes through a rather wide range of experiences when feeding at the breast, and consequently the breast comes to express much more than inserting a nipple into a mouth.

The concept of whole and part objects is useful in evaluating data presented by child or adult patients in analysis; we find that our patients treat analysts as a part object. It may then occur that emphasis is laid on the analyst's communications as feeding or penetrating and not much on the verbal content of what he says. It may be reflected that a baby can not know that an object is a "part object" before he knows a whole object and that raises the question of what a whole object is to a baby? We cannot know but the theory of the self that I am presenting would suggest that a whole object would come first and a part object later as the result of deintegration.

The proposition can be used in observation. The good feed that has already been described (pp. 51f *supra*) comprises a spectrum of experiences beyond and around the experience of the mouth and nipple. That, I would suggest, is an infant relating in a whole object way: the whole of him is engaged with all the mother that he knows at that time.

Can a part object relation also be described? I am persuaded that it can: for instances, some babies are much more inclined to pay attention to taking in the nipple and much less to the penumbra of interchanges that can take place. If a mother colludes in that tendency, the part object nature of a feed becomes evident.

Example

Mother fed the baby

> holding him upright, away from her body somehow crooked in her legs. She held the back of his neck with her left hand and poked the bottle in with her right. The baby had his eyes wide open, staring all the time at the picture on the wall without blinking.
>
> During a visit at nearly three months, L was restless and seemed desperate to have something in his mouth. Some coagulated milk trickled from his mouth – I wiped it away. He seemed to get annoyed and frustrated and started to cry again. Mother took him and put him in his baby rest and gave him a small bottle containing rose-hip syrup. He sucked hard at the teat and gulped the drink with his head turned hard to the side. He drank the whole bottle but did not seem really settled. He fidgeted and whimpered. Mother put him in his pram, placed his head on the side and put another bottle of rose-hip syrup in his mouth. He sucked again vigorously till it had all gone. When the liquid had all gone, he screwed up his face and went on sucking for a little longer, then he stopped and slept.

Lest it be thought that the relation between L and his mother was only on this part object basis, it must be said that whole object relations were much more in evidence during bathing and nappy changes.

My proposition does not cover the other aspect of part and whole object relations in which, as a result of development through deintegration, an infant comes to class experience of his mother as good and bad. It is supposed – and there is some evidence for this – that the good and bad breast-mother are not the same but are two breast-mothers. As experience grows the infant comes to recognize that the two breast-mothers are one and the same. The proposition is combined with a theory of splitting and so presupposes a whole object at the start; that is not usually made explicit. The subject is intricate and I only want to indicate here how self theory can lead to the evaluation of observations.

Ps ⟷ Dp

Another feature of infancy was first discovered by Klein. She found that there were two positions which were first arrived at in infancy: the paranoid–schizoid and depressive positions. These positions were claimed to persist throughout life. Both she and Harris have described them as they occur in infancy.

However, in so far as infant observation shows, it does not appear that they are at all frequent in the babies we have observed, though states bordering on them are frequent. I therefore adopt, provisionally, Bion's sliding scale formulations Ps ⟷ Dp which covers the intermediate states that have been observed.

I am predisposed to accept these formulations because they correspond to primitive identity (Ps) and a first step in individuation (Dp). That proposition I have developed in my book *The Self and Autism* and so will not go further into it. In that book I did not introduce Bion's formula which is nearer to states of mind that can be described, it also relativizes, expands and makes the conceptions more flexible.

I wish to add here that I also find the concepts of projective and introjective identification useful, together with the development of symbolic equation and symbol formation.

The Study of Characteristics in Sequence

By studying characteristics in sequence, it becomes possible to witness the development of a transitory deintegrative action and observe how it comes into relation with other at first discrete behaviour to become a characteristic and persistent behaviour.

Baby N showed a tendency right from the start to look away from his mother's face when feeding; instead, as his mother noted, he looked at her jumper: that began in the second week of extrauterine life. Later, the jumper and other objects became things not only to be looked at but also picked at or picked up: by three months he was picking up bits of fluff between his fingers and putting them in his mouth. Looking soon becomes inspecting. The observer records (when baby N was eight months old): "He found a tiny speck on the floor and put it back on the floor, then he found a long green thread and put it in his mouth. His mother removed it: N cried and hit the table." By nine months he is eating fluff of his mother's jumper and mouthing it; hissing blowing is followed by a vomit, i.e. he removes it as his mother had taken to doing in a different way. By 13 months picking and mouthing becomes related to depression: "he picks fluff off his mother's jumper and mouths it; mother removes it and N becomes depressed and clings." Later in the same observation, "N is grizzly and restless: he pulls threads off his mother's jumper twisting them round his fingers and puts them in his mouth; twitching and making growling noises."

Later N developed scavenging behaviour: scavenging for bits of biscuit on the table or on the floor, looking into and extracting rubbish from bins etc. On the other hand, he became more and more attached to the jumper, sometimes picking at it and rubbing the fluff gently on his skin.

Splitting

Using this method I have come to find it useful to distinguish between deintegration and splitting. The examples I have so far given can be contained within the deintegration hypothesis. However, if the integrative process does not follow, then the term splitting becomes appropriate: the baby's objects become not just good and bad but persistently persecuting.

When N was about one year old, his mother started to subject him to a sequence of teasings about her going away; then quite suddenly she went out for some hours leaving N with a male caretaker. N was inconsolable, neither the caretaker nor the observer could do anything about it, he would have nothing to do with either. Eventually, in a persecution despair, he cried himself to sleep lying up against a large soft pink elephant that was in his cot. That sequence happened twice, but it was not the end of the matter: for weeks afterwards the observer was treated with suspicion – her arrival evidently being associated with his mother going away and subsequently his relationship with his mother, already precarious, degenerated. Further the pink elephant became increasingly important along with the pink jumper which had engaged

N's attention from the age of two weeks. The jumper became necessary for going to sleep.

These events, starting with the mother's teasing and leading up to her going away evidently resulted in N projecting his bad objects into the caretaker and the observer both of whom became persecutory. There was no integration, no depressive position but rather a persecutory depression leading to a sleep which this time was not a sign of integration but was a defensive cutting off using a splitting defence. That state of affairs continued in the need for a comforter when going to sleep. He had split off the comforting mother, replacing her by objects – the pink elephant and the jumper – which therefore had the character of a fetish and not a transitional object.

Self Representations

As knowledge of infancy accumulates, it looks more and more as if an infant has at his disposal many characteristics usually associated with an adult though adapting himself to a very different environment. This statement is needed to counteract the tendency to think that an infant is somehow entirely different from an adult: he is the same self all through life, though the forms of expression are different, especially in their complexity.

We may be amazed at what an infant can do and what he seems to understand through the machinery available for adaptation. He does not know consciously what is happening at first but later he does acquire that knowledge as the self grows an ego.

Much attention has been given to a child's conscious experience of self. It depends upon his capacity to symbolize and so transform his experience. That he develops the capacity to do so cannot be in doubt, and this is reflected in the play and imagination of small children. I have published examples of this in previous publications and in particular have studied it in the case of a small girl aged two. But it is likely that symbolization begins to develop very much earlier. Klein makes it clear that she believes such a process to begin at three to four months and to reach a climax at about seven months in the "depressive position". She also interestingly states that symbolization lies at the root of the infant's mental life.

Theoretically there is no difficulty if it is true that archetypal forms are present at birth: they will regulate the infant's behaviour and they are postulated as having the potentiality for mental representation. Above all it is Klein who, from a wealth of experience and thought, made it possible for us to enhance the credibility of that proposition. We can postulate then that, at some period in development, representations form which give rise to a sense of self: of self as an infant is realistically of self as he would like to be and could be, of wishful selves and ideal self images; he develops a sense of guilt, and of shame which are related to what he ought to be and is not. All these help in organizing a sense of identity.

To develop to these states of mind there are two overriding factors, he must have developed a sense of time and he must be able to distinguish himself from others. That means he must have formed a sense of his boundaries dependent upon the development of a body image.

We are not yet in a position to decide how all this takes place but we can know that the self becomes represented partially in the ego. It is the start of the idea found in Jung's *Mysterium Coniunctionis* and to which I drew attention in Chapter 2 (p. 46).

Inasmuch as the self becomes partially represented in the ego it follows that the rest of it must be unconscious. That is a considerable achievement and involves the setting up of defences of the self. Bion has an ingenious idea that the division in the baby's mind comes about through the formation of a "contact barrier" composed of a screen of alpha elements.

The evidence, as far as I am concerned, is derived from disturbed children and they reveal exaggerations of what may be normal, but, so long as the pathological element is identified, what they reveal may be helpful in understanding others. For instance, in *The Self and Autism* I detailed how a schizoid child developed imagery which made me think that if he had lived in a different age he might have become an alchemist, so complex was the imagery he produced during his manic states. Material of that kind is not absent from healthy children's play and fantasy – they comprise much of the subject matter of play, "let's pretend" distinguishes it clearly from everyday life. That distinction had not been achieved by my child patient.

Thus it follows that magic alchemy and data of mysticism can be seen to have roots in childhood. Later we shall consider these topics with a view to presenting material for comparative reflection.

Conclusion

In this chapter I have applied self theory to the earliest period in life, infancy. To conclude, I will list the ways various investigators have used it in different fields.

(1) Jung had worked out a formula to express the structure and dynamics of dreaming. That formula corresponded to the sequence I had postulated. I illustrated this from a child's dream (Fordham, 1969).

(2) It was used by a number of child analysts and I applied it to the study of infantile autism.
(3) It went far to explain the effectiveness of child analysis inasmuch as it meant that both infants and children had a psychic life distinct from those of their parents.
(4) It led to the study of mothers and infants.
(5) Apart from its use in the study of childhood, it has been used in other fields: (*a*) In Chapter one I suggested that active imagination could be conceived as based on deintegration of the self which produced "objective" data to which the subject or ego could relate. (*b*) It was applied to anthropology by John Layard, Rosemary Gordon and Renaldo Maduro. (*c*) It provided a novel criterion for cure in psychotherapy (*vide infra* pp. xxff). Integration is not enough; it is desirable to ensure that a patient can deintegrate and can pass through integrative sequences. (*d*) The ideas have been used as a central theme by Kenneth Lambert in his book *Analysis, Repair and Individuation*.

From all this it can be seen that the concept of the self that was first put forward in 1947 has been, to use Stein's formula, "doing a job", and has led to becoming less of an abstraction and more of a description of psychic functioning to which meaning is given. It has also found value at various levels of mental functioning and in various age groups.

*Chapter Four**

A possible root of active imagination

Introduction

A considerable literature, mostly expository, has grown up around the subject of active imagination. But little progress has been made in furthering the understanding of it, for which I called in 1958. Dorothy Davidson (1966) has since made an original contribution in "Transference as a form of active imagination" and Plaut (1966) wrote interestingly on the relation between trust and imagination.

In "Active imagination and imaginative activity" (Fordham, 1956), I suggested a difference between fantasy activity in children and active imagination in adults. I proposed a not altogether satisfactory way out of the supposed anomaly that what children displayed was suspiciously like the data recorded by mature persons. Later, I approached the matter differently. In "Active imagination: deintegration or disintegration" (Fordham, 1967a), I reviewed the literature, questioned the validity of some of its features and attempted to investigate its psychopathology further than had already been done – it had only been noted that there was a danger of a psychosis being precipitated if active imagination was begun ill-advisedly. I now noted that it could be used as a shield behind which infantile affects in urgent need of attention could be hidden. As a result the imagery displayed not so much *deintegrative* activity as splitting at the roots of the personality.

A closer study of the origins of active imagination seemed called for on this ground alone, but, it may be reflected, it is also unsatisfactory to be studying and observing data without some idea of how they arise in the course of development. The contents of active imaginings have been referred to the archetypal forms and have been related to the

*Originally published in *The Journal of Analytical Psychology* vol. 22, no. 4, 1977. A postscript has been added.

imagery of myths, but the way in which the manifestations come into being during the lifetime of an individual remained obscure, and it was not until Winnicott (1971) developed his theory of transitional objects and transitional phenomena, which he related to cultural experience, that the problem began to resolve itself.

Transitional Objects and Transitional Phenomena

It is important to understand the difference between transitional objects and transitional phenomena, which I can best illustrate by briefly referring to the events that give rise to the two sets of data covered by these phrases.

In the course of an infant's maturation, his perceptions become related to physical objects and he responds to them appropriately. Besides this realistic adaptation, however, he develops experiences which satisfy his omnipotence and protect him from feeling his dependence up on his mother. In this state, self objects cannot be distinguished from reality and the infant's mother adapts herself to her infant's omnipotence well enough for him to have good experiences of it. When through repeated, but tolerable, frustration combined with growing perception of reality, the infant becomes gradually disillusioned as to his omnipotence, the transitional object may appear to contain the omnipotent state which still needs representation. It is always a real object, e.g. a bit of fluff or rag, to which the infant becomes firmly attached. After a variable time – the transitional object may persist for years – it disappears and its place is taken by a sort of spreading out of its characteristics into mental imagery. Instead of a specific object a whole class of phenomena appears which are transitional phenomena; play expands, stories and creative fantasy emerge and dreams take on transitional features. All are essentially mental states expressed in imagery and, except for play, not in physical objects. It is this sequence, from obsessive preoccupation with an object to play and imagery, that Winnicott defined. The data had been observed for a long time, as Kahn (1967) also noted. To underline this and so throw into relief Winnicott's achievement, I will describe a transitional object which made a strong impression on me many years ago, and then I will consider transitional phenomena in a case described by Wickes in 1927.

Example of a Transitional Object

A small girl carried a doll about with her everywhere and put it to a variety of uses. It gradually began to smell, and this her mother found offensive. So she tried to persuade her daughter to relinquish it, even offering attractive substitutes, but to no avail. Eventually she removed it, presumably when her daughter was asleep, and deposited it in a dustbin. Again to no avail; the little girl retrieved it. A critical situation then arose and it was fortunate that the mother became interested: "Why do you want to carry about that smelly old doll?", she asked, to which came the reply: "You see, Mummy, *you* may not like it, but it smells lovely to me." This story focussed much of my interest in play and toys, so that in writing *The Life of Childhood* (Fordham, 1944) I could consider play as an activity in itself: a derivative of primitive identity in which omnipotence predominates, related to but not identical with the internal images and external objects. I was thus prepared to assimilate the theory of transitional objects and the phenomena derived from them when Winnicott introduced it. I duly included his idea in *Children as Individuals* (Fordham, 1969) where I suggested that the transitional object might be "an early attempt at self representation".

Example of a Transitional Phenomenon

Wickes observed a girl, Margaret, who developed an imaginary companion, Anna (Wickes, 1927). Anna had come into being during an illness, and filled a valuable function for a period in the girl's life. Regressive factors entered into the fantasy, however, and Wickes most ingeniously extracted her from them. Wickes states that demands had been made on Margaret, which she could not meet, but when she retreated from her task she knew that she was making the wrong choice. Anna was "called into being" and she accepted from this other self the truth that she could not accept from the members of her family. Each time that she "went the same road as Anna", the division grew less, until finally she "knew as well as Anna". Then Anna became unnecessary, outgrown; the very continuance of her life now became regressive and Anna was "killed and dead" (ibid., p. 192). Mrs Wickes continues, ". . . do not mean that with the death of Anna the phantasy life ceased. It continued in varying forms . . ." and, she comments, "It would be a great loss if this phantasy life should cease, for it contains the living creative element . . ." (ibid., p. 193).

The episode has the following characteristics of transitional phenomena: it is enacted in mental imagery alone; Anna belongs to Margaret and yet is *not* her; Anna was related to and her statements were final, i.e. omnipotent; she was relinquished in characteristic fashion. It will be noted that Wickes interestingly links the episode with creative imagination.

Winnicott's Thesis

The following description follows Winnicott (1971) closely, though not exactly. An infant sucks his thumb and at the same time enriches his oral experience of pleasure by fingering his lips, nose and cheeks. In the course of his activities, a piece of blanket or a bit of rag may be drawn into the activity. There are many other objects which may be added, such as bits of fluff, string and later soft animals and hard toys which are used by boys especially. Any one of these objects will be taken about by the child and become a treasured possession without which, for instance, he cannot go to sleep. He becomes extremely possessive of the object and behaves as if his existence depends upon it; for this reason it can be called the first not-me possession. It does not belong to the inner world made up of subjective objects and it does not belong to, and is distinguished from, real objects, i.e. his mother as she is and to whom the infant can adapt realistically. It is not experienced as within the infant ego, nor is it external in the sense of a real objective object, though it is related to both; indeed, it can represent almost any part of the infant or the external object mother and all attributions can retain their omnipotence. Thus the object can be loved, hated, torn to bits and reconstructed, it can be made dirty and made to smell and it can be wetted as well as soiled. Through all the multiple meanings the illusion may acquire its unquestioned importance and needs to be allowed. The reality of the transitional object depends, Winnicott says, upon "the mother's special capacity for making adaptation to the needs of her infant, thus allowing the infant the illusion that what he creates really exists" (ibid., p. 14). Because of this situation the transitional object has the characteristic also shown in its derivatives: enquiry into its meaning is resisted and neither its origins nor its place in the infant's life can be gone into without ego debasement. So in analysis it is not to be made the subject of interpretation: that would violate the agreement between mother and infant that the illusion pertaining to the object shall be treated as true and real. By contrast, it would seem that the mental derivatives of the object can be fruitfully used in creative education which would depend on the satisfactory development of the area between the subjective ego and the object world.

When the transitional object has fulfilled its purpose, it is "relegated to limbo", which means that it is not repressed but disappears and is replaced by other mental characteristics: play is one of them and especially creative play; others are archetypal numinous fantasies and some imaginary companions. In addition some dreams have characteristics which are unmistakable. They carry in them a quality which seems to demand that they be taken as whole experience not to be impinged upon by asking for associations or offering interpretations. Among these dreams are the "big" numinous ones which may be remembered over years. I draw attention to them especially because Jung, in his autobiography, links such a dream with a transitional object.

Psychopathology

There is a psychopathology of transitional objects and phenomena. In childhood this is manifested in child psychoses. An example will be found in *The Self and Autism* (Fordham, 1976): "Alan", especially when in a manic phase, showed compulsive symbolic play which had to be allowed as much as possible. I formulated this behaviour as his "living in a mad world". Likewise "Sammy" (MacDougal and Lebovici, 1969), in the early part of his therapy, insisted remorselessly on his analyst sharing the illusion of his omnipotence by forcing her to write down stories to his dictation, resisting any intervention on her part. Fintzey (1971) has studied a border-line child in whom a transitional object persisted, and Greenacre (1960) has investigated the relation between the transitional object and the fetish.

Some work has also been done on the persistence of transitional objects into adult life. For instance, Coppolillo (1967) recorded cases in which intellectual and cultural gifts failed to develop in schizoid persons who continue to use transitional objects when grown up.

Reflections

Winnicott's clear description of transitional objects and their derivatives might give the impression that it is always easy to classify a class of behaviour. That is not always so, and behaviour which seems similar, but is not surely transitional, can be observed: for instance, an object can be important but not characteristically possessed in the same way; it can be taken away and returned to the child later on without objection. In addition, objects take on typical characteristics later on in a child's life without, apparently, having been in evidence in the first few months of life. There are thus still many features of the phenomena which require further observation and research, but it can be said that the need for creative illusion in the discovery of reality persists throughout life.

Another matter which needs mentioning, though the consequences will not be followed up here, is that the transitional object belongs to the period of ruthlessness. There is no indication of sadness or grief on the part of the child over separating from his mother or discarding the object. Therefore it is different from separation resulting from working through the depressive position. This fact, if so it be, has led to the notion that transitional objects should be classed as pathological. Greenacre (1960) discusses the proposition when she distinguishes the transitional object from the fetish, though Winnicott is not as clear as she is about the distinction.

Jung's Childhood Experiences

Winnicott's claim (1971, p. 14) about cultural experiences is a large one which, however, rests upon slender foundations. He contends that transitional phenomena lead, eventually, to the "... intense experience that belongs to the arts and religion and to imaginative living and to creative scientific work". Just how he arrives at this conclusion is not clear, but I believe that analytical psychologists are in a position to provide evidence in its favour. With a view to doing so, I shall consider Jung's childhood and the relation of his early experiences to active imagination about which he is explicit.

Much of what Jung records about his childhood belongs to the era of transitional objects and phenomena, but especially the dream of the underground phallus, the mannikin and the episodes focussing mainly in his fear of Jesus and the Jesuits. Let me remind you of how he presents the dream and the mannikin – the dream preceded the object so I will consider it first.

The Dream

This is related to Jung's doubts about Jesus, the phobic episode with the Jesuit, and his ruminations on death. In the dream (Jung, 1963, pp. 25ff) he was in a meadow.

> Suddenly I discovered a dark, rectangular, stone-lined hole in the ground . . . I ran forward curiously and peered down into it. Then I saw a stony stairway leading down. Hesitantly and fearfully I descended. At the bottom was a doorway with a round arch, closed off with a green curtain . . . [which he pushed aside] I saw before me in the dim light a long chamber . . . Down the middle was a red carpet which ran down the centre up to a rich golden throne . . . a real king's throne in a fairy tale on which there was something standing which I thought at first was a tree trunk . . . it was a huge thing reaching almost to the ceiling . . . made of skin and naked flesh, and on top there was something like a rounded head with no face and no hair. On the very top of the head was a single eye gazing motionlessly upwards.
>
> Above the head there was . . . brightness. The thing did not move yet I had the feeling that it might at any moment crawl off the throne like a worm and creep towards me. I was paralysed with terror. At that moment I heard . . . my mother's voice. She called out: 'Yes look at him. That is the man-eater!' That intensified my terror still more, and I awoke scared to death. For many nights afterwards I was afraid to go to sleep, because I feared I might have another dream like that.

This dream was not communicated to anybody, it was treated as a whole and was remembered and treasured in his memory.

I have deliberately curtailed the account of this dream, and made it rather more as a child would tell it. As written by Jung, there is much that is drawn into it from later years, so that it could appear as if Jung at three years had knowledge of the metric system etc.

Many years later he feeds into it knowledge about the Mass, the "ithyphallic" nature of the object and the mysteries of the earth. There are also personal memories but, and this is striking, nothing of his sexual excitement. Summing up he says (ibid., p. 28): "Who spoke to me then? Who talked of problems far beyond my knowledge? Who brought the Above and Below together, and laid the foundation for everything that was to fill the second half of my life with stormiest passion?" And he adds, "My intellectual life had its unconscious beginnings at that time." Thus he recognizes, had I better say believes in, the dream as lying at the root of his religious, magical and scientific life, as Winnicott says of transitional phenomena.

The Mannikin

When Jung was 10 years old, he carved a mannikin at a period of disunion with himself. Between 7 and 9 he had been playing games. "I was passionately fond of playing with bricks, and built towers which I then rapturously destroyed by an 'earthquake'." (Note that there is no reparation.) There were disturbances in his home atmosphere at the time and besides this he discovered that going to school provided him with playmates who alienated him from himself, they "somehow misled me or compelled me to be different from what I thought I was" (ibid., p. 32). He made a special sacred fire which, in his games, nobody else was allowed to tend. And then there was the stone on which he sat when he was alone. The question arose in his conversation with it: "Am I the one who is sitting on the stone, or am I the stone on which *he* is sitting?" All these events illustrate the disunion that "led me to an action which at the time was quite incomprehensible to me" (ibid., p. 33).

> "At the end of [my] ruler I carved a little mannikin, about two inches long, with frock coat, top hat, and shiny black boots. I coloured him black with ink, sawed him off the ruler, and put it in [my] pencil case, where I made him a little bed. I even made a coat for him out of a bit of wool. In the case I also placed a smooth, oblong blackish stone from the Rhine, which I had painted with water colours to look as though it were divided into an upper and lower half, and had long carried around in my trouser pocket. This was *his* stone. All this was a great secret."

Jung placed the pencil case with his treasured objects in it up in the attic, where he was forbidden to go. Then he says, "I felt safe, and the tormenting sense of being at odds with myself had gone'' (ibid., p. 34). When under stress from internal or external sources, he would think of the mannikin and would visit him. Each time he went into the attic he deposited a scroll written in a secret language. The scrolls made a library for the mannikin.

Jung concludes:

> ''This possession of a secret had a very powerful formative influence on my character; I consider it the essential factor of my boyhood. Similarly, I never told anyone about the dream of the phallus; and the Jesuit, too, belonged to that mysterious realm which I knew I must not talk about'' (ibid., pp. 34–35).

In later life Jung enriched the symbolism of the secret images, representing his secret self, in *The Psychology of the Unconscious* (1912), and with alchemical sources and especially in 'The psychology of the child archetype' (1950c).

I want to pay particular attention to how he worked to assimilate these experiences. They both needed hiding – he told nobody of them, so what did he do? He sought out from books others who could share his illusions and who likewise believed them to be real and true – they were especially the alchemists with whom he shared so much and through whom he came to share with others. This is like finding a mother who would agree that his experiences were both real and true.

Jung is recurrently amazed at his behaviour and the rich symbolic life that he had when he was a child. It is curious to observe how he depreciates the inventive and creative capacity he then had, even though he probably predates the dream for it is unlikely that he dreamed it at the age of three – six is much more likely. He treats it as if he, as a child, had, and could have had, no hand in producing it and concludes that it all came from the collective unconscious. Yet schizoid children have just the capacity he exhibits, they create symbolic imagery sometimes in great and terrifying profusion. Furthermore, it is a capacity that Jung himself understood when he defined ''undirected thinking'' in *The Psychology of the Unconscious*, so why did he depreciate his part in it? With the understanding of transitional phenomena as prohibiting enquiry and as lying at the root of cultural life, it is, I suggest, possible to appreciate his attitude as protective.*

*In a personal communication Joseph Wheelwright writes: ''The casting out of his (Jung's) childhood began the almost total derogation and even denial of childhood in the Jungian world. It was developed by Harding *et al*, who, owing to unresolved transference, slavishly followed the master – totally ignoring infancy and childhood, even denying that a child had a psychology of his own. All this began with Jung saying in effect: 'It was bad enough being a child, let alone perpetuating it as an indispensable part of the life span.' ''

This trend in Jung's thinking which was nonetheless very influential, would appear to have modified later on. cf. his ''Psychology of the child archetype'' (1950c).

The Origin of Jung's Active Imagination

Turning now to Jung's own experience of active imagination, how did he take up the problems with which he was presented on one hand by the loneliness and isolation after leaving Freud and his fascination for culture on the other? In *Memories, Dreams, Reflections* (1963) we learn a lot and there is much of interest in the chapters on childhood; but it was not until "Confrontation with the unconscious" (Chapter 6), in which he tells how he felt the urgent need to play, that our theme can be taken up directly. Feeling under inner tension which neither dreams nor the review of many childhood memories could help, he yet found that one memory of building with building blocks was associated with considerable emotion. It has been noted that, in his earlier descriptions, these buildings were destroyed by earthquakes – that is omitted in the later recording. This time the memory is different and in some ways more developed: "I distinctly recalled how I had built little houses and castles, using bottles to form the sides of gates and vaults. Somewhat later I had used ordinary stones with mud for mortar" (ibid., p. 168). He next conceived the idea of establishing contact with this area in his memory and then that he had no choice but to return to it and take up once more his "childish games". "This moment", he writes, "was a turning point in my fate." Overcoming his resistances, he began to collect stones and built cottages, a castle and a whole village. As a church he made a hexagonal building with a hexagonal drum on top of it and a dome. He hesitated over the altar, but walking along the lake he suddenly caught sight of a red stone, a four-sided pyramid about one and a half inches high. It was a fragment of stone which had been polished into this shape by the action of the water. "I knew at once this was the altar! I placed it in the middle under the dome and, *as I did so, I recalled the underground phallus of my childhood dream*. This connection gave me a feeling of satisfaction" [my italics]. He continues: "In the course of this activity my thoughts clarified, and I was able to grasp the phantasies whose presence in myself I dimly felt" (ibid., p. 169). It was the beginning of his recording fantasies, written down in the Black Book, related to the area between the object world and the inner world.

That is how Jung's active imagination began, from unsolved conflicts of his childhood in which were hidden his true self (personality number two). The childhood experiences seem to have been related to his disturbed family life and to the beginning of school where he found that

More expressive is E. A. Bennet's report of Jung saying with relation to psychoanalysis: "Their view is that when this [infantile sexuality] is realised you must put it away, forget it and be *cured*. But you can't put it away without hurt because childish things are very valuable – the dependence, the interest, the expectant attitude. This is the *puer aeternus* and you need it, especially in old age, for it *keeps people healthy*. So it is a bad blunder to try to get rid of it: moreover you *can not* just dispose of it." (Bennet, 1982, p. 84).

the other children alienated him from himself. The transitional nature of the play and imagery is hinted at but is not clear; however, the secretiveness speaks of separation from others. By contrast, Jung's active imagination was clearly related to separations: it started during his break with Freud. He began to build the Bollingen house two months after the death of his mother and he put the top storey on to the middle tower after the death of his wife because "I felt an inner obligation to become what I myself am". It was also then that he made more sculptures and wrote "Answer to Job" (1952b) and the article "On synchronicity" (1951c) concurrently.

Jung's childhood was infinitely complex and there are atypical features in his use of the transitional object. Furthermore, the dreams, which took on phobic characteristics, and the delusional fantasies of the Jesuits were all, like the mannikin, kept secret and not validated as is usually required. But in spite of these variations the relation between his active imagination and transitional phenomena is clear.

A Note on Terminology

Before going on to consider active imagination as a whole, I want to recall a bit of terminology that is relevant. In considering the ego in relation to the collective unconscious Jung referred to the ego as the subject; it is an idea that corresponds to Winnicott's term "subject ego". Both cover all experiences felt as "me" and my inner world, i.e. all that is felt to be inside my mind, or body. In opposition to this is the real object: mother or reality as she or it is. Finally, there are the transitional objects and their phenomena which correspond to the objective psyche according to Jung.

Characteristics and Management of Active Imagination

If the features of active imagination are studied, as reported in the literature, together with the recommended ways of managing them, they correspond closely with the characteristics of transitional phenomena.

(1) External objects are virtually excluded by deliberately concentrating on images that emerge through the subject ego relinquishing control over them.

(2) So as to conduct it, the ego needs to be felt as the subject and so distinguished from the imagery whose objectivity is enhanced by drawing, painting, sculpting or writing down fantasies. The objective quality of the imagery is emphasized by all writers on the subject. It is often classified under the heading of the inner world, though this is not the

quality of the experience but an abstraction. That the images sometimes take on an inner quality in experience indicates their relation to, but not identity with, the inner world which only truly comes into the picture when the I (subject ego) stands back and reflects before relating to the objective imagery and the dynamic processes going on in it.

(3) Private but active intervention by the subject ego is required in the objective stream of images just as a child has an active relation to his transitional object by doing things with the not-me object (p. 70 *supra*).

(4) The products, pictures, writing, sculpture etc. are prized by the person who produced them, and it is recognized that they belong to him and should not be removed, i.e. they are his possessions. If given away, as sometimes happens, they must be returned to him, because he is held to need them. The relevance of this thesis was illustrated to me rather dramatically by a patient who had been to a previous analyst some twenty years ago. This analyst had taken away the pictures and had not returned them. My patient discovered, in her analysis with me, her fury with the previous analyst, now dead. She wrote angry and threatening letters to the daughter of the previous analyst, demanding their return. The patient believed that they had been stolen and could not have been destroyed.

(5) While the images of objects are separate from the subject ego and in interaction with it, there are procedures which need the analyst's attention and which correspond with the idea that an illusion is being agreed to and is allowed to be psychically real.

(*a*) The process is given prime importance because it contains an evolving pattern which gradually by amplification – the images and processes doing this and not the analyst – leads to the clear definition of a pattern having validity in its own right. It leads optimally to symbols of the self. This is of particular interest if the transitional object, as I have suggested, is an early self representation.

(*b*) Analysis, i.e. interpretation of the data, is not indicated unless the subjective or real object spheres of experience contaminate the psychically subjective ones in a way that disturbs the process. The importance of noticing when this happens and the difficulties of so doing were made the subject of a study by myself (Fordham, 1969). However, even such necessary attention to detail is sometimes deplored, so that analysis of any kind is conceived to be destructive because synthetic processes are deemed to be active (e.g. particularly Weaver, 1964). The distinction between synthetic and analytic is not really as clear as it seems to be but it is emphasized by writers on the subject.

(*c*) As an alternative response to the data, the images may be amplified by the analyst who offers mythological parallels to further a cultural process.

(*d*) A result of the activity may be that original ideas emerge; thus Hubback showed that the contents of the *VII Sermones ad mortuos* were translated into theoretical propositions by Jung (Hubback, 1966).

A Note on Technique

The management of active imagination has been considered. As with transitional data, interpretation is to be eschewed and validation is required. Jung had no person who could have done that for him unless Antonia Wolff performed that maternal function – on this we have no information. Whether she did or not, he had to go a long way round to find alchemy and to research on the alchemists' fantasies: by using these in his practice and publishing his work, he could achieve the needed validation.

Jung followed his own path with his patients, providing them with parallels that can be compared with a mother's story-telling techniques. He probably did so when the imagery became highly autonomous with a view to making a framework in which his patients could feel safer.

At first sight it seems in line with the idea of transitional phenomena being a root of active imagination that Jung held that it, and dream study, made conditions for diminishing interview frequency; he also maintained that long holidays were possible and even desirable. However, that practice differs from what is necessary if a regression to infancy takes place, because the presence of a therapist–mother is required so that the object or fantasy etc. may be accepted and taken as real by "her"; then it is not the absence of the therapist that is useful, but his restrained presence. Therefore, it may be doubted whether Jung's practice can be generalized.

The use of parallels by the therapist also presents problems: his mastery of his subject and ability to adapt his knowledge to his patient's material, can result in the patient idealizing him which, by obstructing and concealing a negative transference (Fordham, 1967a), leads on to initiating the end of the relation between therapist and patient in an undesirable way. Many of the published pictures show this idealization and, in descriptions, fantasies tend to become aggrandized and mystified. That they tend to end with mandala structures also seems unsatisfactory, because these images have a rigidly defensive content. Without detracting from their relative value, it is important that they usually appear in periods of disorganization and that, when this becomes less threatening, the defence can be relaxed. For this to happen the presence of a holding therapist may be essential.

Active imagination, in the form that it is presented in the literature, is not used very often by patients. Not all persons having problems of becoming conscious of their true selves have such vivid cultural interests as Jung, nor do they have his imaginative capacities. Yet the heirs to transitional objects may be expected to manifest themselves in many patients having the inner need that active imagination proclaims, though it is not available to them. Such patients are much more frequent in everyday psychotherapeutic practice. When transitional data, other than creative imagination, become manifest, then it would follow that the question of interpretations, and of when to refrain from using them, arises as a more general proposition. When to interpret to patients in regression and how much is often considered, but no satisfactory answer can be given. It is recognized that therapists vary a great deal in the amount of intervention they employ and the amount of interpretation they give; this is partly a matter of the school to which the therapist belongs and partly a matter of individual style, so not much more can be said about it. However, there is one view which is explicit and frequently expressed: the patient's resistance to interpretations that become persecutory indicates when not to give them. However, as more has been understood about persecution as a means by which a patient evacuates bad objects, thus protecting his own good ones, it hs been realized that persecutory interpretations may perform a useful function and lead on to a new understanding of the relation between therapist and patient (Fordham, 1974b). For this reason persecution alone does not seem a valid reason for a change in tactics.

The theory of transitional objects and phenomena suggests a different approach. If some patients regress and use myth-like material of a complex nature, others regress and display much less complex and often unorganized data, so that it is only by using excessive ingenuity that any interpretation can be devised let alone communicated. In listening to such patients it can become clear that they are not interested in the meaning of their thoughts, feelings, fantasies or dreams which may be told in a jumbled up way as if to prevent understanding. This they do in order to sustain a precarious, but still needed, omnipotence because transitional phenomena are not yet established in the form of play. Such patients are *not* actually playing; their behaviour is rather a tentative attempt to begin so doing. Then it is important for the analyst not to interfere, but only to hold the situation. But it may happen that an interpretation can have a holding effect by acting as a container and for this reason it seems to be the type and style of intervention which is important – a conclusion I arrived at after making a study of interpretation (Fordham, 1975) and thinking about defences of the self (Fordham, 1974b). So it is not so much whether a therapist interprets or not, as whether he interferes with (impinges on) the establishment of a play-illusion which the patient needs as part of differentiating further between reality and his subject ego.

While that condition is found most clearly when there is a delusional transference of the type which splits the analyst into a delusional real person and an unreal interpreter, play activity is to be found in varying degrees in any therapy and is a necessary part of it.

There is a footnote I would like to add before ending. Among therapists there is a recurrent anxiety about rigidity in the analyst; yet it is important that a therapist should interpret with certainty and not be put off if the patient does not accept what he says. For this reason it might be said that too flexible an analyst is a positive disadvantage (flexibility is usually mentioned as desirable when the term rigidity is used). It may be that the anxiety intuitively refers to the area where play is indicated and not analytic work.

Summary

The study of active imagination has given rise to an expository literature, but its nature has been incompletely elucidated. In particular its origins in childhood are obscure. Recent work on transitional objects and transitional phenomena provides a means of filling in a gap in knowledge.

Transitional objects and transitional phenomena are defined and their manifestations related to active imagination, taking as an example Jung's own account of how his confrontation with the unconscious began. It is shown that transitional data lie at the root of active imagination which can thus be related to separations especially from the mother.

Descriptions of active imagination and the current ideas about how it should be managed are then detailed and these are considered in relation to patients who regress to infancy and start to show evidence of early transitional play-like activity. Then the patient requires holding more than active interventions by the therapist. Interference is to be avoided.

Postscript

Since I first related active imagination to transitional phenomena I have come to some modifying conclusions.

In the literature on transitional objects and phenomena there have been two trends. One is to say that all healthy babies should develop by manifesting the phenomena; in consequence it is concluded that if they do not do so it is a sign of psychopathology. On the other hand, the transitional data are themselves considered to be a pathological sign.

There is also a debate about the frequency of the material corresponding to the views of its significance. It therefore becomes difficult to generalize. My own experience is that the transitional matter is uncommon but when found it is quite characteristic.

It does not matter to the argument of this paper which view is taken.

Part Two

Ego and self

Chapter Five

*The self as an imaginative construct**

As has been seen, Jung collected together a large number of numinous images of the self observed first in myth and legend, then in his own active imagination, and he also found them being produced by his patients. Concurrent researches led him to conclude that the unity of God represented the self and that the same datum could be studied in such alchemical symbols as Mercurius, the philosophical tree and the philosophical stone; other studies in mythology led him to conclude that the child images were especially revealing. He also investigated Eastern mysticism, where the self features in a mythical and philosophical context. When he was writing, the concept had not gained much ground in psychology and Jung found reference made to it by only a few authors such as William James; today he would have met with a very different state of affairs. His was an extensive investigation that revealed a common feature in all the diverse symbolic forms: their reference to wholeness in one form or another but especially the wholeness of man in relation to the cosmos.

In addition to this cross-cultural study, Jung developed a historical argument: Lambert (1977) brought the literature on this subject together and developed Jung's thesis at length, so that I only need to consider some ideas in it. Jung thought that Western man had been, and still is, developing consciousness of the self. He conceived that this is, for instance, represented in the evolution of man's images of God. He found the doctrine of the Assumption of the Virgin especially indicative because it seemed to make possible a change in the image of the trinity to a quaternity. Science contributed powerfully to the development of consciousness not only because it has given man greater knowledge and possibilities for controlling his environment, but also because it has made the projection of states of mind into myth and dogma no longer valid.

*Originally published in *The Journal of Analytical Psychology* vol. 24, no. 1, 1979.

A more pressing aspect of it derives from the power of technology, which has made it increasingly urgent for man to gain control over his reproductive capacities, his predatory impulses, his greed and his apparently insatiable destructiveness. The young science of psychology seems to be the new instrument that man has discovered to help in man's need for self development. It has refined techniques through which greater knowledge of his spiritual, instinctual and individual nature in relation to society can be achieved.

Jung's grand conception was elaborated in many essays and books of which "Answer to Job" was the most vivid and dramatic. In these writings the impression can be gained of powerful archetypal images evolving by virtue of man's interaction with them, leading to personal and social individuation. Jung explained his view by asserting that it derived from unconscious archetypal forms, thus defining a field of study without asserting anything conclusive.

Critical Estimation of Jung's Thesis

Jung's thesis has been variously estimated: to some it became an inspiration which led them to devote their working lives to finding out all they could about human beings; to others it has been a thesis that ought to be destroyed because of its imaginative and non-rational features which smacked of fostering religious illusions to the detriment of realistic thought.

Jung never abandoned rational thinking, and he claimed that his conceptions were all based on clinical experience and the witness of patients; as such they were testable and scientific. However, his thesis was attacked by those who asserted that he was not only creating illusions for himself but also fostering them in his patients and his followers to initiate a religious cult. So if the empirical data could be invalidated, the whole structure he had developed would collapse. Aware of this possibility, Jung made efforts to test his data by adopting a cautious and, in a sense, negative approach. He withheld publication of his discovery on mandalas for twenty years lest the information at his disposal should lead patients to produce them because they were expected to do so. He also sent one of his patients to a relatively inexperienced analyst not resident in Switzerland, so that the dreams that Jung surmised the patient would produce, and which he did, could not be said to have been produced by his influence. That patient was the subject of the dream series published in *Psychology and Alchemy* and cited above in Chapter 1.

As scientific procedures, both were naive: in the first place it was known that patients produced material like that of his patient to whomever they went, or for that matter it could be produced if they went to no analyst at all: in the second, it suggests that he over-estimated the effect of transference and feared that he might unwittingly exploit it.

Without doubt Jung's influence was considerable and the setting contributed to it, as I would like to indicate with a personal impression. There was the rather beautiful town around a lake and the mountains in the distance: the two combined to create an especially good atmosphere in which to dream and imagine. Indeed, the parallel with the Greek healing cults of Aesculapius was not infrequently drawn to express the mental state that Zürich induced when the presiding genius of Jung was present. Then there were the seminars, full of rich symbolism, inspiringly elaborated, in which Jung taught his student–patients. Finally, there was the more intimate use of amplification during personal analytic therapy. These were the grounds for suspecting that Jung's method rested more on indoctrination than on the deployment of scientific method.

Though they are worth making, the criticisms of Jung's method should not be over-estimated, especially in that they were all made from inferences. Moreover, the effect of Jung's method can be given a different interpretation: the combined influences facilitated the production of dreams and fantasies, rather than imposing on those who fell under its "spell", and this effect gave rise to a "whole-making" experience. It needs to be remembered also that the effect was made on relatively few persons and especially those who went to Zürich with the so-called problem of our time. There were always a number who could not use what was offered and they went away quite soon but, what is perhaps more interesting, there were others who persisted and who did not produce big dreams or archetypal pictures and who yet progressed towards individuation. They are the best evidence, besides the ubiquity of the data, to show that a predisposition was required for the production of the well-known dreams and images. Finally the material could always be related to the patient's person, his individual and cultural background, which was not necessarily like that of Jung or one of his pupils – the first case in Baynes's (1955) *The Mythology of the Soul* illustrated how significant the cultural background of the patient could turn out to be.

But there was a danger that Jung's methods and influence could engender a false result. For as long as I can remember, there was a question asked among Jungians themselves: how can it be decided whether the experience may be considered authentic or an illusion? Today there is a criterion that can be used even though it is, in a sense, negative. There is a class of patient with a strong false self organization to their personality for whom the experiences become unreal. They produced what they divined was required of them through a delusional transference which it was particularly difficult to work through, as, at the time that Jung was working, it was not known how to analyse that transference; the patients suffering from it drifted from one analyst to another or ended up in a religious cult. Today more is known about the false self and so we are in a better position to deal with that situation by penetrating into its infantile roots. So if that group be identified, Jung's teaching and amplificatory methods can be seen as they were intended, to feed the patient's symbolic function with what it needed.

Characteristics of Symbolic Thought

Symbolism is a complex subject and I shall not embark on considering it as a whole but select only symbolic archetypal imagery. It is of the kind that does not follow the rules of rational thought. Archetypal imagery, inasmuch as it becomes thought, is much looser in its structure and jumps to conclusions based on similarities; dissimilarities are ignored and likenesses emphasized in such a way that the imagery can draw together all sorts of different elements in to one. A symbolic image, when functioning positively, is thus synthetic in the sense of being a container of mental contents that appear inimical – that is its transcendent function (e.g. Fordham, 1957a). Its activity can promote cultural and spiritual life and enters into scientific discovery as Pauli (1955) probably suggested in his "The influence of archetypal ideas on the scientific theories of Kepler". However, its effects are not always so fortunate and then the process can lead to confusion and to mystification of the kind that is often found in alchemy. Whether it functions in one way or the other depends, to a large extent, on the capacity of the person to make use of the symbolic process; if he can relate to it without being engulfed by it, he can assimilate it and it will lead to personal development and the increased effectiveness of any scientific, artistic or religious gifts that he may have.

The Sense of Mystery

The experience of symbols, when closely related to the self, often carries with it a sense of mystery. It has been much emphasized. The nature of what symbols represent is felt to transcend comprehension, and so what is being sought for cannot be discovered in the symbolic expression. It is this mystical element in imagination that can give rise to a religious possession in those who identify themselves with it.

That fault is not what Jung intended; and his adherence, to the end of his life, to the scientific nature of analytical psychology meant that a mystery is a challenge to discovery rather than an unresolvable end-point. I shall consider Jung's relation to religion in Part 3 of the present volume and shall also discuss differences between him and Freud, reflecting upon the proposition that Jung no less than Freud criticized the illusion that religion could become, but showed that he did so in a more subtle way so that the value in religion (not denied by Freud, let it be noted) could be extracted from its illusions. I will now approach the subject from a different angle.

The sense of mystery, and awe too, may not be transcendent; both may be evoked when a human being starts to investigate himself. Then he may well be astonished by what he finds and come to understand that there is much more to him than he can perceive, think or feel. Some are relatively content with this realization, but others are not and start to invent ways and means for becoming more aware of themselves. It is then that they may reach the sense of the self as ultimately unknowable and so essentially mysterious.

That is what happened to Jung after his separation from Freud. Then he initiated himself into a world which, so to speak, attacked him and compelled him to make often desperate efforts to control and hold his person together. Being highly imaginative, he had from childhood onwards, in dream, play, hallucination and delusion, been making symbolic imagery himself or studying the myths and religions of the world, so that when he came to enter his own psyche he was presented with a long sequence of complex and dramatic images which led to an end-point defined as realization of the self in a particular image – the mandala.

Jung never capitulated to the sense of either awe or mystery, but took both as a challenge to "know". Thus he retained and applied scientific method to the end and began to construct a conceptual account of the self, defining it as the totality of conscious and unconscious. I have already discussed that definition in Chapter 1 in connection with his tendency to call the self an archetype. The two definitions are apparently a contradiction since the second places it in the category of unconscious structures. For present purposes it is better to follow the first proposition and define the self as the whole person, psychic and somatic. It must then be outside the categories of conscious and unconscious and thus becomes a concept which makes sense of the mystical experience, since the wholeness of the person cannot be represented and perhaps never will be. I say this though there are indications of how mental and physical forms might be related in a common language, as Stein has so brilliantly indicated using the unlikely field of immunology (*vide* Chapter 8). Yet psyche and soma often appear as irreconcilable opposites and a symbol, in the sense that it is the best possible expression for an unconscious content, can refer to a state in which they are united. Jung studied such symbols in the *Mysterium Coniunctionis*. He found that the alchemists were concerned with the problem and defined its solution as a mysterious union between the *unio mentalis* and the *unus mundus*. That view left us with imaginative constructions, i.e. symbols conceived as the best possible, though inadequate, means of understanding the nature of the psychodynamic self.

It can not be emphasized too often, however, that a symbol can only express parts of the self which, we infer, are more or less related to its wholeness. A symbolic expression can never represent the whole self because in order to form images the self has to divide up to produce two part-systems, the one that creates the imagery (this is rather loosely called the unconscious) and another that records and interacts with it (the ego). It is the images referring to the self, but only representing parts of it, that become numinous and induce feelings of awe especially when, we assume, they come close to representing the whole self.

The Construction of Images

I will now consider some ideas about how images are constructed. I have already indicated that both affective and intellectual processes are involved. I believe that I can develop that idea best by starting out from an example provided by a child whose analysis I have detailed elsewhere (Fordham, 1976).

Example

Alan, aged seven years, played a great deal with water. The water represented babies' urine, felt by him to make floods: this was rain, which was God urinating, and so babies were good like God. Rain–urine was dangerous and in crises it would be released as urinary incontinence, which once or twice happened in the interviews. God [he thought] flooded the world to drown people, just as babies imagine they could drown parents and especially mummy. But urine could be good and be drunk like milk; on the other hand it could be evil and full of poisonous germs, which brings death. So God could be good or bad.

> He used the water to make the biggest sea in the world – "bigger than the Thames or the Atlantic Ocean." And in the sea there "were storms and floodings"; in contrast, water was also soft and plastic, so it became mother whom he caressed and stroked. It was mother's milk and became an ocean inside babies; he sucked in the water-breast so that he came to possess a "minick breast", which could be an unlimited number of babies and restore damaged parents (Fordham, 1976, p. 206).

In this sequence different objects are equated, i.e. urine = rain = milk = water, because they have likenesses. In addition, the child's mind jumps from one line of thought to another often by the juxtaposition of opposites and he draws conclusions on the basis of such jumps. This thinking has been given different names according to the context in which it appears: omnipotent, undirected, analogic or mythopoeic.

It is from body imagery that other abstracts and impersonal forms develop by incorporating analogous material. Thus Alan's fantasy material already contained a number of ideas that he had been told about and which he had assimilated: God, the Flood, the river Thames and the Atlantic Ocean are interlaced with images, breast, milk, urine, babies etc., from everyday experience.

Thus, Alan's material showed a sophisticated imagery emerging. Indeed, it had characteristics also recorded by alchemists. These I collected together in *The Self and Autism* using some texts cited by Jung (Fordham, 1976). I remarked that had Alan lived in a suitable environment he might actually have become an alchemist. In fact he became a scientist.

The tracing-out of these "body-myths", which Alan developed, in relation to a child's life, and the working-out of their roots in infancy, has gone far enough forward for child analysts to begin constructing a picture of how it develops. In this it has been possible to gain help from psychoanalysts, especially the Kleinians whose theories of symbolic equations preceding symbolism, and the idea that symbolization underlines the development of thought, have been illuminating. Then there are longitudinal studies taking place. Patterns of infant behaviour are followed through into childhood. In this way a simple pattern can be shown to develop into rich symbolic play (e.g. Hoxeter, 1977).

Another example of the method was contributed by Winnicott, who suggested an origin for some forms of archetypal imagery in transitional objects and transitional phenomena, a subject I have already taken up in Chapter 4.

Alan's capacity for symbolic thought was very considerable and it only occurs in such profusion in disturbed children. But it is there in many others, though its quantity varies within wide limits. In normal children it is limited, in schizoid children it can be prolific especially in their manic states.

What is the essential difference between these children? It can be expressed psychiatrically, but it can also be approached by considering the theory of self-representations. In a schizoid child, self-representation is precarious, even fragmented, and so he creates links with which to hold his fragmented self together. In the case of a normal child with a well-established self-representation, that effort it not required because the self does not fragment. Thus it is understandable why a schizoid child makes so much use of symbolic thought: he tries to pull the self fragments together by emphasizing similarities and equating opposites so that he can prevent some sort of disaster taking place – a feeling of non-existence, perhaps, but it is not known with certainty what it is.

Returning now to the idea that the self is ultimately not representable, we may approach it from a different direction. A healthy child assumes a self and so he appears self-assured: he feels that he is somebody whose wishes and achievements will be taken into account and whose anger will have effect on those others in his environment who have charge over him. Basically he can trust them even though they have to do things that he does not like (or objects to with more or less violence). He is capable of love and does not have to use his mind to make an imaginary world full of symbols that will help to hold him together. In short he assumes existence and gives quite realistic though, from an adult point of view, limited accounts of what sort of a person he believes himself to be. He feels himself located in space and time with a group of characteristics, physical, mental and perhaps spiritual.

Ordinary Self-representation

A simple empirical approach can equally well be applied to adult persons by enquiring superficially how ordinary people commonly express views about themselves. Their views can be examined and grouped together so as to be made into a self-assessment inventory. Then a number of selves appear; physical, moral, ethical, personal, social etc.

At first sight these make a striking contrast to what we have been discussing. They are nothing like the seemingly inaccessible mystical self and nothing like the symbolic part selves. But are they all that different? Consider the parts of the self that Jungians regularly define. What of the persona? Is not this the kind of person that an individual needs to be recognized as being within his social setting, i.e. a social self? And the old wise man, is he not the ethical and moral self of the self-assessment inventory? There are other selves not included in the inventory but they could be. Why not include a question about what sort of person you are that you do not wish others to know of – would not that indicate the shadow? And if it were asked in a more discreet and subtle way, the anima or animus could be elicited. The person might have to be rather sophisticated to ask about the woman that a man knows himself to be internally or the man a woman knows she harbours inside herself, but it would be possible. According to analytical psychologists there are a number of other selves in this sense, not usually referred to as such, but often indicated by calling them the archetypes of the collective unconscious. These I think, would be much more difficult to contact through a questionnaire. They are more vague and ill-defined and seem to run into each other so that the image of chaos seems to cover them better than any other.

We have moved a long way from the grand archetypal forms that were said to influence the course of history, and from the mystical indefinable self, descending to a pedestrian level quite out of keeping with the grand conception of the self that has been generated by the complex personalities commonly treated by analytical psychologists. But the notion of parts of the self felt to be "myself" are essential in an ordinary person living an ordinary life, so that he can distinguish himself from other selves (persons) and the objects in the real world of which he can make reliable images by using sensory input constructively.

In varying ways the parts of the self can cohere and then a sense of identity or wholeness and continuity with the cosmos can emerge. It can be represented in images or it can be an imageless state that ordinary people assume or about which mystics inform us and to which they later on give names, such as union with God, nirvana, ultimate truth, purusha, atman or the zen states of enlightenment. Claims to attain this absolute sophisticated and unchildlike state require, with good reason, special conditions not provided by ordinary social living. However, less absolute and more relative states of wholeness are achievable and are increased by holidays, sexual intercourse and love, while we are given to believe that mothers and infants achieve quite a lot of it.

The Forms of the Self

I have postulated two forms of the self: the whole self and part selves. They are the result of two kinds of self functioning – integration and deintegration. It is apparent that deintegrated part selves can become sufficiently stable to be revealed in a self-assessment inventory. Thus both forms of the self tend to stability though there is oscillation between the two – more in infancy, less in adult persons.

The model is abstract, it does not value one self experience more than another; whether the self be integrated or deintegrated each has its place in differing cultures. Our society favours deintegrated manifestations for, if everybody devoted themselves to integration, there would be little room for the kind of culture that we have at the present time, which requires a person to make operational assessments of himself in varying situations and to act accordingly; so the stability of the whole self is difficult to realize. Perhaps that is difficult in any culture, but the more introverted cultures of the East seem to have given it greater status. However, it does not appear to be more within the reach of ordinary people for whom a religion of gods and rituals is provided.

I now want to apply the model to infancy and this will lead to the subject of individuation. Thinking from observations on children backwards into infancy and applying the idea of integration means that an infant began from a state of unity – a primary unity of the self. This conception leads on to seeing a number of quite obvious facts in a way that had not been possible before because an infant was conceived, among Jungians, to be in all essential respects a part of his mother. The hypothesis of a primary self leads in quite a different direction: the foetus can be seen as essentially separate from his mother and so also can the new-born child. This being so, then coming into relation with his mother becomes an achievement worked out gradually as maturation progresses. It begins with behaviour which involves deintegration out of his primary integrated state.

The unity of the infant expresses his individuality and it is attractive to think that it could provide the motivation for individuation as follows: just because the primary wholeness can never be achieved again once individuation has taken place, there is a drive to regain what is impossible. However, it can be approximated to in sleep, in blissful experience; later on it can be represented in omnipotent, wishful, ideal and holistic imagery. But in all these the original condition can only be sought for, so that when self representations are developed as a creative imaginative act, individuation is facilitated. As a psychodynamic principle this formulation may be justified, but when we start to apply it there are difficulties.

I derived this proposition by analogy, from Freud's ingenious derivation of the ego ideal from primary narcissism (Fordham, 1971). The idea that I found especially interesting was that, since the earlier state of primary narcissism could not be regained, but continues to be desirable, it leads to the construction of an ideal which refers to but does not repeat the original condition. Individuation, though conceived of as a process, is also thought of as an ideal state that can never be reached.

But is there a persistent period in the life of an infant that can be called primary narcissism? The idea that states of satisfaction, of unity, fusion or bliss have their root in a natural "stage" in the early life of an infant is very persistent. The idea that there is a stage in infancy when there is no conflict because there is no ego, and the mother's provision is so good that there is no conflict and the infant is always satisfied, is elaborated by Neumann (1973) as the "primal relationship". It is supposed to be the essential condition for satisfactory later development. It is sustained during the first year of life and is given up through the action of "automorphic" trends which lead to separation from the all-good Great Mother. Conflict then begins to be experienced as a result of ego development. The hypothesis includes the rather odd idea that the mother becomes the infant's self.

Neumann's thesis suffers from the disadvantages of Freud's stage of primary narcissism, though he is at pains to differentiate himself from that conception (Neumann, 1973). Non-conflictual states can be experienced from time to time by children and adults, and it seems likely that infants experience more of them, but that is as far as it is possible to go. It is of course true that the infant's relationship with his mother is his earliest one, but it is a rapidly developing one, often conflictual and essentially complex. The thesis that a mother becomes her infant's self is no more than a rationalized fantasy which takes little or no account of careful theoretical work, the analysis of small children, mother–infant observation and observational and experimental studies of the mother–infant relation. All these are brushed aside and replaced by generalizations.

Individuation

Individuation was originally conceived by Jung as a process of self-realization that took place in later life. It was related to the cultural development which has been referred to at the beginning of ths chapter. It was not related to childhood and it was not conceived that children individuate in the same sense at all. He held that a child needed to develop his ego with a view to adapting himself to the social milieu into which he had been born, and that it was the duty of parents and educators to foster these requirements of society. With their help the child could exercise his ego preparatory to achieving the limited aims of earning of livelihood, marrying and having children. The aim of becoming whole and realizing the self was relegated to a later phase. The thesis is a curious one for Jung to put forward for he never had a serious problem, because of his gifts, of finding a place in society and he could make his own choice and pursue his own interests throughout his life – true, much of himself had to be kept secret (personality number two) but it was always there. In later life, if we are to believe Jacobi (1967), he modified his view but her book still follows the earlier account to a large extent: the first half of life demands adaptation, the second requires introverted reflection and individuation proper as if this was not in itself an adaptation to ageing and the requirements of society for ageing people.

In *Children as Individuals* I put forward a rather different view, i.e. that a small child individuates before he comes much into relation with society which then exerts its influence so as to emphasize aspects of the self but not the whole. Thus a child specializes various parts of himself, and if other parts are less used, this is not necessarily at the expense of his individuality. Which parts are developed depends upon the culture pattern, the collective conscious and its correlate, the collective unconscious. Adaptation, let it be remembered, is not the same as conforming.

A small child or infant is of course influenced by the culture into which he is born, but it is through the styles and methods of upbringing adopted by his parents. The styles begin from childbirth, infant care and provision, continuing in the way his parents behave themselves and train him to behave. Later his teachers continue the process and school living inducts him further into social life. However, to all this he reacts as an individual if he is healthy, and so he is not just as it were ironed out by his education into a cultural norm. During a child's maturation there will be periods of introverted reflection and he will paint, draw, mould substances into shapes and use his imagination in all the ways that will be familiar. So in these respects he is like the individuating adult.

Of course he is different, and the differences lie mainly in the focus of his interest: it is directed to objects and persons and grow out of his relation to physical bodily objects which gradually coalesce to form whole persons. The rather portentous phrase "realization of the self", which involves a lot of purposeful introversion and often considerable intellectual activity, is not there; it is all more playful, so that becoming philosophical in the antique sense or forming an individual philosophy of life is meaningless to a child.

If I were to single out one difference among many others, which is decisive, I would point to the different form of the identifications involved. For a child these are based on his parents. It would be absurd, therefore, to talk of him as being identified with his profession, his parental role or an ideal business, political or religious philosophy. Yet it is those identifications which, having served their purpose, become no longer meaningful to individuals in later life and it is they who found that individuation provided a solution to their quandary. When social (alternatively called collective) identifications broke down they did not become children again when a regression took place to the underlying primitive identity, they became childlike through establishing a relation to the child archetype.

Once the differences have been specified in this fashion, then it can be seen that the basic underlying process of individuation in infancy, childhood, adolescence and adulthood is identical. It is a progression from states of primitive identity and magic thinking to separation from that state and a resulting release of creative imagination leading to maturation of the ego expressed by saying that an extension of consciousness takes place.

If we consider how this occurs during early infancy and early childhood, an extra step needs to be added because the infant state is first of all one of integration. Soon after birth deintegration takes place as the infant develops approach and attachment behaviour which brings him into relation with his mother to form an experience of her which is percolated with omnipotent feeling and fantasy of an archetypal kind. When he achieves this, he has arrived at the state of primitive identity which underlies the adult's mature identifications. Its imagery is more physical and it is far less sophisticated, as I indicated by describing Alan and his alchemical-like fantasies, but it is essentially the same. Out of this state individuation takes place whatever the age of the person.

Conclusion

We have considered groups of experience which carry the feeling of being myself. They can be quite personal and can be quite easily located or can, as it were, expand by the development of imaginative constructions to cover a sense of being an individual and part of the cosmos.

These experiences begin in early childhood, ripening and changing their form as growth proceeds. I have also introduced some abstractions from these experiences and that of the self as the whole person is the main one. As an abstraction it leads on to considering the nature of man – I gladly feel that I have done my duty in mentioning that, and have no intention of going further into the subject. Therefore I can restrict my conclusion by repeating the notion, which appears to stand on firmer ground, that a human being needs to develop ideas, feelings and concepts of himself and what he is like in different situations so that he can orientate himself in relation to others. In addition, he expands those experiences to material and spiritual life and finds, in the end through imaginative constructions, a way of relating himself to the cosmos.

Chapter Six

*The ego and the self**

Introduction

As I shall now consider some writings of psychoanalysis, a preliminary comment on my method may not be out of place.

In studying psychoanalysis and searching especially for concepts of the ego that can be useful to analytical psychologists, it is necessary to keep in mind that the orientation is different – more so historically than at present. For instance, even when analytical psychologists are using "reductive" analysis, they tend to be more on the outlook for synthetic processes than are psychoanalysts. That leads to differing orientations towards ego defences; these are thought of more as psychic structures, so that they are not something to be done away with, as psychoanalysts sometimes think. That sharp dichotomy is not truly valid today, and the Jungian view of defences has been taken into or developed independently by psychoanalysis, while there are Jungians who currently believe that defences, particularly repression, are undesirable and should not exist. Nevertheless the broad distinction remains because psychoanalysis, in contrast to "classical" Jungian practice, is essentially occupied with tracing out the infantile roots of symptoms and personal characteristics.

In consequence the idiom is different: one does not find the same emphasis on awe-inspiring imagery in psychoanalysis. How that comes about is very well illustrated by Jung in his comparison between reductive and synthetic interpretation in *Two Essays on Analytical Psychology* (1926). A view of numinous imagery from a psychoanalytical stance is to be found in Hans Sach's analysis of "A dream of Bismarck's" quoted by Freud in *The Interpretation of Dreams* (Freud, 1900–1, p. 378).

*Originally published as "The relation of the ego to the self", in the *British Journal of Medical Psychology* vol. 37, no. 89, 1964. The present chapter has been added to and revised.

Other quandaries arise from time to time. The recent studies of narcissistic disorders by psychoanalysts with the introduction of self theory has some striking similarities with my own conclusions studying the same field, but I would not have thought of the conditions described as being primarily narcissistic. In so far as many of the features are evidently narcissistic – the grandiose self and the mirror transference as described by Kohut – I would agree, but I would be disposed to interpret the narcissism as a manifestation of an introversion neurosis and to conclude that the narcissism comes about through identification with the often exalted images derived from the archetypes of the collective unconscious. I do not want to argue again the long contested question about the nature of libido, but only wish to point out that psychoanalysts can use the extended theory of narcissism because of the sexual theory of the libido. Consequently any inturning libido is automatically narcissistic. For Jung the libido was not exclusively sexual and so narcissism cannot be used in the same extended sense.

There are also other differences between concepts of the ego. In psychoanalysis all data that are not more or less inchoate drives, emanating from the id, are states of the ego which is divided up into the ego, super-ego and more recently the self has been added. Thus the ego can be unconscious as well as conscious. By contrast, Jung defined the ego, originally at least, as the centre of consciousness and so it did not extend into the unconscious except in so far as a part of it could be repressed.

I am deliberately making stark contrasts which are now largely historical to the thinking of both disciplines. Neither can claim the same theoretical solidarity; indeed, the confusion is something at which to be amazed. Nonetheless, history is not dead but still colours our deliberations and, if not kept in view, makes far more confusion than is often necessary.

I am persuaded, however, that a common pattern can often be found both in the data and the formulation of the two schools even though the idiom is more or less radically different. The common ground is much more obvious in later developments of psychoanalysis, especially in the English school of psychoanalysts whose members have studied the same clinical field of border-line and psychotic disorders.

In pursuing my line of enquiry, I am following Jung's method in so far as he compared numerous disciplines, searching in them for common archetypal patterns. The procedure I adopt will not always produce a logical structure, though there is both a theory and a model of the self in my mind all the time. Comparing the literature of psychoanalysis with that of analytical psychology results in an amplification, an attempt to clarify what is obscure by a comparative method. I see no reason to regret either occasional ambiguity or obscurity, though one should endeavour to limit both. In writing about the psyche and particularly the self, one is trying to comprehend a system that may be essentially obscure and ambiguous, so that anything like formulating clear theoretical statements and testing them with precision is only occasionally possible. Such a proposition would make it understandable why attempts to build a coherent theoretical metapsychology by psychoanalysts have resulted in a regular babel of voices and lead to a detachment from analytical experience with patients which is the despair of clinicians.

It is usual to contrast what is Freudian with the ideas and practices to which Jungians subscribe. So far I have followed that classification, though I no longer consider the distinction valid. Psychoanalysis has developed in a number of original ways which will be considered in the following chapter, selecting those changes which include self theory. In that there will be an omission: the work of Melanie Klein though Clifford Scott, Winnicott and Margaret Little were all powerfully influenced by her.

It was Melanie Klein who followed a parallel path to Jung in penetrating behind the oedipal conflicts into the mother–infant relation, thus opening up the child's inner world from which Freud was debarred. Her achievement was fiercely contested and is only now becoming better evaluated and developed. It was she that, without using the word much, introduced a psychology of the self to psychoanalysts and it has been with Kleinian psychoanalysts that discussions have proved most fruitful to me and other members of the London school of analytical psychologists.

This chapter is divided into three sections: the first enumerates some of the many efforts made to build a concept of the self based on empirical data; the second discusses the relation of the self to the ego; the third suggests ways in which the concepts developed can be used to elucidate analytic practice.

Since radically different data are being observed which are supposed to represent a single concept or entity, I have paid attention to some varying methods used to obtain the data, only, however, entering into those methodological details that are relevant to the rather general style of presentation.

PART ONE

Some Definitions

In his book *The Principles of Psychology*, William James (1950) devotes a chapter to "Consciousness of the self". There he considers the subject at length in the light of philosophers' deliberations and then with current psychological knowledge. Naturally, much of what he says has dated, but his general thesis is found among us today. In masterly fashion, he ranges over a wide field to define the varying selves – now material, now social, now spiritual – among which we live. In this changing scene there is an overriding self, expressed in the sense of continuity of being and of personal identity. This he can call "the pure ego", a change in terminology which caused him no trouble.

Since then the term "self" has taken on rather different but contiguous usages. When hypostatized, i.e. expressed as a model, it means an entity which organizes separate parts of the personality into a whole and is the embodied personality, psyche and soma. Becoming aware of it is the goal of a particular life and, because each life is different from any other, the individual alone can become conscious of its unique characteristics. For this reason no true assertion can be made by a second person about another self and accurate knowledge of it is outside empirical observation.

However, all this need not prevent ideas being developed about the self so long as they are recognized as approximations, nor does it obstruct analysts acting as if the ideas were true. Thus the behaviour of analysts regularly accords with the assumption that they cannot decide what is ultimately right or wrong for any particular patient. Expressed anthropomorphically, they work on the principle that the self alone knows what is right for the individual.

Winnicott's use of the terms true and false selves seems in line with this thinking; a true self represents the real nature of a person and can be experienced by him in the way he lives. If I understand him rightly, the true self does not need analytic dissection and is therefore irreducible. At first sight, the differentiation between true and false self follows Jung's distinction between self and persona. Winnicott, however, gives much more weight to the false self as a pathological formation, whereas analytical psychologists conceive of the persona as a sub-system in the self which facilitates adaptation to the requirements of social living. Only when the ego becomes identified with the persona can the condition be thought of as pathological.

Clifford Scott's concept of the body scheme also belongs to this area of study. He defined an entity which covers the total picture of the cosmic and personal situation of man as follows:

> Let us assume there is a more or less conscious integrate of sensations, perceptions, conceptions, affects, memories and images of the body from its surface to the depths and of the body from its surface to the limits of the cosmos. Let us assume that it is an integrate that is concerned not only with what is inside a boundary but also with what it outside a boundary as well as with the boundary itself.

. . . This integrate is a scheme, or to use an old English word, a plan; and as the boundary or interface has not a peripheral but a central position, for our purposes, perhaps, it can best be called a body scheme (Scott, 1949, p. 142).

He instances a patient who called the scheme "my enigma":

He was [35 years old and] reared a Roman Catholic. At 25 he had lost his soul and had felt better. He felt he could call his experiences either mental or physical. At 30 he ceased to feel any essential difference between body and mind. He felt an improvement in his ability to deal with work, children and adults. What he had in place of mind, body and soul he called "my enigma" – the enigma of growth and development. His growth is continuing (ibid., pp. 142–3).

The patient's account introduces "growth and development". Scott makes explicit the cosmic element frequently found in writings on the self. To exemplify it, he cites a number of disciplines in which he conceives the body scheme to be relevant: embryology, neurology, academic psychology, parapsychology, religion, psychiatry, psychoanalysis and poetry. I am sure he could have added more.

Jung's Empirical Research

Jung advanced the study of the self in a way which is close to Winnicott's empirical writing about a true self. His conclusions are also like Scott's, in that the self is a scheme, with a centre, a boundary and a cosmic dimension; it also embraces the psyche–soma and remains ultimately an enigma. Jung, however, claims more than either Scott or Winnicott. He not only formulated ideas about the self but studied empirically how the self could be made conscious. With this aim in view, he observed patients in whom symbolic images, which took the form of configurations, or structures, referred clearly to a single totality (*vide* Chapter 1).

Jung's Method of Eliciting Data

Since Jung's formulations are abstractions derived from his experience, we can neither estimate their reliability nor evaluate them without being clear about the method he employed to elicit his data. I have already considered some of these in Chapter 1 but will now go into them further.

He studied dream sequences and extracted recurrent archetypal themes from them. Alternatively, he used active imagination (Jung, 1916; also Fordham, 1958a).

Active imagination is a method which builds on the capacity of patients, usually of middle age and showing rather marked schizoid or depressive trends, to treat their inner world as if it were objective. An object is deliberately imagined; it may be painted or modelled but, in whatever medium it is expressed, the aim is to establish an inner subject–object relationship. If proceeded with consistently, the method leads to individuation.

There is also a trend in Jung's discussion of his method which I believe is much more important and does not get the attention it deserves, though it is reflected in the common anathematization of technique (*vide* Fordham, 1967b). He believes that "the doctors habit of 'knowing beforehand' is a disadvantage to a psychotherapist and that in any thorough analysis patient and therapist find themselves in a relationship found on mutual unconsciousness" (Jung, 1946, p. 176), and elsewhere in *Memories, Dreams, Reflections* he writes after agreeing that an analysis therapist must be familiar with "method", "in general one must guard against theoretical assumptions . . . In my analysis they play no part. I am unsystematic very much by intention" (Jung, 1963). His procedure was very much interactional and involved the unconscious of the analyst. In addition, he sought to diminish the analyst's influence by giving the patient the means of analysing himself and reducing the frequency of meetings between analyst and patient. Whilst I have criticized some of the applications, I believe that Jung did much to introduce an attitude of not knowing on the part of the therapist. Of course that attitude may be seen in Freud's "free floating attention" or in his recommendation that the analyst use his unconscious as an instrument of cognition in the analysis, but I think that all these rest upon a fundamental unknowing – the unknowing about the self expressed in the totality definition of it. That state cannot ever be known, only its manifestations and deintegrates can be observed; thus "unknowing" constellates the self.

It is of course obvious that Jung published studies involving a vast amount of knowledge about the psyche and a method of studying it and I find it impossible that all that had no influence on his analysis and other therapeutic endeavours. It inevitably lies as a reservoir of knowledge to be consulted as the analysis proceeds. It is not complete and any particular patient will more or less frequently produce material which falls outside its competence. The act of unknowing to which I refer sometimes simply involves scrupulously detaching from it and sometimes dismantling it. The attitude which Jung aimed to induce by using active imagination reminds one of that described by Kris in terms of a "good analytic hour".

In the "good analytic hour", the ego regresses and at the same time observes until the analyst "can put what he has to offer into a question and the patient himself can do the summing up; the patient's participation is thus maximised" (Kris, 1956, p. 451ff.). Continuing, Kris says: "The principle involved is, I believe, fairly stated when we say that when interpretations are offered, the controlling part of the ego over the state of temporary and partial regression, is expected to expand into an observing one." He proposes that "The object of this observation is the *self*"!*

All this occurs within the interpersonal setting of the psychoanalytic set-up and differs from Jung's attempts to initiate a method in which such observation was made by the individual in isolation. My object in taking an example from the experience of a psychoanalyst is to show that different methods can interdigitate. Whilst strictly speaking results cannot be separated from the method of attaining them, yet it is of particular interest if comparable observations can be made using different methods.

Kris gives us a warning about the pitfalls of self observation:

> [it] may become symptomatic of obsessional scrupulosity or narcissistic introspection "the self admiration of the mirror image" . . . but [self] observation as autonomous function tinged as it may be by both self critical and self-loving components, is essentially characterized by its detachment, or, as one might say, by the individual's ability to achieve objectivity in his perceptions about himself. It is a goal never to be reached . . . but . . . at least a tendency towards detachment may be all important (Kris, 1956, p. 452).

It has been made a reproach that Jung's method leads to both the faults mentioned by Kris and, indeed, some of the literature displays them. All that need be said here is that, if his methods of observing dream and fantasy opened the door to obsessional scrupulosity or narcissistic preoccupation, these are not results which Jung himself would have agreed to countenance except as transitory states of mind.

Besides these dangers there are, I think, others which need consideration because of Jung's contention that he is studying objective data which cannot be assimilated by the ego under the conditions he set up.

(1) It could be that his methods increase tendencies to depersonalization and that consequently the objects are not fundamentally objective but are the result of their alienation by the ego (*vide* Federn, 1953).
(2) The method may foster splitting in the ego or even ego disintegration.

*Though Kris does not refer to anything like the symbolic material which Jung details, Aigrisse (1962) shows that mandala symbols can be found in a case treated along psychoanalytic lines. She saw her patient twice a week and analysed childhood memories using free association.

It is known that active imagination can occasionally precipitate psychotic reactions, but the cases in which this happens invariably show evidence of a previous or a latent psychosis. That Jung's case material often gives a rather dissociated picture is largely due to his method of extracting archetypal contents from the material as a whole.

Characteristic of Jung's work is the combination of clinical observations with ethnological parallels. He elucidates the historical dimension in the following way: he defines the more stable components in the inner world by finding out which recur and which do not. Then he relates the recurring themes to their historical parallels and thus his clinical data are set in a matrix of historical antecedents. Combining this dimension with his emphasis on prospective ongoing developments in time, it is easy to account for his interest in the sophisticated complex structures which his data show. They contrast sharply with the simpler object relations revealed by analytic reduction of these structures to their origins in infancy and childhood. It may be necessary to point out here that partly because of his ongoing, prospective interest, Jung's studies are not analytic in any sense of the term which is meaningful and were not intended to be so. He repeatedly insisted that he aims to study the synthetic processes in the psyche (Jung, 1953).

It was to implement this aim that he limited the analyst's influence by reducing the frequency of the interviews and diminishing his interpretative efforts as well. Both procedures were intended to increase the patient's active interest in the parts of himself that can be treated objectively and handled individually with minimal assistance from anybody else. Thus he kept in mind that realization of the self is ultimately a private uncommunicable state and even the presence of an analyst is an intrusion on that state.

However, his demarcation between synthetic and analytic treatment is not so convincing today as it was when he first elaborated it and cannot be maintained with the rigidity sometimes implied, for instance by the idea that therapy can be divided up into two parts: the first being reductive, the second being synthetic. Furthermore, his procedure is not so different in principle from contemporary "psychoanalytic" techniques of interpretation as it was believed to be at first. He aimed, for instance, to reduce anxiety by linking up the experiences with comparable ones recorded by other people and introduced educational methods, such as selected reading and seminars, so as to give information about the imagery which becomes conscious and which is otherwise confusing. He recommended myths and religious ritual – as used either today or in the past – so as to show the patient that he is not alone in his experience and that others have survived it. In principle this is also an aim of interpretations which differ, however, in being intentionally made more personal by including the transference.*

As it may be supposed that these reflections detract somewhat from Jung's work, I want to leave no doubt as to my own position. I consider Jung was the first to evolve a method whereby the self could be systematically observed and experienced.

Integration and Deintegration

There are two features of Jung's material which have been of particular interest to me:

(1) Though the data show an inner consistency, their content varies greatly: anything from a small dot to an elaborate structure does to represent the archetype of the self, and only when a reasonable degree of organization has taken place do the symbols show characteristics already referred to above. They thus represent states of organization or steady states which are more or less conscious.
(2) The integrated states shown by the symbols are periodic.

What is going on in between the steady states and how and what dynamic process makes it possible for their content to vary by increasing in complexity? These two questions suggest that the concept of the self needs revision along the lines that I first put forward some years back (Fordham, 1955). I outlined an idea that only one function of the self is to organize and integrate; it also divides itself up, and for this event I proposed the term deintegration. Thus I introduced a new view of the subject; the self is no longer conceived of as a static structure, instead the steady state represents one phase in a dynamic sequence: integration is followed by deintegration, which in turn leads to a new integrate. The sequence is conceived to repeat throughout life and lies at the root of maturational development.

In formulating this process theory, I also had in mind the tendency of integrated stable states to be sterile in that they could now allow adequately for the incorporation of new components. I was confirmed in this idea by the studies of creative activity undertaken by Marion Milner (1957) in her book *On Not Being Able to Paint*, and in Ehrenzweig's (1957) paper "Creative surrender". Both contained ideas which came close to what I was wanting to present.

*An interpretation implies that the analyst has experienced in the past, and is now able to manage, something like the patient's present experience and which the patient fears that he cannot survive. There are clearly great differences between education, learning and interpretation, but there may well be an untapped field of study by comparing the two procedures more carefully.

PART TWO

Ego and Self

Quite early on in his career, Jung defined the ego as the centre of consciousness. This conception was part of his theory of complexes which rested on experimental evidence (Jung, 1906–9).

In his later empirical work, particularly when using active imagination, he found it essential to distinguish the ego from the archetypes because of the need to keep the archetypal experience objective and so preserve ego boundaries and avoid inflation of the ego, as manifested, for instance, in the grandiose self that has received increasing attention especially by Kohut. He therefore underlined his definition, repeatedly and sometimes emphatically, by asserting that the self is different from the ego in that it includes unconscious processes which the ego does not – a formulation which contradicts later ones – and refers to his idea of "confrontation" between conscious and the unconscious. Keeping as close as possible to his observations, he also thought of the ego as a subjective personal datum in contrast to the objective archetypes and the self.

In this context it is possible to understand his assertion that the self "is completely outside the personal sphere" (Jung, 1954b, p. 30); a statement, however, that also combines with his interest in the study of those religious experiences which have social, historical and anthropological implications.

However, as his work developed his ideas changed. He discovered that some of the archetypal forms, particularly the shadow, contained ego structures which had been split off and needed re-assimilating into the ego. Later he went further and recognized an unconscious aspect to the ego; indeed, in the *Mysterium Coniunctionis* (1955–6, p. 117) – his last important book – he developed a basically different concept (*vide supra* p. 46). The ego is phenomenologically identical with the self and, since the self is a union of conscious and unconscious components, the ego must be made up of these two elements also. Here, then, the concept of the ego has become deepened, but all the same he still maintained that the self was to be distinguished from the ego, rather in the sense that God (the self) made man (the ego) in his own image. Though contextually different this notion is not basically so different from Freud's formulation (where Id was Ego shall be).

Jung demonstrated a synthetic process in the personality reflected in symbolic forms: he described his method clearly and demonstrated his results, but his account of the relation between personal and archetypal experience is unclear or lacking (*vide* Chapter 1, pp. 16f; Williams, 1963a). This was one motive which led me to study the work of psychoanalysts:

perhaps they could help to fill in the gap Jung had left. We have already referred to the work of Winnicott and Scott, but Federn's struck me as the more relevant for the purpose I had in mind.

Jung, it will be remembered, approached the subject of the self from the study of schizophrenia. Federn also investigated the same realm and had become a psychoanalyst after starting as a psychiatrist. He studied the empirical sense of "Ich Gefühl" which is translated as "ego feeling" or "self feeling". In these investigations the ego concept was more comprehensive in that anything that was not id, comprising more or less unstructured drives, was ego or later super-ego. Federn's work, is a first attempt by a psychoanalyst to study the self empirically. The result was different from Jung's findings. Nothing resembling active imagination is found in Federn's studies and it seems that he had not thought of the symbolism found in schizophrenia as thereapeutic in any sense that Jung meant it, though Freud had arrived at the idea that "*The delusional formation, which we take to be a pathological product, is in reality an attempt at recovery, a process of reconstruction*" (Freud, 1911, p. 71). It remained for Jung and, after him, Perry (1957) to work out some of its implications by taking the psychotic manifestations as a distorted form of active imagination. Federn was consistently in favour of preventing the manifest schizophrenic disorder by reinforcing the ego against the disease process. Therefore he concentrated his interest on ego boundaries and the relation of these to depersonalization and estrangement (also called derealization). This makes a link with observations by analytical psychologists in that it is recognized that as the archetypes emerge into consciousness – and especially the central archetype of the self – feelings of strangeness or mystery are registered. Federn, however, emphasized their negative meaning and investigated them in terms of narcissistic cathexes as the psychoanalytic metapsychology required: an advance on Jung's thesis in that it is more dynamic and explanatory; a retreat because there is no room for the concept of a central archetype which seems to be of value when studying the psychoses.

It may be tempting to consider Jung's observations on the self in terms of splitting in the ego and do away with the necessity for operating with two entities. To do so it must be shown that a concept of the self is unnecessary. It has been shown above that, on empirical grounds, there is much against such a solution. If Jung's and Federn's work is compared, that conclusion is reinforced. Federn distinguishes two kinds of estrangement, that applying to external and that applying to internal objects, but he develops his observations and ideas only in relation to the former. This ties in with his negative evaluation of the symbolism in schizophrenia and there is little doubt that he devalues the inner world in the terms it is studied by analytical psychologists in such detail. Nonetheless he agrees with the need to preserve ego boundaries.

It is no surprise to find that Federn ended up in the metapsychology of ego cathexes and the subjects of primary and secondary narcissism. If we accept the idea that theories can represent archetypal forms (*vide supra* p. 7), it then seems probable that, in his theories, he was unwittingly representing the inner processes under consideration. The form was abstract and so the value of the imagery behind it eluded him.

Relevant interest in ego psychology has recently expanded and with it seems to have come an interest in a self which is different from the ego. Hartmann was one of the psychoanalysts to distinguish between the two. He states:

> . . . in using the term narcissism, two different sets of opposites often seem to be fused into one. The one refers to the self (one's own person) in contradistinction to the object, the second to the ego (as a psychical system) in contrast to other substructures of the personality. However, the opposite of object cathexis is not ego cathexis, but cathexis of one's own person, that is, self cathexis . . . (Hartmann, 1950, p. 84).

He thus began to differentiate the self from the ego and others have followed him. It is, no doubt, on the basis of this work that Sandler (1962) defines a self schema having the following characteristics:

(1) It is not the same as the ego.
(2) It contains conscious and unconscious components.
(3) It has a shape which can appear in the representational world and can change.
(4) The shape gets built up gradually.

How does the self become represented? Spiegel (1959) introduced theories based on experimental data. He thinks that the idea of pooling perceptual data can be useful and says:

> In the beginning of mental life, separate states of tension and discharge succeed each other, such as hunger, thirst, diffuse sexual tension, bowel-bladder tension; these leave traces in the form of mental representations; the pooling function establishes an average representation of each separate representation of these states which, as a result, possess permanence and continuity in time. . . . In the normal individual these average representations become interconnected and grow into a steady frame of reference to which we give the name self (Spiegel, 1959, p. 96).

Whereas he considers that the pooling process is a function of the ego alone, it may also be contributed to by the functioning of archetypes in the unconscious. These may be conceived to order and arrange perceptual data on average lines rather as the gestalt psychologists propose.*

To conclude this part of my thesis, it is clear that a number of research workers agree that, though they may not know very well what the self is, they have yet ways to define it in terms of clinical or experimental data. All of them discuss the relation of the ego to the self. I have assumed that they all refer to the self as a single entity. It would also be possible to develop the alternative thesis that several contiguous entities are being referred to, but I shall ignore that.

PART THREE

Analytic Observations

Approaching the self from Jung's standpoint, I have become interested in applying his ideas and observations to analytic practice so as to include personal components and development from infancy onwards. Jung paid little attention to either of these and I have tried to supplement his work by applying his thesis to observations made in the transference setting. Instead of looking at the problem in terms of symbolic imagery reported by the patient, it is my object to define data which can be observed directly. In passing we may note that Jung (1946) himself had included the transference in his studies of the self and its manifestations, but he had done so mainly in terms of alchemy and of the structure of society.

Regression

An influential factor in what I have to say now has been the positive attitude which Jung sometimes adopted to regression. He went so far as to state that: "The regressive tendency only means that the patient is seeking *himself* . . ." (Jung, 1930a, p. 33).

This statement combined with his essay on "The child archetype", especially in the section "The child as beginning and end" (Jung, 1951a, pp. 117ff.), suggested to me that one object of regression could be to realize steady states noted in discussing the self conceived as the central archetype.

*It may be of interest here that Spiegel draws on the work of Helson, who suggests "a neurological model to account for pooling" (Spiegel, 1959, p. 96, n. 7). Jung (1958a, pp. 370ff.) also considers that the self, as central archetype, has a neurological basis.

It is not at all difficult to find examples of steady states: the "good analytic hour" described by Kris is one, but his description is incomplete so I will supplement it. After, or during, a good piece of analytic work there is frequently a favourable change in a patient. Matters which had earlier been the object of intense anxiety get talked about as shades of their former selves. Memories from childhood change so that aspects of a parent come to light which had before been uncommunicated or denied. The patient himself seems more self contained and able to relate to his analyst, to have an identity of his own, and at the same time boundaries become firmer and more resilient. When it first appears, this state is almost certain to be unstable and will give clear indications of the lines future deintegration will take. But when the steady state occurs, particularly in the analysis of psychotic parts of the personality, it is a significant event because, once it has been achieved, and the patient retains a memory of having felt whole, later disintegrations are likely to be more easy to handle.

Steady states often depend upon reaching, through regression, an affective balance which the patient can manage. Thus material presented in terms of oedipal patterns, with a great deal of persecutory anxiety and idealization, can become relatively unimportant when a further regression is made to a two-body relationship. The oedipal conflict has not been resolved, it has been abandoned by regressing from the genital to the oral phase in which the object relations become positive because of a preponderance of good over bad objects. It is a stage in development which has been relatively successful and so makes good point of departure for dealing with bad objects.

States of wholeness may occur with nobody else present. Jung, I suggest, may have found a non-analytic way to make these truly worth while because he showed his patients how to be with themselves, alone, and find it productive. States of wholeness also occur with one other person present. Then a relationship is possible if the second person is stable enough. Once this has been achieved, the infant or patient can go on to manage three or four body relationships. Once a four body set up has become possible (self, mother, father and one sibling), it is usually assumed that other more complex object relations will present relatively little difficulty. Today, however, research suggests that a group, for example, is more than a family and introduces different conflict situations.

If some self realization, and so a relationship, has become possible, then analysis is possible; when achieved, quite a lot can be done about less developed states in which the patient needs to be alone (and a unit) so long as the analyst is willing to be treated as non-existent.

Dimensions of Ego and the Self

Reading Federn's book (1953) with Jung's thesis in mind, it became increasingly clear, however, that two dimensions were involved; that of the ego and that of the self. If the "Ich Gefühl" be considered from the dimension of the ego, then the self appears as part of the ego. But looked at from that of the self, then it would be conceived as manifesting the central archetype of which the ego is a part. I now want to approach the subject of the two dimensions from a different angle by considering further the subject of regression.

When Little published her thesis "On basic unity" (Little, 1960), she described the management of regression to a state of fusion with the analyst, a state to which the patient needed to regress and had to be accepted. Her paper was followed by another in which the authors (Nacht and Vidermann, 1960) asserted that regression to this state should be firmly controlled, since it led to abandonment of the ego in favour of fusion with the analyst. Here were two attitudes towards regression to a state of unity through fusion. At first, they seem incompatible but they can be seen in terms of the two dimensions under consideration.

To elucidate further what is meant by the two dimensions reflected in the two papers, I introduce the postulate of a primary integrate or original state of the self. It corresponds to the state of Scott's patient (*vide supra* p. 98) in that there is no relevant distinction between mind and body. In order to derive psychic structure I assumed that the self deintegrates; when the first deintegration occurs was left an open question. However, in view of increasing knowledge about intrauterine life, it we may think happens before birth. The flood of stimuli provided by birth itself produces anxiety, the release of breathing, and crying activities that must certainly suggest an early deintegrative state. It is assumed that the infant reintegrates again before he starts his first feed, in which further instinctual release (deintegration) occurs.

The primary integrate is, subjectively, a phenomenonless state. I have used this idea to comprehend autistic children and assume that basically they are so integrated as to be inaccessible. Their ability to express themselves is primary and so is conceived to depend upon a hard core of the personality which cannot be reached, there being no means with which to express what is there.

I can illustrate my idea by an example: an autistic child never made much improvement over a period of several years. I kept in touch with him for 10 years. To my recurring surprise he always insisted on coming to see me, but never said a word. I can only say with confidence that what I said or did on two occasions had any influence. On both occasions it was dramatic and was due to an interpretation: one stopped him getting fevers, another made it possible for him to relax and look at me directly with love.

Another example: an adult patient, who nearly died of a severe illness many years before she had started analysis, stated that she felt her emptiness at the time of her illness was full of a power without form, so she could not express anything. She had told me of a state that I inferred lay at the root of the child's pathological stability.

Margaret Little reconstructs the healthy unity as follows:

> within an individual both survival and the ability to find objects with which relationships can be formed depend upon the existence of a unity . . . From it a rhythm of differentiation and reassimilation or integration comes. It provides the "stillness at the centre" which allows of movement and perception; it is the *sine qua non* for living continuously in one's body, for having an identity, and for being identical with, and able to make assertions of or statements about oneself (Little, 1960, p. 125).

That important statement looks like agreement with the notion of the self integrating and deintegrating, but when she explains the states of mind by attributing them to an original "mother–infant unity" I would question her explanation. The relation between a mother and her baby is far too complex to consider one supposed state of mind to be decisive in any psychopathological construct.

My own earlier investigations and speculations were published in *Children as Individuals* and *The Self and Autism*. In those books I accepted a stage of primary identity because I had not taken sufficiently into account the studies of Klein and Bion, nor had I grasped the significant data revealed in mother–infant observations. The correlation of infant–mother observations with constructions made during the analysis of adults and children leads to the conclusion that the stages or positions hypothesized are partly successful attempts to describe states of mind that an infant may experience: they do not do more than that. Thus the state of unity between mother and infant is not an especially useful idea to describe states of mind of observed mothers and their infants.

Long ago Kant postulated a transcendental ego which William James discusses and quotes from Kant as follows: "At the basis of our knowledge of ourselves there lies only 'the simple and utterly empty idea: I; of which we can not even say we have a notion'" (James, 1950, p. 362). Substituting self for "I" reaches what I have in mind: an original self integrate without phenomena. It is first manifest in infancy and is also represented in philosophy and religion, for instance in the Oriental doctrine of maya.

The original phenomenonless self is assumed to develop by deintegration – instinctual release is one manifestation of it. It is commonly assumed, though without evidence from studies of infancy, that this leads to a primary identity with the mother. It first occurs in the early stages of breast feeding: the original integrate being reflected in oral identity with the breast.

The essence of deintegration can thus be conceived of as part of a progression brought about through the breaking down of integrates and dissolving previously established unities. It follows that in normal development the "delusional" state of primary identity – or unity – with the mother can only be transitory and the formation of a new integrate, a new dynamic equilibrium within the infant, corresponding to, but more differentiated than, the original self unit. It is a development in the sense that part of the original self has become ego.

Returning to the dramatically different attitudes adopted on the one hand by Little (1960) and on the other by Nacht and Vidermann (1960). It is clear that, conceived from the dimension of ego psychology, primary identity can only give opportunities for the ego to abandon all that has been established later (this is the position of Nacht and Vidermann (1960)). Looked at from the dimension of the self, a different attitude is possible towards regression. If the primary identity with the mother is a development, an early deintegration, it is an ongoing process, a step forward and the model for deintegration in general. This conception accords with Little's findings and attitude about the need for some cases to regress to "basic unity" with the analyst.*

In my understanding Little's argument means that if primary identity with the mother has never been reached, then there is nothing that can be done analytically. If it has been achieved and everything following is precariously balanced, then it will be necessary to regress to the state of primary identity before the processes of growth and development can proceed satisfactorily, but it will mean the analyst being ready to feel treated as non-existent in the sense of being replaced by a delusion of unity with the patient. Since some schizophrenic children have got far enough to let analysts function as parts of themselves in this sense, it may be assumed that primary identity with the mother has been achieved by some of them. That explains why they are accessible if given forms (interpretations) which they use increasingly to express themselves (see Fordham, 1976). Once again I consider this attractive but too facile an explanation.

Countertransference

In an earlier paper I stated that the self "controls and has controlled all my thinking about countertransference" (Fordham, 1960a, p. 6).

*The concept of basic unity alternatively called primary identity is global. It is experienceable in some patients as a rather fixed state of affairs, but that is a state which is not simple. If it is studied as a term to cover all the early states of mind in infancy, then a complex picture emerges.

I would now like to record some notes amplifying what I then meant. My statement was made with the following idea in mind: to conduct analysis on the basis of a theory and its corresponding technique could mean an analyst barricaded within an abstract system into which the patient is "found" to fit. That conception is not entirely absent from accounts of analytical and analytically orientated psychotherapy and, when based on "scientific" considerations, can give a glow of omnipotence to the therapist.

That conception of analysis belongs to the days (still present in many quarters) when it was thought that interpretations could and should be correct. If they were not, then it was customary to suspect the activity of countertransference on the part of the analyst.

It is true that there is a wide field of analytic practice in which an analyst may be able to understand a patient well enough for the patient to gain profit from his interventions, so that changes take place in the patient's flow of associations or other behaviour, indicating that his resistances become less and more manageable (see Wisdom, 1967). Such criteria are rough though important to observe, but it is daring and probably unjustified to believe that what he says is correct; he is on much safer ground if he decides, with the patient's collaboration, whether or not his interpretations are useful. The situation between analyst and patient consists in the interaction between two personalities. The analyst's theory and technique expresses, in generalized form, that part of himself which has in the past proved useful and so can be put to the service of the patient. Theory is understood, not as an autonomous impersonal structure upon which the analyst bases his technique, but as the abstract expression of the analyst's own self or parts of it in so far as he relates to his patients as a whole.

According to this idea, teaching techniques and theories of analysis rely upon the common archetypal basis of the human personality, and upon the like nature of the structures that have been built upon it through identifications made in the course of development. However, there are also the individual characteristics of the self to be considered: these ensure that any theory of analysis or psychotherapy is incomplete, and represents the common pooling of experience with the individual characteristics shorn off it. In analysis itself the individual characteristics are reinstated, and so each analysis is unique and, as Jung evocatively put it, requires a new theory.

So far these ideas are an interpretation of accepted ideas current in analytical psychology based on Jung's concept of the dialectical process. What does the idea of the self as a deintegrating and integrating system add? It implies that the process of analysing a patient depends upon the analyst having gone through a sufficient number of integrated and deintegrated states to reduce his anxiety to manageable proportions about changes occurring in the self, and be capable of not knowing in a fundamental sense. We can now consider countertransference.

An illusional or delusional countertransference (Fordham, 1960b) depends not on deintegration of the self but on disintegration in the ego. By contrast, in an ideal analysis without any countertransference illusions a transitory regression will occur when an analyst puts an unconscious part of the self into the service of the patient. If the self deintegrates, there is no necessity for splitting in the ego so long as the self is distinguished from the ego. The term syntonic countertransference differentiates this state of affairs from the illusory countertransference. The syntonic countertransference depends on the self boundaries dissolving without the ego disintegrating; then deintegration will be followed by integration. The ego, distinguished from the self, is enriched and strengthened in the process without its boundaries being seriously disturbed. Under these circumstances the ego acts as a recording apparatus for unconscious states and as the instrument which can communicate them to the patient.

This conclusion accords with the clinical experience that it is safe either for a normal projection by the analyst to take place whereby he may enter into the patient, or for the analyst to introject parts of the patient. Each will be respectively withdrawn or ejected again later on, without the analyst needing to exert the kind of control which is associated with conscious processes (see Fordham, 1960a; Money-Kyrle, 1956). It may also be added here that these processes are effective because a good analyst will inevitably link is interpretations with his own affective processes, so making it possible for him to participate in the affect of his patients without danger to himself.

The processes described above are illustrated by a frequent sequence of events which occur in the training of analysts. A new candidate may start off with apparent confidence only to find, with the help of his supervisor and analyst, that his interpretations are off the mark and reveal fantasies relevant, not to his patient, but to himself. They thus reveal an illusory countertransference – the result of splitting in his ego. There follows a period of disillusionment and depression in which the candidate becomes excessively cautious. Finally, he regains his confidence by discovering that he can gradually rely more and more upon his responses to his patient without exerting conscious control. Then, when projection and introjection occur, the result is on the mark, reliable and a true expression of that part of the self which can be used in analysing patients. The candidate gets much more free in his work and can "let himself go" in a way that was also possible at the beginning and which needed to be regained. Now, however, since he is no longer producing illusions, interpretations become increasingly useful. At the same time he becomes much more able to take in and digest his supervisor's ideas and comments adapting it to his own style of analysis.

Motivation for Analytic Therapy

It may not be out of place to make a note about conceiving the self as motivating analytic therapy. What makes a patient decide that there are certain parts of himself that he wants to get rid of, transform or become more tolerant of? At first sight they were enormously variable and not only a matter of distress or displeasure, nor is it guilt or shame alone which motivates them. Furthermore, it is something different from what a patient conceives that he comes for at the beginning of treatment. In that he is comparable to a child who is brought to therapy for reasons with which he does not agree at all, though he may have his own secret intention.

If the analysis begins in the right way and the patient feels understood, he develops a good therapeutic alliance which usually contains transference elements, and so his motivation to continue his analysis, whatever that may mean to him, is sustained or increased. His symptoms may diminish or even vanish, but he still continues, and to the therapist that indicates that the transference has become important: what was in the symptoms has now come into relation with him and that is in need of recognition. As the analysis proceeds, the patient indicates that he needs help over distressful conflicts with which he is struggling etc. But just what makes him select what is important? In it all transference interaction and its interpretation features prominently.

Jung's finding that there were certain patients who "hung on", they would not go away in spite of the transference being adequately understood, was seen by him as the patient challenging the analyst: The situation was that they sought to bring out "the whole man", though whether that meant the analyst or the patient or both is not clear. For purposes of my own I will assert that it does not matter so long as patient and analyst recognize the demand being made.

It is a practice of analysts to generalize a feature that they discover. That may later prove unjustified but has often proved fruitful. I will therefore extend the observation which was Jung's first but which has since been experienced intensely by others. In this way I propose that the effort to bring out the "whole man" is the tendency in the individual to find out what is an essential part of himself and that to live according to his "true nature" is more important than anything else. May not this be the element in motivation for treatment and in the patient's selection of matter for investigation? In the end he wants to know, never mind how agreeable or disagreeable that "knowing" may be. Though

I shall consider the subject of therapeutic results in the next chapter I shall now refer to it briefly.

It is disconcerting that the individual characteristic of the self puts all estimates of its dynamic activity outside generalization, and makes all estimates of therapeutic results approximate for ever. I do not think, however, that this conclusion need deter us from ignoring the individual component until it makes general statements manifestly absurd.

Suppose then, we grant that the self is a general frame of reference to which results can be referred. As a dynamic system, we would have to include stability and instability as necessary variables. Normality, currently defined as a steady state, can no longer be treated as a criterion by which to estimate a satisfactory therapeutic result; on the contrary, any assessment would have to include the capacity of a patient to negotiate abnormal as well as normal states (see Fordham, 1960a). Only making longitudinal assessments in time satisfies this more exacting requirement. A cross-section assessment giving the state of a patient at any particular time must be insufficient.

Chapter Seven

*Mental health**

It was not so much the concept of mental health as that of mental disease that transformed our mental hospitals. The diseased patients became those who suffered unreasonably from psychic pain, often expressed through their bodies, or who challenged ordinary standards of behaviour or who were possessed by ideas, imaginings etc., which seemed strange unacceptable or menacing.

To conceive of these as deviations from a "norm" and not as crimes and moral defects (possession by spirits of one kind or another) opened the door to their scientific investigation and to a more humane and rational treatment of patients. Released from legal restraint and moral condemnation, they came under the umbrella of the medical profession.

Of course, the recognition of mental disease implied that of mental health and a majority of any community considered themselves mentally fit. To be mentally well was to be normal, and it became so regarded: any suggestion of mental failing soon became met with resentment – the standard of mental health had become a social judgement. Whatever may be thought of that prejudice, it underlines the notion that mental health is largely a matter of judgement and that judgement may be wrong with serious consequences. The social criteria lack depth and become a prejudice. To compare it with a physical condition it is like saying that a person with certain symptoms or malignant disease asserts that he is normal and will not allow further investigation.

More penetrating criteria of health have been made. One of these was put forward by Freud who said that cure of a neurosis was to exchange mental pain for tolerable unhappiness. Jung for his part, by introducing the idea of individuation, set down a different and more

*Originally published as "Ego, self and mental health" in the *British Journal of Medical Psychology* Vol. 35, no. 3, 1962.

complex frame of reference. Melanie Klein later considered it was possible for those who reached the depressive position.

Both Jung and Klein stressed the operation of inner mental processes as decisive. While Klein could be more specific, Jung could be more individual: the person was healthy who was living according to his real nature, which expresses itself through imagery and the inner sense of what is right for him. Such conclusions could cut across ordinary estimates of mental health. For instance the content of delusional systems of psychotic patients expressed archetypal themes and so must be regarded as normal manifestations, albeit in a more or less disintegrated psyche; in addition he thought that it might be more desirable for a patient to remain neurotic than to have his neurosis "cured" (that is to say removed) by ingenious techniques whether psychotherapeutic or not. Such a conclusion presupposes detailed knowledge of a patient's psychic organization.

Jung was not the first to introduce such challenging conclusions, for Freud also had thought that paranoid delusions might be considered an attempt by the individual to re-establish contact with reality. So the distinction between mental health and mental disease has become increasingly difficult and, indeed, has led to denying the whole concept of mental disease (Schafer, 1976). It was a development that led some analysts to question their ability to decide when the therapeutic possibilities had been reached. They held that the outcome of analysis could not be decided by the analyst alone, and in some cases it may be the patient's decision which has to be taken as final. That conclusion is in line with the concept of individuation and the essentially unknowable nature of the self.

All that does not absolve analysts from struggling to define what they conceive mental health to be. My attempt in this chapter is to explore whether the concepts of the ego and the self have anything to contribute to their endeavours. Both the ego and the self as theoretical entities define ways in which distinguishable psychic structures and functions are subjected to regulation, and this occasion provides an opportunity to review some tentative formulations of their interaction.

The concept of the ego is related not only to consciousness and so to perception, but also to the organization of psychic contents; it is a system which has affective roots in the unconscious. If it is defined as the centre of consciousness (i.e. of conscious systems), what the relative independence which the ego could achieve is emphasized. The organized state to which it refers is indicated in the *Collected Works* by the use of the term "conscious mind". However, consciousness is not the only attribute of the ego, which is the agent of repression as well, and can also be combined with the idea of defensive systems which ward off external and internal dangers.

This discovery makes the first definition inadequate since parts of the ego are essentially unconscious, i.e. it has a shadow. In using that term, Jung follows the contention that unconscious contents can best be expressed in metaphor. The relation between the ego and its shadow is important for the stability of the whole psychic organism in that if the two become separated, the ego is seriously weakened; likewise if the ego is not sufficiently differentiated from the shadow, it cannot perform its integrative function as the organizer of those psychic systems having consciousness as their main characteristic. The shadow extends far into the unconscious and, since it has an archetypal foundation, the ego must be part of and interrelated directly or indirectly to all the other psychic systems.

In early infancy the psyche is relatively homogeneous, though structure is perceptible, but gradually mental life becomes differentiated in various ways. For instance, the distinction between the external and internal worlds is gradually built up; it is the developed ego which discriminates between the two and exerts a controlling, mediating and modifying influence over each. However, because of essential differences between the ego and the archetypes, the part of the ego which gives rise to consciousness cannot integrate the archetypes into itself any more than it can integrate the external world. It is held that the two functional systems, the conscious ego and the archetypes, as parts of a total organism, relate to each other in a compensating manner.

Rejecting the consideration that the ego cannot assimilate the archetypes gives rise to the question: are these archetypes themselves organized in relation to each other, and if so how? Part of the answer to this question is not difficult: inasmuch as they conform to instinctual patterns they must be largely self-regulating, yet if the archetypes are more than instincts and appear to be at the root of acausal, unpredictable but nonetheless meaningful connexions, their activity is not just instinctual in the modern sense. Turning to the possible ways the archetypes may be related to each other, we at once think of the possibility of a hierarchy subservient to a central organizing system, as Jung suggested when he referred to the self as the central archetype of order. That sounds almost like the ego inasmuch as it is an important organizing principle in the psyche. So what is the relation between the two? It is obscure. However, Jung says:

> The term "self" seemed to me a suitable one for [the] unconscious substrate, whose actual exponent in consciousness is the ego. The ego stands to the self as the moved to the mover, or as object to subject, because the determining factors which radiate out from the self surround the ego on all sides and are therefore supra-ordinate to it. The self, like the unconscious [archetype], is an *a priori* existent out of which the ego evolves. It is, so to speak, an unconscious prefiguration of the ego (Jung, 1958a, p. 259).

It is a statement which is in line with and foreshadows my own more detailed hypothesis of a primary integrate in infancy which may be considered the original state of the self. This deintegrates, and instinctual experience is one of the results. That experience leads to more or less intense perceptual input which goes to foster ego development. That is furthered by the integration of the self which ensures that the rich experience of the infant is digested and integrated.

By processes of this kind, it is conceived that the self becomes differentiated out into separate structures with specific functions. These become delegated and develop through the interaction of the organism with the environment. However, all the developing systems are still part of the whole and they all remain subordinate to the self, connected intimately with all its parts. Self images described by Jung symbolize a central integrative system. The essential principle in this theory is analogous to our knowledge of the way separate organs of the body differentiate out of the zygote and are all subordinate to control systems, of which the central nervous system and the endocrine glands are the most important.

Building on reflections such as that which I have just quoted, Jung came to hold that the ego could take over if not all the forms of the self, yet an increasing number of them, maintaining, nonetheless, subordination to the self. That ego growth is characteristic of individuation. If that is so, it would appear that the development of the ego and the extension of its control over the other psychic systems represents an achievement with almost unlimited possibilities. This formulation would clearly fall in line with those concepts of mental health that involve not only adaptation to the norm but a creative interaction between on one hand the ego and on the other the inner world. These dynamic processes lead to recurrent modifications in each, especially as the personality as a whole is conceived to continue emergent development throughout the recurrence of the twin processes of deintegration and integration.

Any concept of mental health must include the consideration of variables and emergent possibilities in a periodically unstable system. What is healthy, and what not, will depend upon the dynamic deintegration of the self into the component structures of the ego and archetypes and the integration of them into the whole organism. The two processes lead to the development of an ego whose growth must involve periodic experiences of disorder felt as dangerous or even chaotic. These states, however, need to be negotiated and can be rendered creative if they function healthily. Only the periods of integration can be relatively stable and, it might be added, adapted, in the sense that the organism fits into the environment and influences it effectively. The states arising from deintegration are often unadapted in the first place, since they arise when a new development is required under the stress of internal or external dynamisms. Therefore mental health must be considered in relation to externally unadapted as well as states adapted to social requirements and in relation to the inner growth processes known as individuation.

Chapter Eight

A clinical study*

One way of thinking about the self is in symbolic images. But since the self comprises the totality of the psyche, another way would be to make an inventory of its parts adding an "*x*" for what is unknown and unknowable. Thus one can indicate that united the self comprises more than the sum of its parts formed by deintegration; all the known or psychically speaking unknown (unconscious) parts of the cosmos, inasmuch as it could be perceived and known about, are to be included. It is usual to assert that the self comprises the internal world formed by deintegration and perceived by the individual in his known and unknown aspects together with the external world as likewise known and unknown by the individual. It is clearly different from and more comprehensive than the ego and the sense of being oneself which, as I have said, is a self representation only.

It is impossible to consider the self without reference to those unconscious and paradoxical elements that are most different in their nature from the rational ego. They are said not to have the properties of space and time with which man is ordinarily familiar, and it is probable that there is no clear distinction between psyche and soma. These apparent conclusions are all based on inference, but they are useful in considering synchronistic data (*vide* Chapter 9). The experience of irrational meaningful coincidence depends upon a lowering of energy in the ego. When the conscious threshold is thus lowered, the active archetypes become prominent enough to disturb space–time perception: then a different order may seem to take over sometimes clearly discernible sometimes to be only inferred. The following example contains ego and synchronistic components – the latter are inferred to imply constellation of the self.

*Originally published as "Ego and self in analytic practice" in *The Journal of Psychology* (Lahore) vol. 1, no. 1, 1964. Revised. (As far as I know this journal is no longer in existence.)

Example

When I was asked to deliver a paper to a group of psychoanalysts on the subject of the relation between the ego and the self, I at once accepted with excitement. Such an invitation had seemed to me impossible: I am a Jungian analyst and a senior psychoanalyst friend had once told me not so long before he had tried to mention Jung's work during a scientific meeting of the Institute of Psychoanalysis in London. The ensuing silence, he told me, made it clear that he was not to do so again! At the time of the invitation, I had been studying the subject they asked for and had been completing a chapter on individuation to be published in a book which was due to go to the publisher. In the middle of that work, the draft of a paper "On being alone" had been sent to me by D. W. Winnicott which had provided a clue to studying states of integration related to the self and individuation. His ideas had been partly assimilated and they had also led to my incorporating them in another essay on countertransference which I felt was important. In that paper I had discussed a case of a woman who induced a very intense sense of being alone; I will come back to her later. The sense of being alone had by that time become related in my mind to the conditions under which active imagination took place and that, if continued, could lead to the emergence of symbols of the self.

Then I realized that I would need some clinical material to discuss. Next day a patient I had been analysing for some time came into the room and remained silent – she had nothing to talk about. But as the interview developed she seemed somehow different, it was not the silence itself for she began to talk but it was empty – there was something I could not define.

When I pointed that out to her relating it to her first statement, she told me the following dream: "I am floating on the water, on the surface of the sea; I am undressed and have nothing on at all, my genital was like a flower, only not so beautiful." I at once felt this was the material I was looking for, and without waiting for associations I met the dream with the following interpretation: "The dream seems to have a sense of being alone that you have experienced in the past after a satisfying orgasm in intercourse with a man you loved."

The patient was quite startled and responded with: "How did you know that?" and she went on to talk about my states of mind, that sometimes I seemed right on the spot, but not often and this was one occasion; today I was in a very good state, sure of myself, and she liked it. In retrospect I believe the interpretation to have been only partly correct, and rather startlingly avoided the transference implication.

The image of a flower had associated in my mind with the self which emerges from the conjunction; I had in mind the symbolic nature of actual intercourse. It also linked up with Winnicott's paper and with being asked to give a paper at all. This material was, I felt sure, the material to be given in my talk. I may say here and now that I am not asserting anything about the truth or falsehood of this sequence but describing the elements of it. To draw conclusions and analyse them further would be to emphasize ego activity. Yet it would not take us too far to see in this episode a conjunction: what I said was penetrating, a phallic interpretation, entering her receptive containing "genital". It was a conjunction generating wholeness in the unity of sexual opposites.

Something linked all these events into a sequence as if there were a unity in them outside my control. This something is what is meant by the self. It is as if bits of my internal world were not separate from the outer and other people but both were part of a whole which was not myself only.

This way of experiencing events could be magical or narcissistic if I conceived that I had done it all, instead of taking part in it, or if I thought or felt that the people in the outer world were subject to manipulation by *my*self, not a manifestation of *the* self. The sequence contains meaningful coincidence (synchronicities). In it they are part of *the* self which is the unity of events behind or transcending my external and internal worlds. The internal and external worlds have been constructed in the course of years and so are mainly ego constructs.

Analytical psychologists usually work in terms of complex processes or images; they do this because they are primarily interested in the interrelation of objects which the images represent.

It has been understood that there are two states of the self; deintegrated and integrated ones. The two may be thought of as occurring in sequence and this makes the self a rhythmic dynamic system. The advantage of conceiving the self thus is this: if you start to make diagrams of a system which has a relatively static partial system (the ego) and a dynamic one in which there is a rhythm of integration and deintegration, it is possible to explain how persecutory and so called splitting processes can soon occur in the ego more or less inevitably. These will occur because the ego cannot always detach itself from the self at times when deintegration is active – then the self may seem to the ego to be an alien aggressor ready to tear it to pieces, hence the anxieties connected with supposedly destructive processes.

I will now go on to describe a case to illustrate the value of the proportions elaborated in previous chapters. In this case ego functioning predominates, but both my patient and myself felt each other as violating our personal integrity. What takes place or what is inferred in the patient cannot be described apart from my internal world.

The early part of the analysis of a woman in the middle thirties proceeded uneventfully: she recorded events in the external world. She told me dreams which she was adept at analysing – she had been in analysis before. The transference was not particularly in evidence because she was conducting a "Jungian analysis" in which she held (in fact wrongly) that the transference was not a part. Gradually the material began to decrease and there were periods in which she had nothing to say. It was clear that she was not saying all she wanted to and it took her some time before she was able to make an announcement: she said that she was perfectly well and that she did not need any more analysis. Then she went a step further to say that the analysis *had* stopped. Still she went on attending, though once or twice she said she was not going to come again. Her acts did not live up to her words. Then followed a group of statements about my decency, what a good analyst I was, until eventually there emerged a conviction: she was quite sure that I was in love with her, but was prevented from declaring my love because of my personal and professional integrity.

She stopped detailing her dreams, she said little about anything that occurred between interviews and nothing about her past life, of which she had told me little anyhow. The whole time was filled with concentrated attention upon the conflicts which she was certain were going on inside me. Partly because I did not talk much, every movement of my body was interpreted by her; on the other hand, nearly all statements by me were understood as projection or concealed love. I understood what was occurring as projective identification.

I now want to turn to what went on inside me as a result of her behaviour. My patient's attitude made me feel very separate from her, and led to my wondering what could be done. The answer was very little or even nothing. It was no use telling her that I was not in love with her for this would be interpreted as an aspect of my integrity. It was no good trying to relate the projection to her history of which there was in any case little to use. It was no use pointing to the subjective nature of her feeling and almost but, as we shall see, not all interpretations were unprofitable. Gradually much more came to light: according to her I was going through a crisis and I needed her, so she continued to come to see me out of "mature" love for me; she emphasized the maturity of what she was doing. Gradually I discovered that the only interpretations which were called for were those which clarified the transference projection; any bits of the projection that she did not tell me openly or had not got conscious were interpreted.

This situation – a general one – resulted in my being placed under a maximum of strain because I was virtually left alone with my thoughts about what was occurring. In such a case no gratification at all is provided by the patient, no recognition is given to the notion that something useful is being done. No improvement is admitted, no change is to be seen. This can lead analysts to construct illusions and making mistakes.

When the patient made an interpretation about me which was near the mark I was tempted to believe what she said was true. Indeed she made a number of statements which were remarkably accurate, not so much about my feelings, for she was entirely beside the mark here, but in terms of facts. For instance, she correctly surmised the month in which I was born; she was interested in astrology, had decided that I was a "Leo type" and then decided that I was born in August. Some of her statements were naturally the result of picking up information about me, but it would have been an error to assume that her ideas and interpretations were significant to me even though they appeared correct. This was one of the ways in which my patient subjected me to strains which could easily have led to *folies à deux*. Feelings of persecution in me came from the belief that I was not succeeding in being what is usually called an analyst, or because nothing of what I said was accepted; in addition a feeling of robbing the patient became very persistent, partly because she was paying almost half her salary for her "analysis", which she believed was over.

Under these conditions I tended to develop a feeling that I was two persons so that there was, as it were, my body into which she was projecting everything of herself and of which she had taken possession. I became separate from it, listening, paying attention, trying to spot what was hidden, and at times becoming exasperated. I know in introspect that the deintegration took place because of the sense of having my body invaded and taken possession of by the patient, and this led to the fantasy of abandoning my body and locating my conscious self outside in space or in the room. Gradually I came to realize the importance of my developing a greater capacity to be alone, and at the same time to be with the patient. As this occurred my fantasy worked.

I now want to consider a bit of my experience which I feel confident was what I was then defining as syntonic countertransference. The patient used to start her interviews by questioning me, and for some reason I never replied. My not replying made her more and more provocative; I did not make interpretations about these questions. She then talked at length about how she wished I would come to her flat, how she wished I would go to the theatre with her, wouldn't I come out for a walk, wouldn't I listen to some music; endless supposedly attractive possibilities were put before me, always as questions. I did not reply, and then in spite of all sense and analytic theory about the patient's more and more deliberate attempts at what appeared to be seduction, I began to wonder why not; there was no possibility of any of these things happening, mainly because the overall picture she made of me, apart from the correct facts, was so unlike me that there was nothing that I recognized. Therefore, when she asked me to do things with her, I did not feel I was being asked at all.

As time went on I began to point out more and more firmly how she never made any reference to the past; at length she began to talk about it, largely to please "me". I went on to point out to her that since she saw us as lovers she might do what lovers often did; talk not only about what was going on now but also about the past, about what their life had been as much as what it was now. One day she arrived at the following set of memories. She described how her father used to sit in a chair and she used to go and see him. He was fond of her, she knew that, but he seldom made overt contact with her. She had come from a well-to-do family and much of her time was spent with the servants, particularly her nurse, to whom she talked about her father. The nurse used to suggest to the patient ways of persuading her father to go out with her, because he never did so. So she used to suggest anything that she could think of with a view to inducing him to come with her and enjoy her company as she "knew" he would, but he never replied. This made me understand why I never answered – I was acting as he had done. When I pointed out the similarities between what she was doing with me and what had happened with her father, the questions stopped almost once and for all. When she did it again, I reminded her of it and she broke into a rage. The point I wish to make is not the obvious interpretation but the fact that she went on for months during which I behaved in a manner which I knew to be unusual for me.

It had taken me a long time to discover this. I had no chance of making an interpretation before, not having the material to make it with, but if I had not wondered why I never answered her, I should have missed the significant element in my reactions. It will be agreed, I think, that there were a number of platitudinous interpretations which might have stifled this feeling. When her memories emerged I could interpret with a conviction which would not otherwise have been possible.

At first sight, it would seem that this phase of the analysis led to another, and gave me new ideas of what was meant by the projection screen. I had become a screen and I was led along it by giving as little justification as possible for her projection, keeping as quiet as possible, concentrating in awed fascination on the gaps in her talk. Rather over a year before writing this paper originally, I wrote that the thesis of the analyst as a projection screen current in psychoanalysis holds no charms for analytical psychologists who unanimously reject it because the concept of the self renders it untenable. This patient has shown me the charm of it, for it was entrancing to watch a projection, to discover how extraordinarily unimportant you are in it, that nothing makes any difference to it and that everything is turned to serve the purpose of the projective process. However, there is an essential difference from the classical idea of the projection screen, in which the analyst passively reflects processes in the patient with the aim, as Ernest Jones says, of "getting the transference in pure culture". My behaviour was not a policy, it was an attitude that grew in the analysis, something discovered and which the patient unconsciously needed; it was thus dependent on needs and was not a pre-ordained technique; or, to put it another way, it was part of the dialectical relationship. I think this is true in spite of the patient's belief that I was ruining her life in not having intercourse with her or that I was causing her to become diseased internally for the same reason. She needed to bring these fantasies into consciousness.

The current objection, in analytical psychology, to the projection screen technique is that it rests on the notion of any analyst *not* being himself. It was only gradually that I appreciated the possibility of being *myself* and alone with the patient, though this must have been the predominating feeling all the time; only gradually did I become conscious of its importance to the patient as well as to myself. The feeling of being alone involved being at one with myself, and with the cosmos, ready all the time to take the patient in or to enter into her psyche when required. Being alone can initiate a very large number of experiences which happen to the analyst; if it is lost, the projection becomes intolerable, a division occurs and so one becomes two, as I have described.

There were definable consequences of being disintegrated and alone, some of which I have mentioned but which I will now complete. There was feeling of persecution based amongst other things on her complaint of being unable to get anything out of me. She tended to become a persecutor who was being attacked by me; I was aware of this and controlled it but my hostility probably appeared in tones of voice. An alternative to attacking was to withdraw more or less completely. But if I succeeded in containing the persecution I deintegrated internally.

Another tendency was to identify with the patient, that is to feel with the patient, and, realizing in part what she needed, to try and fulfil the need. Another one was to despair with or without persecution. The signs of this were feelings of hopelessness about the lack of progress; the patient was not getting better, she was not doing "analysis", I felt that I was being a bad analyst and inadequate in many ways. This same led, when persecution was minimal, to the desire to make restitution by reducing fees, changing or reducing the times of attendance etc. All these I resisted.

Directly the need for being alone with the patient was realized, it led to a state of integration, but one in which I was also ready to follow up deintegrates when they occurred. Being alone meant to be in relation to the self in a state of integration outside my control, but this cannot be maintained for ever and deintegrative processes will occur. These are also outside ego control, and the various possibilities which I have enumerated become actual if the manifestations of deintegration are not conscious. One manifestation of deintegration is the making of interpretations with conviction. I assume that because I became related to the self, I reached a need of the patient.

I have described a reaction which contained the essential features of the paranoid–schizoid and depressive positions as described by Klein. I have left out my patient's oral sadism which could easily be inferred, because I wanted to underline that these cannot be analysed in a patient unless they are first known in experience with each patient by the analyst. I realize that once an analyst has been through these experiences often enough, he can manage them later on without too much trouble, but the patient's experience and the analyst's are in my conception based on an ultimate unity which in analytical psychology is called the self. This is one of the basic reasons for the analysis of the analyst. It is the object of analysis to create conditions under which this unity can be realized.

Having said this, we must return again to the beginning and recall that the ego has boundaries and so the main part of analysis is usually conducted on the basis that these boundaries between analyst and patient are there. They also remain essential after analysis is completed, but in the process of analysis a paradox gets brought into being that the ego becomes more and more like the self, which, in becoming more and more capable of consciousness, gets boundaries itself, as the pictures of mandalas indicate. Thus we arrive at the roots of the intuitive metaphor:

> "Man (the ego) was made in
> God's image (the self)",

but also of the converse that God becomes man in the process.

Chapter Nine

*An interpretation of Jung's thesis about synchronicity**

In the previous chapter, reference was made to synchronicity and an example was given illustrating some features of it. The matter needs further discussion.

It is well understood today by many scientists that the concept of causality is inadequate in their discipline and that probability theory and attention to the future (prediction) are more important. In this development biologists have played a leading part (e.g. Bronowski, 1960). But scientists are loath to consider whole situations. They select a single or a small number of data, isolating them so as to exclude undesirable variables. They can thus make experiments under controlled conditions.

That does not provide a method for assessing situations where such control is impossible and where apparently arbitrary events rule the day. I am reminded here of Tolstoy's account of war, in which unforeseen events are so frequent that the conduct of a battle seems more determined by them than by thought out plans of action. The total situation in all its rapidly changing aspects eludes rational order.

Jung was much interested in that total situation and in events for which no cause was conceivable. There can be little doubt that he thought of these as being related to the self in its cosmic dimension. His scientific intellect was challenged and he resolved his dilemma by studying specific instances of events for which no cause could be found and which yet had great significance for the individual or had far-reaching effects of one sort or another. At first he classed these as irrational facts: unable to explain them by applying causal principals, he attempted to build them into his thinking, inventing, when necessary, new means of doing so. Synchronicity is one of his conceptual inventions. It is a way of

*Originally published in the *British Journal of Medical Psychology* vol. 35, no. 3, 1962.

thinking about irrational data; it penetrates and orders total situations. Therefore it is conceived as standing in opposition to causal thinking, in which parts of a whole situation are isolated for inspection.

The definition of synchronicity is as follows: it is an acausal connecting principle based on a meaningful relation between two or more otherwise unconnected events – one psychical and the other physical. The connexion is unpredictable and spontaneous and seems at first sight to be dependent on chance. However, this becomes incredible because the events have too much significance or meaning to the person or persons experiencing them. The term suggests that there is a correspondence in time between the events but some of the examples show that this is not necessarily so. It is therefore not surprising when, near the end of his discussion, Jung conceives synchronicity as a special instance of general "acausal ordering" in nature. Furthermore, in a footnote he says that the data under consideration may possibly occur "without the participation of the human psyche . . . in this case we should have to speak not of *meaning* but of equivalence or conformity" (Jung, 1960, p. 502). On the other hand, though it is not explicitly stated, it can probably be applied to meaningful coincidences between two psychical systems, of which so-called thought transference could be an example.

The history of our topic begins when Jung started collecting striking examples of irrational data in 1900 or thereabouts; his first published case (Jung, 1902), the hysterical medium, provided what seemed to be startling evidence of her powers. Jung then appears to have been thinking in terms of energy and hence magic, for she seemed to have broken a carving knife and split an old walnut table without taking any destructive action, while being far away from the event. Then there was the occasion when, during a discussion with Freud, a formidable crash occurred "as if the whole book-case had come down" (Bennet, 1961, p. 34). According to E. A. Bennet, it was heard by both men and, in violation of his later thesis, Jung correctly predicted that it would happen again! Freud for his part sought to establish more reasonable conclusions.

Jung did not publish any of these data and others of the same kind for many years, though he went on collecting them, and a number of examples can be found in the literature. However, it is worth noting that he read a paper to the Society for Psychical Research on "The psychological foundations of belief in spirits" in 1919. There he stated that spirits were projections of unconscious archetypal contents. It was not until 1930 that he first used the term "synchronicity" and then only in an "Obituary notice to Richard Wilhelm", the sinologist, his collaborator in the short volume on yoga, *The Secret of the Golden Flower*.

The first time he said much on the subject was in his "Foreword to the *I Ching*" (Jung, 1950d), when that book was published in a new translation by Cary Baynes. There he consulted the oracle as to the book's reception and recorded his interpretation of the hexagrams.

In 1952 he found the time and confidence to elaborate his position at length in "Synchronicity: an acausal connecting principle", which appeared in a small volume together with an essay by Pauli (1952) called "The influence of archetypal ideas on Kepler's theories". There is little doubt that the combination of these two authorities was intended to suggest a much closer relation between unconscious processes and scientific investigation than is usually supposed, for in his own essay Jung introduced a conceptual schema, arrived at in discussion with Pauli, the Swiss physicist. It gives a place to synchronicity as a complement to causality. There is little doubt that, in formulating his ideas, the conclusions of theoretical micro-physicists had considerable influence on Jung.

Setting aside complicating reflections which these introductory remarks must raise, it will generally be agreed that there are a large number of events occurring within us and around us which happen only once and so cannot be subjected to controlled investigation. Many of these are really caused and the rest are usually interpreted, rightly or wrongly, as chance. A few of these "chance" events can become highly significant in the sense of numinous or meaningful, and among them are the phenomena of so-called parapsychology. If I have understood him rightly, Jung's formulation aimed primarily, though not exclusively, to deepen our understanding of parapsychology and to bring it into relation with his theory of archetypes. By doing this he joined those who contributed towards taking the magic out of a subject hedged around with illusion, hallucination, delusion and fraud. In doing this, he risked the misunderstanding that the data were caused by the projection of archetypes into events thrown up by chance.

The genuine manifestations of parapsychology are regularly linked up with a supernatural world in which ghosts, spirits, poltergeists and the like abound, in themselves strongly suggesting the activity of archetypes. Since these are defined as organs of the psyche, Jung was inevitably predisposed to think of this difficult subject in terms of the psyche rather than some supernatural or parapsychological agency.

One reason for considering parapsychology as a discipline distinct from psychology is that physical objects can take part in the manifestations; in any case this happened in Rhine's (1948) experiments which Jung accepted – to my mind wrongly – as supporting his own ideas, rejecting current explanations of them. His argument here is as follows: even if Rhine's results are statistically significant, this cannot indicate the operation of energies in the parapsychological sense. It will be remembered that Rhine's subjects made significant predictions when hundreds of miles away from the cards or dice. Furthermore, the predictions could be made a long time before the cards were turned up. In writing about these data Jung is most emphatic: (1960, pp. 433, 434):

> If, in the spatial experiments, we were obliged to admit that energy does not decrease with distance, then the time experiments make it completely impossible for us even to think of there being any energy relationship between the perception and the future event. We must give up at the outset all explanations in terms of energy, which amounts to saying that events of this kind cannot be considered from the point of view of causality, for causality presupposes the existence of space and time in so far as all observations are ultimately based upon bodies in motion. (Jung, 1960, pp. 433–4).

Though agreeing with this argument, I cannot follow Jung when he uses Rhine's experiments as especially good evidence of acausal patterning. He pays insufficient attention to the nature of statistics, so that this part of his thesis is developed in defiance of its basic argument: Rhine's data claimed to be statistically significant and this makes a cause not less but more probable. Since the cards and dice are randomized the cause of the experimental data must be in the psyche, which is then only too easily assumed to have some improbable capacity. It is because the evidence cannot be explained that terms like extrasensory perception get invented, supposedly to help in solving a quandary. That there is no adequate theory to account for the data then easily gets overlooked.

In his own rather misnamed "Astrological experiment", on which I have commented at great length elsewhere (Fordham, 1957d), Jung used an ingenious argument that involved statistics. I argued, and Jung supported me, that if it is desired to look for meaningful coincidences, they are best sought in data which are not statistically significant and so where causal laws are improbable.

After this brief examination of Jung's excursion into statistics, we may now consider how he integrated synchronicity into his general theory and in particular into his ideas of the reciprocal relation between the ego and archetypes. It is worthy of reflection that, though he did not explicitly develop a theory of object relations such as we have today, Jung was in fact a pioneer in this field and the study of object relations was a major feature of his researches. Synchronicity is an extension of his position. It is indeed a means of studying meaningful, uncaused subject–object relationships. Once it becomes apparent that no cause is conceivable, the sense of purposive behaviour on the part of objects is important because, Jung says, it gives affective processes in the unconscious a chance to express themselves. As a consequence the archetypes become active and can be experienced because their independence can be allowed in a projection. In short the ego defences are loosened or broken down, and Jung means this when he says that an *abaissement du niveau mental* is a necessary condition for the emergence of synchronicities. In support of his view he instances the affective states in which the data appear and develops his argument by saying that the space–time continuum ceases to operate efficiently and becomes more or less dislocated. In this he keeps rather close to the phenomena and so succeeds in avoiding the improbable explanations commonly advanced, including the idea that the archetype causes the synchronicity. But how can the space–time continuum become, as he says, relativized?

There is a correspondence between the external event and the archetype itself, which becomes manifest in meaningful relations with the material object in the external world. It appears certain that it is the archetypal imagery which makes the correspondence meaningful, but the synchronicity is essentially the correspondence and is *not produced* by the projected archetypal image. Jung's argument may also be stated in another, negative, way: unconscious processes do not take the same account of space–time – and so causality – as does the conscious mind. Space–time and causality thus become characteristics of ego structure and function and not of archetypal activity.*

Though it is quite clear that Jung did not think of archetypal imagery as the cause of synchronicity itself, yet he seems to have thought of it as a means of registering the synchronicity by a symbolic perception. This would mean that the projection is not only an illusion but also a way of getting at the otherwise unconscious event. However, to my mind, the important element in Jung's thesis is not so much this possibility as that it makes the whole subject of parapsychology accessible to analysis in terms of the relation between the ego and the archetypal objects. Thus the door is opened to studying the data in terms of individuals.

We can now consider some clinical data with the idea of briefly studying the kind of states in which synchronicities may reveal themselves. These examples will also serve to show what is and what is not synchronicity and how synchronicity may operate behind and so influence the analyst–patient interactions.

If we look at the accounts of synchronicity given us by Jung, it is striking that only one occurs in a patient. She was, he says, particularly difficult to analyse, but one day she was talking about a dream in which she was given a golden scarab. Suddenly he heard a noise at the window, and there was a real beetle which was only very rarely found in Zürich and was of a golden-green colour. He showed this to his patient and her rationalistic defences were punctured. This interesting example is unique in Jung's publications. It clearly needs more critical discussions,

*When considering this argument, it is important to keep in mind that the term archetype as used here is an abstraction. Any manifestation of archetypal activity requires space and time. The notion that the archetypes are "timeless" is based on the tendency for there to be disturbances in space and time as experienced by individuals when in regression or under the influence of archetypal activity.

and I have broached it elsewhere (1957d) by pointing out that the transference implications are not considered. It could have been the transference effect of Jung's act which created a meaning that would not otherwise have been there.

There may very well be a reason for the relative rarity of analytic observations. A main analytic aim is to increase the strength of the ego; therefore, though an *abaissement du niveau mental* may occur, i.e. though ego defences may be relaxed, they are handled under relatively controlled conditions. The manifestations of such control comprise the regular attendance, the continuing existence of the analyst, his room and finally his interventions based on close attention to what the patient is saying or doing. In most analyses these are enough to ensure that regressions are sufficiently controlled, and unconscious elements, in Jung's sense, do not break through without soon being made conscious.

Therefore we may expect synchronicities to appear most clearly in the analysis of more disintegrated or psychotic patients, or if one or more of the conditions for good analysis is not fulfilled. For instance, if there are countertransference difficulties, they might become manifest; in discussing a paper by Servadio (1955) in which there is a so-called extrasensory perception, Balint (1955) states that this kind of experience happens when the analyst is pre-occupied with matters outside the analysis and fails to reveal his pre-occupation to his patient. The patient senses what is happening and tries to bridge the gulf by giving the analyst a shock.

In the following cases there were difficulties which made for a rift in the relationship between analyst and patient. They derived from projective identifications made by the patient which evoked a countertransference that was difficult for me to handle. I shall discuss whether these factors are a sufficient explanation or whether synchronicity may not be in action as well.

The first patient became pre-occupied with some ornaments on my mantelpiece. They kept changing places, moving about between interviews and the patient became convinced that I was deliberately doing this to test him and play on and stimulate his passive homosexual trends. It was true that the objects were changed and I was unable to control them, but it was due to the activities of a cleaner who defied, or so it seemed, my repeated requests to leave them where she found them. Later, when I tried to make sure that they had not changed places before the interview, I could not remember where they had been at the last interview and so the horrid persecution continued which made analytic work very difficult. There is nothing synchronistic about that. At one time, however, the behaviour of objects began to excite a countertransference, and it would not have been at all difficult for me to believe with conviction that some spirit or other was deliberately playing tricks and to suppose that he (or she) had got into and was controlling the cleaner – that would be evoking an archetypal image through which to perceive a synchronistic event. It will be observed that this conclusion arrived at by deintegration covers the total situation better than the analysis of the separate component parts in the situation to which I actually confined myself. The spirit can be conceived of as the unitary being, evidently intended to create a confusion in the patient and myself by using the cleaner for his purpose – that conclusion would still be in the field of causal explanation.

If I had started looking at the overall pattern and had been able to see through the magical projection, then I might have arrived at synchronicity, of which the spirit could have been the symbolic perception. But I should have needed to deintegrate far enough for the synchronicities to become conscious. In retrospect I could not do this for fear of being disintegrated by my patient's projective identifications.

Here is another example. My Pither's heating stove accumulates gas and periodically discharges itself up the chimney with an audible bang. More then one patient of mine had been convinced that these bangs occur at periods of stress in the analysis; sometimes the bang is said to be due to me discharging my emotions or sometimes to spontaneous meaningful activity by the stove which is conversing with us. On these occasions I was unable to judge whether the stove really did discharge more often than at other times, but Jung's thesis supports me in not minding and concentrating on the meaning of the pattern in the transference–countertransference set up. One patient clearly thought this was a meaningful coincidence, i.e. a synchronicity, and wanted me to believe in it also. On the contrary, I suspected she was using the idea of synchronicity as a weapon.

Both these examples illustrate the kind of data which can be used to suggest the idea of synchronicity as it were behind the scenes, but in neither case did I assume them to be the consequence of the activity of entities separate from the persons involved, i.e. I did not indulge in parapsychological speculations. In the first case, one cause of objects moving in an arbitrary manner was the cleaner, and in the second, the cause of the bang was the accumulation and discharge of gas. The intrapsychic causes can be traced out in the patient and me, but something seems to be lost when the whole pattern is reduced to physics and psychological mechanisms. What is omitted is expressed, in some measure at least, by the fantasy imagery, i.e. the spirit, which, though it contains an explanatory element, takes the whole situation more into account. From this point of view, the tendency for me to get drawn into the total situation – countertransference – becomes increasingly significant because I am part of the total pattern as the patient's analyst.

In these examples the states of mind were temporary and occurred in the analysis of non-psychotic persons. In 1963, Mary Williams recorded observations on a schizophrenic man who told her about the activities of a poltergeist (Williams, 1963b). Both Mrs Williams and the patient heard noises at critical periods of the analysis and on one occasion a cupboard door swung open; it had never done so before or after that occasion.

Noises are commonly not registered but remain below the threshold of consciousness. This can become conscious and subject to projections into them, if, for various reasons, the threshold of consciousness is lowered as in regression. However, the opening of the door could not be explained in this way. It had no cause but it had a meaning. The patient "knew" it was the poltergeist; Mrs Williams started, she says, getting resistances.

These examples all illustrate the way in which the behaviour of objects becomes linked up with projected unconscious contents, and this was confirmed by further analysis for which the projections became integrated. Then the implied or manifest synchronicities ceased and tended to become incredible.

The question which all these cases pose is whether the events could be explained in terms of integration and deintegration, projection and introjection? Jung would say no, there is a basic meaningful unity behind it all and we need to drop our causal way of thinking to get the hang of it. Of course, he might very well have reproached me for failing to produce striking examples. But I have not intended to do this, though I have done so in my earlier essays on the subject. Here I rather wanted to underline the different attitudes involved in thinking causally and synchronistically.

Are we to think of the examples cited by Jung and others as unusual or are we to think of synchronicity as a common, but overlooked, kind of object relation? Jung clearly believed he was observing a common event which was usually unconscious. It may be that the study of analytic material will show them up. There are many features of analytic interviews which are puzzling other than those that I have outlined. Spontaneous reactions by the analyst occur and prove useful then or afterwards in defiance of all rational sense; these may very well spring from meaningful coincidences. In addition unusual events outside the consulting room, when heard by analyst and patient, can be highly charged with meaning.

No account of Jung's thesis would be complete without giving some idea of the ways that his idea has been applied.

(1) In *Aion* he uses his studies of astrology, which he understands as a product of synchronicity, to show how it influenced, or revealed the effect of synchronicity on the development of Christianity and its heretical movements.

(2) The idea of synchronicity is the basic assumption of much Chinese thought, expressed in Taoism and such extraordinary volumes as the *Book of Changes* or *I Ching*.* In all these spheres a way of thinking in terms of patterns in which no causal chains are displayed.

(3) Then there is the question of psychosomatic medicine and the wider issue of whether the psychosomatic set-up is not based on synchronicity. Jung, at least, went so far as to suggest that it was. This would mean that it becomes necessary to drop all idea of a psychic event being caused by a somatic one or vice versa and we should have to be content with looking for meaningful correspondences between the two. This thesis would make it wrong to think, for instance, of the psychic manifestations of General Paralysis of the Insane as being caused by brain damage – both are needed for the condition to arise but one does not cause the other; the two synchronize.

I hope that this short account of Jung's daring, original, even revolutionary thesis, together with my own reflections, will recommend it for serious consideration. It clearly needs further study and its conceptual basis may well need revision in the light of further analysis. For instance, it is not always clear what Jung means by causality – an idea which has been subject to considerable discussion in recent years by philosophers and scientists. Furthermore, his examples do not always make it evident in what his idea of meaning consists.

I can not close without recording a suspicion. The study of the causes of a patient's distress has a part to play in his analytic treatment, but such causes have too many overtones to make them very reliable instruments: for instance, when a cause is found in infancy, this can be used to imply that a patient should now stop behaving in the way he is doing ("don't be a baby"). Moreover, meaning is much more important than are causes and we do not plan an interview as a scientist does though there is a framework in operation which excludes social or sexual intercourse. It is the meaning of an often very diffuse collection of data which leads to the emergence of a conscious expression either found by the patient or made known to him in an interpretation. It is also a matter of interest that most of the formulations of analysts are not of the kind which renders their conclusions suitable for statistical investigation. These reflections give a special cogency to the idea of synchronicity – it may be that we work much more on the basis of meaningful coincidence than we like to admit.

*The *I Ching* is an assembly of organized symbolic statements to which commentaries are added. They can be studied in their own right as well as be used for mantic purposes.

Chapter Ten

*Countertransference**

In this chapter I shall approach the subject of countertransference starting from Jung's conception of analytic practice as a dialectical process between two involved persons (selves). By implication he advocated an open systems viewpoint. A closed system is one with clearly defined limits or boundaries; two persons may stand in relation to each other yet function as distinct entities. In their conversation words have an agreed meaning or, if there are disjunctions in their communications, these can be clarified by reference to the psychical system of one or the other. Open systems, on the other hand, are those in which boundaries are not fixed, with the result that the two systems - patient and analyst - interact, change and transform themselves in relation to eacn other. Difficulties or confusions therefore require a change in *both* psychical systems before validation is possible.

Developments in psychoanalysis appear to have led psychoanalysts close to conceptions being worked on by analytical psychologists, particularly in London. I have used the work of psychoanalysts extensively and recognize that many of my propositions were considered before I thought of them. However, I shall not refer to their specific publications but will content myself with making a general acknowledgement to the following: Bion, Heimann, Klauber, Langs, Little, Meltzer, Money-Kyrle, Racker, Searles and Winnicott (for a complete review, see Langs, 1976).

Jung has laid great stress on the patient's individuality. He believed that each analysis differs in essential respects from every other.

*Originally published as "Analytical psychology and countertransference" in *Contemporary Psychoanalysis*, the journal of the William Alanson White Psychoanalytic Society and the William Alanson White Institute, vol. 15, no. 4, 1979 and is reprinted with the permission of *Contemporary Psychoanalysis*. It was also published unchanged in *Countertransference: the Therapist's Contribution to Treatment* (Epstein, L. and Feiner, A. H.), New York, Aronson, 1979. It has been subject to revision in the present chapter.

> Psychotherapy and analysis are as varied as are human individuals. I treat every patient as individually as possible because the solution to the problem is always an individual one. . . . A solution which would be out of the question for me may be just the right one for somebody else (Jung, 1963, p. 130).

I read that statement as indicating the central importance of the self in analytic practice. He placed less emphasis on method than on interaction. In later years he even adopted a sort of non-method:

> Naturally a doctor must be familiar with so-called methods. But he must guard against falling into any specific routine approach. In general one must guard against theoretical assumptions. Today they may be valid, tomorrow it may be the turn of other assumptions. In my analyses I am unsystematic very much by intention. We need a different language for every patient (ibid., p. 131).

These remarks were Jung's last statements on psychotherapy, but for many years their spirit had influenced the development of analytic psychotherapy, in my view to its detriment. I believe the study of the analytic situation was seriously delayed because there did not seem any point in describing what happened with one patient since, in principle, it would not apply to others. Thus Jung's statements lent themselves to an abhorrence of any general theory of technique, since any such theory could in this view only foster a misunderstanding and be used as an intellectualized defence against the patient as a unique individual.

However, if Jung's expositions are studied in context, a different picture emerges. While Jung was consistently suspicious of theoretical abstractions, this did not prevent his developing a number of theories: e.g. the theory of types, of archetypes and of the collective unconscious. Moreover, he was a master in their application, as a study of his analyses of dreams shows. The Tavistock Lectures (1935b) revealed his method of amplifying symbolic dream material. That procedure, which Jung used when studying alchemy, aims at elucidating symbols by placing them in their historical and cultural contexts. The method derives from the notion that there is always a penumbra of mystery around symbolic data and it is desirable to make that as explicit as possible while preserving the context of the imagery. In view of all this, Jung's final statements should be taken not as a denial of the value of the theoretical guidelines for psychotherapy, but rather as a suggestion that they must leave space for the self.

The development of Jung's conception of the analytic situation (see Fordham, 1957a, 1969, 1974b, 1978) may be said to have started when he emphasized the need for the analysis of the analyst. He thought that it was the influence of the analyst as a person that was the decisive therapeutic factor, a conception that had been formulated in the deceptively obvious idea that no analyst can help his patient to progress farther than he has himself.

I have never been happy with that statement because it seems to depreciate the capacity of analysts to learn from their patients both in an emotional and mental sense. I think it likely that in any good analysis the analyst's psychic life is enriched, and if he does not understand his patient, he can act as a container while his patient works on seemingly incomprehensible matter.

In line with this position, Jung held that transference could often be the result of interaction between analyst and patient. He thought that transference, though ubiquitous in everyday life, is intensified in the analytic setting in reaction to the analyst's behaviour. The real attitudes and personality of the analyst play a significant part in the form and intensity of transference. Furthermore, he held that when the analyst is incapable of empathizing with his patient, an intense transference develops, representing the patient's effort to close the gap. Jung further believed that transference can also represent an effort by a patient to adapt to an analyst who, endowed with the qualities of a parent, can act as a bridge so the patient can move from his regressed state back to reality.

A conception more relevant to my thesis is that Jung recognized the analyst's capacity to introject his patient's psychopathology and become confused or disoriented.

> The doctor by voluntarily and consciously taking over the psychic sufferings of the patient, exposes himself to the overpowering contents of the unconscious and hence also to their inductive action. . . . The patient, by bringing an activated unconscious content to bear upon the doctor, constellates the corresponding unconscious material in him. . . . Doctor and patient thus find themselves in a relationship founded on mutual unconsciousness . . . [and] the unconscious infection brings with it a therapeutic possibility – which should not be underestimated – of the illness being transferred to the doctor (Jung, 1946, pp. 175–6).

All these ideas are related to the theory of archetypes, which suggests that there is a substrate common to all human beings. It is conceivable that the archetypes are virtually the same for everybody. It is this archetypal activity that sensitizes analysts to their absorbing and "taking over" aspects of their patients.

In Jung's writings there are a number of other observations which imply his interactive approach.

(1) He believed that a patient's resistance could be thought of not only as intrapsychic but also as related to the therapist's conflicts (Jung, 1951a, p. 115; see also Lambert 1981).
(2) He implied that a patient might be ahead of the analyst in understanding and lead the therapist into appropriate functioning. In a lecture only published after his death, Jung described how he had

become depressed at his inability to understand what was happening. With his patient becoming more and more ill, he offered to refer the patient to someone else. To his astonishment she said she thought everything was fine, and added that it did not matter at all if Jung did not understand her dreams. Jung continued the treatment and gave evidence that he learned from her, in that she introduced him to the study of Yoga.

(3) He made it clear that in his relations with his patients he would from time to time express strong emotions openly, and that he did so because he thought they were needed by the patient.

In his writing Jung hardly mentioned countertransference, though he seemed to refer to it often in its current sense. In addition to his idea that the analyst absorbs the psychopathology of his patient, he though of the analyst as just as much in analysis as the patient. If the patient was to change or transform himself, the analyst must also be prepared to do so, and should previously have experienced the essential nature of this process in his own analysis.

I have argued previously in favour of developing a theory of analytic practice and that such a theory would facilitate interaction rather than imposing a system of ideas on the patient. The individual nature of the analytic situation can be preserved by careful attention to the patient's communications; understanding by the analyst of the patient's participation can be facilitated by the former's own analysis and his capacity for transformation. The concept of countertransference is useful in this regard since it relates to the apparent subjectiveness in Jung's ideas and helps in distinguishing between their valid and invalid aspects (Fordham, 1957e). Countertransference theory has been developed by classical psychoanalysis. The earliest view was that an analyst can develop illusions about the patient based on residues of the analyst's infantile neurosis or on disturbances in the analyst's personal life having no relevance to the patient. These data are to be treated by the analyst just as he might treat his patient's transference. That is, they must be analysed and mastered intrapsychically. To classical psychoanalysts, it is all related to the notion that transference and countertransference originate in the unconsciouses of separate persons with firm boundaries, that is, not as open systems interacting with each other.

Though it is convenient to think of transference and countertransference illusions emanating by projections or displacements from essentially closed systems, there can be, at the same time, unconscious interactions. The contrast between the open and closed systems models, each of which has its relevance, does not necessarily mean they are antithetical. The differences can be related to stages in analysis or even to the requirements of different patients.

Analytical psychologists have worked extensively with border-line cases, as well as with a fair number of psychotics. Also, one of Jung's special contributions was his encouraging the treatment of persons in the second half of life. With older patients he engaged in a form of therapy which included considerable personal interaction and more or less frank education.

With the severe as well as with the less disturbed, the analyst's affective reactions to the patient may contain some validity. I have suggested that as a result of some patients' effects on their analysts, the latter tended to introject their patients' unconscious fantasies or archaic objects. Consequently I surmised that the analyst is in a position to study further his patients within himself. This impact of patients on analysts I originally labelled *syntonic countertransference* (Fordham, 1957e). Unlike countertransference illusions, which should be mastered and resolved by the analyst, syntonic countertransference provides valuable information about patients. The concept of the syntonic countertransference was derived from Jung's observation that an analyst can introject his patient's psychopathology and the idea that it is has therapeutic potential. Accordingly, an analyst might find himself behaving in ways out of line with what he knows of himself, but syntonic with what he knows of his patient. Moody (1955) observed that this kind of response by an analyst might have a significant influence on the progress of analytic therapy. Plaut (1956) studied the influence a patient had upon him and showed that the analyst might, as he put it, "incarnate an archetypal image"; he then worked through that situation with the patient.

Later I came to think that something similar might be contained in countertransference illusions. This idea was developed in a paper by Kraemer, who described the case of a depressed patient who was treated by a therapist who in turn came to him for analysis because the therapy was at an impasse. Kraemer's therapist patient had developed a countertransference love for her patient, whom she actually inhibited from doing the analytic work because she had dreamed about him in a positive light. She insisted on expressing her positive feelings to the patient despite his strong objections. Such behaviour obviously needed analysis and the therapist knew it. Yet some depressed patients tend to evoke loving feelings in their analysts, and it was conceivable that the therapist's feelings could have been used to advance the patient's treatment had the therapist's compulsion not stood in the way.

These two forms of countertransference are rooted in projective and/or introjective processes, although other defence systems also enter into their formation. For example, the analyst may identify with the content of his introjection and then inadvertently play out a role for his patient, which is actually a powerful way of perpetrating his patient's neurosis. Or the analyst will crudely or subtly force a compliant patient to fit in with his projection. These are deviations from the therapeutic process but are destructive only when they become inflexible, remain unconscious, and are not used as sources of information on which to build interpretations or interventions.

The question remains as to how countertransference data can be utilized. A countertransference illusion may have one useful characteristic: it demonstrates the fallibility of the analyst. Though optimally the illusion does not last for long, it does seem to place the analyst on the same level as the patient. In addition it reminds the analyst of his tendencies to become undesirably involved. When countertransference does interfere with the analytic attitude and with technique, the analyst must struggle to find some solution. These occurrences can be quite subtle. Minor manifestations of countertransference illusions may seem unimportant. Some may derive from the analyst's life outside the analysis, so that he will inevitably go through periods of stress which in turn influence his work. Overtly he may proceed consistently, but with an underlying mood change his participation will be coloured. Sometimes this goes unnoticed. With others the effect is repressed, or it may be observed and reflected upon without being communicated. However, it will influence the course of patients' associations. I do not call this countertransference proper, in the sense that it is a reaction to a patient. However, if a patient consistently induces a specific mood in the analyst, then it is countertransference and must be understood, interpreted and brought into consciousness. I mention this because they are human attributes. They are to be expected. Otherwise they can be the springboard for pathological countertransference reactions.

A criticism of technique centres around the tendency for it to become divorced from an analyst's affects, especially his love and hate (and their derivatives) for his patient. If an analyst believes that being loving, tolerant, kind, understanding and long-suffering is enough for the relationship, he is mistaken. An attitude of that sort can be supported by demonstrating that the patient's transference behaviour is only to be expected because of his developmental history and by implying that it has relevance to him, the analyst in the present. An alternative is to refer the "projection" to archetypal sources, and again it has nothing to do with either the patient nor the analyst as persons. Having understood the genesis of the transference, the analyst interprets, though that may not happen, and then waits for the working-through process to complete itself. Unfortunately, all this can conceal contempt for the patient which reinforces the patient's detachment by increasingly splitting, so that the patient becomes isolated and frustrated – in reality. This is liable to occur usually with the more severe character disorders, the narcissistic neuroses, and the border-line cases. These patients will then attack the analytic frame as a whole (Fordham, 1978) and try, in a delusional way, to engage in a "human" relationship. Since the analytic frame is threatened, the analyst may decide that the patient is untreatable. Then he either terminates the treatment or clings to technical clichés long after they have proved fruitless. I suspect that it is this that gave rise to the anathematization of technique in Jungian circles. Such consequences suggest that descriptions of method are incomplete in that they fail to pay sufficient attention to the affective states that the analyst goes through during the application of a technique. I am impressed with Bion's description of transformation in "O" and transformations in "K". When using techniques the analyst is looking for transformations in K, whereas he should be looking for transformations in O, but that would mean divesting himself of memory and desire. These would be expressing themselves as preconceptions about the therapy and the patient and not knowing what could or what ought to be done or thought.

At one time the *syntonic countertransference* was seen as providing a clue to the patient's psychology, in that it defined a condition from which an analyst could gain information about the patient without the patient's awareness, thus giving greater access to the patient's affective state. It was soon learned, however, that in order to accomplish this the introjection had to be reprojected, for only then could it be perceived as part of the patient. A *countertransference illusion* led to the converse conclusion. Before any positive content could be defined, the projection had to be withdrawn and assimilated. Thus, the concepts of projection and introjection and then more primitive forms of projective and introjection identification came to be viewed in a different perspective. Could it not be then that in any analysis there is a sequence of projections, introjections and identifications that provide affective information which, when transformed, underpins the conscious use of the analyst's skills?

Take the interview itself. When a patient comes into the room, how does an analyst behave? Does he immediately know the state of his patient? He may but usually he waits until the patient tells him what is in his mind. But this does not answer the question: What is the analyst's state of mind in the interim? While it will vary from patient to patient, if he discards "knowing beforehand", he will make every effort to empty his mind of what he has learned about the patient on other occasions. In this way the patient is approached by the analyst on each occasion as if they had never met before. Having emptied his mind and divested himself of memory and desire as far as possible, the analyst waits to see what happens both in his patient and himself. Since he has discarded "knowing beforehand", he will make every effort to let his observations, thoughts and fantasies develop in relation to the patient's communications. Then they may link up with material from past sessions which he can recall spontaneously and without effort and give rise to the matter of interpretations etc. Thus a series of changes (transformations) takes place in the analyst.

Bion has given a sophisticated account of the processes I have described. It is highly complex and I will only extract one segment of it. Once (the "ultimate") O has been reached it will lead first to transformations leading in the direction of K (K being knowledge resulting from sensual experience). I translate this formula as the desirability of starting from the self at first without characteristics, but later developing characteristics through processes of deintegration. Bion asserts that this involves faith in its scientific (not religious) sense is cogent, as is also his formulation that O→K involves transformations in O (leading to symbolization of the self as I understand it).

Clinical Example

A patient, over fifty years old, gets up from her chair when I come into the waiting room. She looks bright, with eyes sparkling like a little girl's. I feel annoyed at something hungry about her and think that she wants to be met with a hug and a kiss. It seems inappropriate and I do not want to do it. She lies down on the couch and says nothing. I feel a growing frustration and become aware of my hunger. She is not going to feed me with associations and I reach for my pipe. Then she starts talking and I put my pipe down. I am able to listen comfortably as the interview proceeds.

These incidents and reflections would not have become conscious had I not emptied my mind. This patient had been in analysis for some time and I could know quite well what this was about. I could have documented each of her actions. She was a somewhat narcissistic personality and easily felt angry if her virtues were not appreciated. I knew enough about her childhood to know why she had regressed when she came to her sessions and could have interpreted without difficulty. I might even have made an interpretive construction later on as the occasion arose. In short, instead of transforming my own state of mind, I would have proceeded on the basis of a concealed countertransference so as to establish, falsely, that I "knew beforehand". If I had done that, none of the affective content of the meeting would have been felt and my underlying irritation would have been missed. Also, my projective identification, and the way it was withdrawn to discover my own hunger, would have been lost sight of. Finally, I might very well not have noted that she started to talk out of competition with my pipe. My technique had aims in addition to the ones considered here. These were

(1) to individualize the meeting with my patient,
(2) to proceed in a sequence from unknowing to knowing.*

*This episode might be considered by reference to Bion's vertex. The progressions from O result in the emergence of beta elements to which attention is paid (horizontal grid 4). The result is

The Analyst's Errors

Many errors by an analyst are ascribed, with good reason, to countertransference. But in order to make judgements about errors, it is desirable to know when an intervention is sufficiently correct to be useful and when it is not. Indeed, to work with any degree of refinement on countertransference requires some such criteria for judgement.

Some criteria are derived from the patient's response and these are important (Wisdom, 1967). But those stemming from the analyst are more relevant to the thesis of this paper. How is the analyst certain that an intervention is relevant and needs to be made? He listens and arrives at a hypothesis of the unconscious content of his patient's communications – the projective and introjective identifications playing an essential part in stimulating it. Though the idea is tentative at this stage, it stimulates interest in what is going on. As the analyst continues to listen, his idea may have to be discarded as faulty. If it is confirmed, he reaches the conviction that it is relevant. Then he may communicate it to the patient. When the analyst has done so, he listens again to see what use, if any, the patient makes of this contribution. A useful interpretation will refer to what is unconscious in the patient. In that sense it may be relevant but incomplete. Therefore, it will not be accepted immediately. Indeed, it may be energetically rejected and only afterwards stimulate reflection or change in the patient's associations. Interventions are best thought of as a part of dialectical exchanges.

Flagrant errors usually but not always indicate the presence of countertransference. But its presence is also suggested when the dialectical process is interfered with, especially

(1) when the analyst experiences difficulty in listening to his patient's response to an intervention so that he cannot estimate whether it is being digested, accepted or rejected;
(2) when he becomes aware that he is failing to pick up indications his patient may give that the intervention has been appropriate or not; and
(3) when he misses what is happening or discovers it when the patient begins to guide him to a relevant or better formulation.

transformation through alpha elements to a grid row higher up the scale so it can not be determined at what level the patient started to operate, but I would estimate that row D (preconception) was arrived at.

Deviations from the Analytic Attitude

There are a good many instances in the literature where analysts have expressed their affects forcefully and I have discussed some of these elsewhere (Fordham, 1978). They are all non-analytic and, as responses to the patient's transference, may be classified as countertransference. They are usually aggressive and seem to be common with patients who are border-line, have psychotic traits or are frankly psychotic. Often they take place when the patient threatens the analyst's posture and self-definition, either by consistently acting out or by frustrating the analytic process or by attacking the analytic frame.

Some of these responses seem to be related to establishing the frame of analysis. Jung (1935) gave a dramatic example of an obsessional woman who had the habit of slapping her doctors in the face. He relates an instance when she threatened to hit him: "'Very well, you are a lady. You hit first – ladies first! But then I hit back!' And I meant it. She fell back deflated before my eyes. 'No one has ever said that to me before!' she protested. From that moment on therapy began to succeed." An example given by Giovacchini (1977) illustrates this as well. His psychotic patient's delusions at first involved Giovacchini in protective actions, but to no effect, and his patient eventually ended up in jail. In the course of the subsequent treatment Giovacchini told his patient that he would absolutely "not get involved again and if he found himself in trouble, he would have to depend only on his own resources."

Little (1957) illustrated what she called "R" – the analysts's total response – in the case of a patient who told repetitive stories about children. Little told her that she was "as tired of them as [the patient] was of the children's behaviour. The patient 'did not know' and went on into another story." Little then said, "I meant that; I'm not listening to any more of them."

No doubt many of these are states of the analyst which will not be repeated. Giovacchini (1977) infers as much when he describes another patient who made excessive demands upon him. He became furious and told him so. "I felt that I had over-reached. . . . But I did not become further distressed and the patient has not made any further demands of me. Undoubtedly he will, but I now believe I can reinforce the condition I set up without becoming upset" (ibid., p. 438). In this statement there is an implication that the exchanges involved a transformation in the analyst.

Patient A

Mrs A developed a delusional transference and did everything she could to break down my analytic posture. This was clearly expressed by her question, "Can't you stop being an analyst and become a person?" It was followed with great ingenuity and vigour. My reaction tended to be passive, to suspend my analytic efforts, and sometimes to retreat masochistically. Occasionally I found myself projectively identifying with my patient: the analytic method had no validity at all and I started looking at myself through her eyes.

In the face of her consistently negative reactions, I reflected guiltily about what had gone wrong. Had my diagnosis been at fault, and should I never have taken on this patient? Had my technique been inadequate? Had my interpretations been wrong too often or badly directed? Had I failed to analyse defences adequately? Had interpretations been too numerous so as to drive the patient to hopelessness and despair? And so on (Fordham, 1974b). During this period of self-scrutiny I felt very much more like a patient than an analyst. And the patient reinforced this by making attempts to analyse my state. Occasionally she was right. For instance, she believed that my infantile traumata had emerged, but she consoled herself with the thought that I would eventually mature into a state in which I would be able to be of help to her. Despite what appeared to be a predominantly sterile, even destructive process, she showed no signs of wanting to terminate. The lengthy process that my patient and I went through did produce a satisfactory therapeutic result although I had to initiate its ending. The analysis was not as complete as I might have wished. During it I learned to sustain my analytic stance much better with such patients so that when comparable situations arise I am no longer inclined to react the same way.

Patient B

Mrs B was concerned about her tendency to see penises everywhere. She apparently suffered from mild hallucinations, not to be thought of as clinically psychotic but making her concerned lest she be on the edge of psychosis. In this context she told me a dream in which there were long objects on a couch. She was uncertain as to whether they were faeces or penises. The dream had occurred many years ago and she told me that she had taken it to her previous analyst and together they agreed to call them "faecal penises." Some days later I had occasion to remind her of this incident. She adamantly asserted that she had told me nothing of the kind, that I had "gone mad" and that the incident was a figment of my "fertile mind." In various contexts similar situations had earlier arisen, when the patient, in addition to her denial, asserted that I had confused her with somebody else. On this occasion she inferred that I was in need of analysis, indicating that she would be ready and glad to undertake the necessary work. Like Mrs A, she implied that only when that had been completed could her own analysis proceed.

On previous occasions I had bypassed this quandary, unable to find a way of resolving it. Here it presented itself again. This time I emphasized that there was a difference of opinion which, distressingly, did not seem possible to resolve, and I made no further attempt to do so. She made further objections and the interview ground to a halt, giving me time for reflection. I did not give serious thought to the possibility that she was correct (as I had done at length with Mrs A). I was at a loss until I became convinced that an intervention was required. I told her that I thought the idea or feeling of a penis as faecal was relevant and I would tell her why I thought so, emphasizing the word "I" to indicate that it was offered to her as my idea and not necessarily one to which she need agree. It might, in short, be treated as part of my bit of "madness". There had been a number of times in her life from childhood onwards when she had been frightened or repelled by penises as disgusting or otherwise undesirable objects, and I summarized these events as some length. After considerable reflection and further objection, she came to agree that what I said felt true, but that her intellect kept producing arguments against such a mad proposition.

Which elements of this interchange are relevant to this discussion? There was the period after my patient's assertion that I was having an illusion about her which must have felt more to her like one of her "hallucinations". During this time I did not know what to do and was forced back on myself as with the countertransference to Mrs A. Here was food for thought, and it was digestible. Introjective identifications were contained in this and hence some uncertainty about whether she was correct. Looking back, it is clear that I had also identified with my patient's attitude in a projective way, and this made it possible for me to respect and empathize with her contention and temporarily to identify with it. Though these affective processes tended to make for a feeling of confusion, I was still able to reflect. The conviction that I had to intervene actively was not accompanied by the knowledge of what I was going to say. Indeed, I was still under the influence of what I believed was a countertransference when I started to speak. When I began to talk, however, I found it surprisingly easy to develop my theme in such a way, as it turned out, that my patient could understand its sense so that a shift in her transference took place. If, as on previous occasions, I had not been able to respond adequately, then there would be no doubt that I had developed a countertransference which had interfered with the progress of the analysis. But what of the rest? The affects roused by my patient are the consequence of her attack and they counter it. There was introjection, temporary confusion and after that the intervention came out of me, reflectively, but also as a spontaneous interaction. I had a certain feeling of surprise and satisfaction. It would be possible to consider all this part of a syntonic countertransference and to conceptualize it in terms of my reprojecting the introjected content with the intervention. This might even account for the spontaneity of my communication. But is the term *countertransference* necessary? It was an interaction in which projection, introjection, and identifications took part. Between these two clinical experiences I conducted a good deal of "self-analysis". This paid off in my personal and social life. Since this occurred in relation to a patient, it also facilitated the therapy. There were also other contributing activities: discussion with colleagues, writing papers (Fordham, 1969) and reading the literature, thereby discovering that my experience was not unique. I ended up developing a new hypothesis about defences of the self (see Chapter 11). I had apparently embarked, more or less under compulsion, on a research project. Such a project was to a large extent personal at first, and required my affective states of transformation. This seems to me to be an essential ingredient in all analytic research, and here affective complications entered into it. Once completed, I needed to discover whether it was a contribution to the body of psychoanalytic knowledge.

Additional consequences of this research were that I re-evaluated some patients' need for statements about the analyst's own affective states and also gained further insight into the notion of an analyst as a child.

A Concluding Statement

Looking back on the development of the concept of countertransference, one can see it as having gone through various phases. First it covered a set of undesirable data, arising from the analyst, to be controlled, analysed and resolved by him. It fitted in with the aspiration of analysts who hoped to achieve objectivity so as to know correctly what went on intrapsychically in their patients. Their own psychological states were to be thought of as essentially irrelevant. Not much attention was paid to Freud's (1910) view that the analyst uses his unconscious as an organ of perception, nor to Jung's emphasis on the importance of the analyst's personal influence. Next the term was expanded to cover the analyst's intrapsychic states. This had an important consequence: the analyst's personality, not only his psychopathology, could now be brought under review. In light of this approach, the analytic situation came under close scrutiny and thus led to a far more detailed description of what goes on between analyst and patient. There is the holding capacity of the analyst, as well as his capacity for projective and introjective identification with his patient. This is necessary for arriving at sufficient comprehension as to the processes going on in the patient, and between the analyst and his patient. A further study of how to validate the analyst's interventions led to understanding that a patient might work out mistakes, guide the analyst to a better formulation, and facilitate the analysis of the analyst.

It seems to me that these issues can all be brought under one heading, the analytic dialectic, and that they lead toward a view of the analytic situation as two open systems interacting. In the course of the development of the theory, the terms *transference* and *countertransference* have been expanded and generalized. Thus an analyst's appropriate feelings and affects about his patient have been included so that the original concepts, to which the terms refer, are in danger of losing meaning. Now the whole analytic situation is to be thought of as a mass of illusions, delusions, displacements, projections and introjections. I would suggest that, apart from an analyst's appropriate reactions, his transitory projections and displacements cease to be called countertransferences since they represent the analyst acting on and reacting to his patient. These actions may contain false perceptions, fantasies, illusions or even delusions, but these can be contained by the analyst till they are resolved; they can then be utilized to extract appropriate interventions. It is when the interacting systems become obstructed that a special label is needed and, to my mind, it is then that the term *countertransference* is appropriate.

I have suggested that rigidity be used as a criterion indicating countertransference, but I must qualify this. There are areas in analysis where there is rational rigidity: for example, the frame of analysis into which projections are made needs to remain stable until termination. In addition, there is a need for the analyst's stable style.

I believe the theory of countertransference has performed its main function. It has had the most desirable effect of taking analysts out of their ivory towers, making it possible for them to compare notes on what they really do during analytic psychotherapy. The pathological reactions of the analyst, comparable to the patient's transference, may be called *countertransference*. I would call the rest part of the interactional dialectic.

In that, the need for the analyst to transform the complex information he receives both from himself and the patient is included.

Many years ago now Jung defined such a "stage of transformation". I find that any analytic encounter with a patient involves transformation, whether it takes place in a single interview or whether it takes time over weeks or months. When it fails for too long, then one can speak of a countertransference in its deeper sense. To facilitate transformations, the analyst's capacity to reach the self is important. Bion's formula that the analyst divest himself of memory and desire means that he starts from a state at which there is no past and no desire for change, especially desire to change a patient in a social or intrapsychic direction. He can then receive the patient's impact and start to transform that. Hopefully he will arrive at a state when he can digest the patient's material and feed it back to him in a way that facilitates the transformative processes in the patient. Countertransference occurs when the analyst's transformation fails to take place.

Chapter Eleven

*Defences of the self**

This chapter is largely descriptive. It defines the "total defence" exhibited by patients in a transference psychosis. In this everything the analyst says is apparently done away with either by silence, ritualization of the interviews or by explicit verbal and other attacks direct to nullifying the analytic procedure.

Ego Defences

Before starting to study this condition, it may be useful to glance at the history of defence theory, so that the subject may be put in perspective. Defences were originally postulated when patients resisted analytic work. When transference analysis was introduced, the resistance took on a new dimension. Nonetheless they persisted: interpretations – especially those which referred to instinctual and infantile drives – which seemed evident to the analyst were at first denied by the patient. However, it was held that, as long as the analyst did not capitulate, resistances could be overcome so long as time was given for working through: the unconscious content would emerge from the unconscious and become accepted. These findings were based mainly on the analysis of hysterical patients, and they are still relevant to much analysis of the transference neuroses: we still pay attention to repressed contents and endeavour to make them conscious by following and interpreting the patient's defensive use of symbolization, displacement, compensation, conversion, reaction formation etc., with a view to making conscious what is unconscious.

Since then there has been a development in analytic technique by ego psychologists, particularly in the United States where it is held, to put

*Originally published in *The Journal of Analytical Psychology* vol. 19, no. 2, 1947. The present chapter has undergone additions and modifications.

it all too briefly, that the essential feature of analysis is defence analysis. If that is well conducted then unconscious processes in the id will become conscious in a way that can be satisfactorily assimilated. The technique is subtle and interesting, but if that technique were used without identifying the unconscious process against which the defences are constructed, it would leave the patient with no idea about what his resistances were all about.

As time went on it was discovered that the postulate of other defences of a different kind was record. They were observed in the compulsion (obsessional) states and were called "isolation" and "undoing". Here the affective element defended against is conscious, but its significance is not accessible because of its isolation from the rest of the personality.

Finally, there are the more primitive defences against bad objects; splitting, projective identification and idealization directed against part or whole objects. In the case of part objects there is no unconsciousness, but rather more or less violent attempts to attack and do away with the bad object – they can reach a level at which one must speak in terms of annihilation. It is this last group of defence systems upon which I shall focus, for it is in this area that total defences are mobilized.

Transference Psychosis

I first became interested in transference psychoses when investigating delusional transferences, because I was made aware that the patient never took what was said to him at its face value but reinterpreted it in the light of the projective identification that held sway at any particular time. An alternative way of putting it would be to say that there was no longer an agreed meaning assigned to words upon which ordinary discourse depends.

First, I proceeded on the ordinary basis that it would be enough to name the projection and suggest, even if I could not prove how it had arisen in the expectation that the analysis would then proceed. However, since the interpretation itself was submitted to reinterpretation, this did not work and, I found, could be read to mean that the analyst was defending himself against the truth about himself and was trying to force his own anxieties into the patient. In a variation on this theme, in the patient's view, the analyst was using his technique as a shield behind which to hide himself. Thus the transference interpretation was nullified.

Partly as a result of this situation, confusion arises, and it struck me more than once that this became very much worse if common sense was appealed to or if reference was made to reality – then the patient became convinced, as one patient put it, that his analyst had gone mad!

In its more dramatic forms the syndrome can develop so that the interview becomes filled with negative affects and confusion, until the whole of the dialectic seems to break down. The time may be filled with denigrating the analysts interventions, ending up in loud groans, screams or tears whenever the analyst speaks: the patient seems to use every means at his disposal to prevent the analyst's interventions from becoming meaningful, or alternatively or concurrently a meaning is given to them that is so distorted as to create confusion if not identified. Almost everything is reversed, turned upside down or subtly distorted so that direct communication becomes impossible.

Perverse destructive aims dominate the picture: the attack on what is good and the conversion of good into bad objects and vice versa, the delusion that the analyst in concealing himself and depriving the patient of himself, that he is ill or is himself so pathological and infantile that he needs the patient for his emotional survival; all these can be prominent features of the transference. At the same time the patient's efforts to preserve the delusional true person of the analyst or foster his growth can lead to the construction of a destroyed or perverted world outside the analysis. Parents are denigrated because of the transference situation, and their failings may be rigidly held to have caused the patient's condition. The denigration extends to relatives, siblings and to society politics and religion.

All this can be understood as an attempt to ward off destructive attacks on the good person of the analyst, and to project the split-off destructive processes into the past, society and the cosmos. Therefore, in the situation on which I am focusing, the attack on the analyst, by dividing him into a bad technical machine and a good hidden part, which it is the aim of the patient to unmask and obtain for himself, is a step forward in therapy even though the terror of the destructive aim is greatly increased.

A correlate of this situation is disturbance in the sense of time. There is no true historical dimension and, as a consequence, past and present are the same. This is the affective state of affairs, though references can be made to the past and be understood during periods when the delusions recede. However, they lack cogency and are treated as academic niceties; and if the historical reference is accepted, it is because it fits the patient's delusional system. When outside its scope, it is denied: the analyst is said to have "got it wrong" and the memory may be repeated with the necessary emendations.

It is characteristic that any memories of childhood that have been revealed do not alter and expand as analysis of the transference proceeds in any progressive analysis. The content screen memories are not accessible; they remain emotionally isolated from the setting in which they are known to have arisen.

I think there is a true running-together of past and present, and the patient will exploit this with a view to putting maximal emotional pressure on the analyst, aiming to split him up, or wear him out, sometimes going on to reversing the analytic situation so that the analyst "becomes" the patient. It can be on this basis that reconstructions are treated as an evasion of the analysts fear of his own infant self.

Countertransference

The pressure to which the analyst is submitted can produce characteristic effects:

(1) That the analyst can be led to participate in the confusion was held to be, if not desirable, at least an inevitable state of affairs.
(2) He can be pushed into masochistic acquiescence to become persecuted and guilty at not being able to help his patient, whom he may feel he is robbing, especially if the patient is relatively poor. This can lead to splitting along the lines that the patient is trying to achieve. If his guilt becomes too strong, he may even make attempts to stop the analysis as Jung (1937b) reports he once did, characteristically, without success.
(3) Feeling frustrated and inadequate in his efforts to help his patient, the analyst can seek to do something that mitigates the situation: he may more or less abandon analysis, submit to the patient's seductions by excessive use of tokens, or allow the patient to take more and more possession of him physically. This can lead to a sexual relation being started. As far as the countertransference comes in here, sexual acts, usually of a polymorphous kind (Meltzer, 1973), may be introduced to frustrate the patient's efforts to induce a regression. The transference contents are, as I have suggested, directed towards inducing helplessness in the analyst and this can change the patient into a threatening, persecuting beast. Such a regression may be stopped by adolescent sexual activity.

If I lay stress on these effects, it is because they can become indicators of the patient's attempts to split the analyst and force his way into him. If this is not detected he will succeed, and the analyst may collude with the delusion that it has happened. Thus an amalgam of analyst–patient is set up, and it can be very difficult to dissolve: it is a malignant form of countertransference.

All these states of the analyst avoid helplessness, despair and depression on his part, so he can begin to consider whether it is not these feelings that are the state of the patient contained in himself. It cannot be underlined sufficiently that the patient remorselessly plays on any weak points he may discover in his analyst, the effect being to destroy the mature, nurturing, feeling and creative capacities of the analyst.

Technical Faults

It is interesting to review theories that the psychotic transference is due to faults by the analyst with the countertransference in mind:

(1) The diagnosis was in error; the patient should never have been taken on for analysis.
(2) Technique has been faulty and in particular:
   (*a*) Interpretations have been directed towards the patient's bad objects and treated by the analyst as though they were really good objects. As a result, the analyst becomes the "devil's advocate".
   (*b*) As part and parcel of this faulty procedure, the patient's defences have not been taken sufficiently into account, or even not at all.
   (*c*) Interpretations of whatever kind have been so excessive as to induce malignant persecution in the patient. It is these that drive him to hopelessness and despair.
   (*d*) The analyst has made so many wrong interpretations that the patient's trust in him has been undermined.

These faults cannot be excluded; indeed most of them happen from time to time in most analyses and can usually be detected and rectified: the development of ego psychology amongst psychoanalysis has done a good deal to help in avoiding them.

The feature of the syndrome described, which makes the argument about technical faults inadequate, is that the patient does not go away; on the contrary he often contends openly, but more often by implication, that his whole life depends upon the continuation of the analysis and its successful outcome. He so contends, even when he insists, that for a solution to come about the analyst must mature or cure himself first of the illness that he has (in the patient's delusion). Therefore it is hardly likely that the analyst's real faults come into the picture much.

Analytic Method

In the literature there is confirmation of the effects that patients have on their analysts and there is a consensus that some change in technique is required. The work of Little (1981), Balint (1968) and Searles (1965) (though the latter's views are set in a more pathological framework) favours changes. In my experience (and I mean just that; it is apart from anybody else's) it has been difficult to sustain my analytic attitude and so it became doubly necessary for me to be sure of my position. "Technique and counter-transference" (Fordham, 1976b) was largely an attempt at digesting experiences of pressure from these patients: in conducting his work an analyst needs to keep aware of his inner real feeling of self in relation to the patient. With this clear the patient's demand that you stop being an analyst and become yourself can be shown as part of his delusional system that is being worked on.

Thus, the analytic attitude needs to be maintained, so that it is not desirable for the analyst to try "being himself" any more than he is already so doing by making confessions or giving information about himself etc. Nor is it desirable to become excessively passive or guilty at the amount of pain, terror and dread that the patient asserts the analyst causes. It is important that the analyst should control any guilt he may feel about the patient's claim that he causes confusion, is sadistic, cruel and destructive etc. It is important also to recognize a feature of the pain: it is a sign that the patient is struggling and of his will to live. It is even secretly valued by the patient as such, so it is mistaken to try and take it away from him.

It is most revealing that if the condition starts to resolve, the patient may say how all along he has secretly valued and made use of those interventions of his analyst about which he has been most negative and was relieved by the verbal continuity as a manifestation that the analyst had not, in reality, been damaged. Thus all along there had been a secret ally of the analyst within the patient. This gives me an opportunity to refer to the need for interpretation of the positive aspects in the patient's behaviour: it is easy to overlook them, but it is most important not to do so. It is also important never to treat the patient as though he really is an infant, but to keep whatever contact there remains with the adult part of the self and, if it is not accessible, to continue as if it were. This attitude I have again found is appreciated when and if recovery takes place.

Tokens

Though tokens may have short-term beneficial consequences I am very dubious of their long-term positive effect: they can prevent analysis of the very situation that needs analysis by focusing the delusion in them. So I conclude that they should not be given in any case when the patient is actively demanding or pleading. When doing so he is conscious of his need and is near acting on his own – the problem here is that it is not the act, but the anxiety associated with it, that needs analysis so that the compulsive impulses can be brought under greater control. However, this is not to deny that the patient, without having been given permission, will from time to time touch, get hold of, hit or bite his analyst and may break or steel objects in the room, so that it is important to have no objects around of much value. I believe, however, that there are occasions when the annihilation turns against the patient so that he becomes so broken up that physical contact initiated by the analyst may be justified – at least I have not found a way round doing so.

Infantile Roots

I cannot convince myself that a bad start in life will account for the syndrome. Though there is often evidence of one early catastrophe or more, and though that can look as if it has been all important, this cannot be extended to cover the whole picture, and later traumata can be even more important at any particular time. Nevertheless, early disasters such as manifest in disturbed breast-feeding, illness and traumatic hospitalization can be most relevant. A special situation arises if the family is reasonably good for children; it may even be unusually rich and satisfying as the child grows up. I have met this combination of early trauma with subsequent good family life in other cases and it seems to make access to the infantile root in a historical sense particularly difficult. However, there are instances in which it looks as though the birth of a sibling was far more important, perhaps because mother and infant had been excessively close so that, and in consequence, insufficient self representation had taken place in her child. The excessive projective identification that takes place in these circumstances would provide the conditions for self representations to be faulty. In consequence the pregnancy of the child's mother is more than usually disturbing to the elder child, and the birth of the younger sibling is severely traumatic. In addition, owing to the closeness of the mother to her elder child, the father cannot fulfil his role of deepening his relation to the elder child: he is treated as alien and so the child's development is further blighted. Thus the scene is set for the accumulation of traumata which build up in disaster after disaster.

I find it impossible to sort out in detail what originated in the infant and what can be put down to the real parents, because in many cases the force of the child's needs impels him to seek out the failures of his parents, and raise them to monstrous proportions and if, later on, it becomes apparent that his family was not worse than others, then it can be the structure of society that is at fault (compare "The angry brigade").

I therefore fall back on a mixture, and this seems to serve analytic purposes well enough. However, this position presupposes a constitutional component in the self.

The ravages of envy and jealousy are all too apparent as well as the enormous need for projective identification. There is also arrogance and omnipotence which can cover feelings of emptiness, formless terror and dread. All this becomes built into a system of false maturity so that it is extremely difficult to sort out what is secondary regression and what is primary; it is important to do so as far as possible.

As to the confusion, I must repeat that there can be little doubt of one of its aims; it is to maintain an infantile perverted state of mind. It draws on distortion of the body image so that any one zone can be combined, replaced or identified with any other (so-called confusion of zones). The more stable delusional structure is reparative and is to be understood, with Jung, as containing archetypal forms aiming to re-establish relatedness, although seemingly in a malignant form.

A Note on Theory

Much work has been done in this field by psychoanalysts and I have found that of Klein, Bion, Rosenfeld and Meltzer illuminating. It is clear that all these patients have not developed an adequate self feeling, and indeed seem to have largely emptied themselves into the analyst. In doing so, they operate powerful defences against the not-self part of him seen by the patient as technique, method etc. This has led me to think about their condition in terms of the self and its defences against not-self objects, a subject elaborated some years back by Stein (*vide infra* pp. 167ff). I will not enter here into this theoretical suggestion because I intend to keep close to the more important clinical features I have described.

In this paper I have aimed at clarifying a particular syndrome. It is on the basis of the experiences contained in this chapter that I have profound doubts about the procedures adopted by Kohut. He and his associates base their method on the view that the self is so damaged that it has to be repaired through the analyst's capacity for active empathy. I believe that he would have explained my data as due to my lack of empathy and failure to allow adequately for the mirroring and idealizing grandiose transference. That may be, but it became evident that, as I worked on the data, I was able to metabolize the projective identifications better and better; I was also developing my interpretive skills with pleasing results. Thus I think it valuable to continue analysis of the delusional transference, however destructive it may appear.

My work depends upon the view that the self in its ultimate sense is indestructible, since it does not belong to the realm of sensual experience. However, its deintegrates can become split up and distorted: these can then be expressed (experienced) in projective identification which forms the basis for the delusional transference. In health, the creative and destructive deintegrates of the self are required for growth, so even when we deal with pathology there must be a question as to whether it is empathic, in the deeper sense of the term, to repair the good aspects of the self at the cost of leaving the bad ones untransformed. So it is not enough to act as a reflector (mirror transference), it is necessary to take in (projective identification) and metabolize the material by digestion until it can be returned to the patient in the form of interpretation usable by the patient. In my view the mirror, which has become such an attractive metaphor, is liable to deceptive misuse. For instance, the study of infants indicates that they are greatly puzzled should they see themselves in a real mirror; but if they see their mother's image in it, there is a familiar image and it is easily enjoyed. It is the newness of the experience of seeing themselves in a mirror that can be investigated. I interpret that to mean that in this instance the mother does not mirror the self image and this is something that is strange to the infant.

Chapter Twelve

*Jungian views of body–mind**

In this chapter I will explore further the defences of the self. They will be considered from the vertex of psyche and soma.

The motives which led Jung to become a psychiatrist reveal why his main interest became the psychology and not the physiology of human beings. There were powerful influences, both familial and temperamental, impelling him in this direction, as *Memories, Dreams, Reflections* records. Therefore his investigations of the relation between body and psyche mostly stopped short of employing physical methods. And today in analytical psychology the diagnosis of physical disease is generally made on negative grounds: if a mental or psychic cause cannot be found for a particular symptom complex, then there is likely to be a physical one. It also follows that the contribution of analytical psychologists to the problem of body and mind have been largely speculative.

It was early in his career that Jung, in collaboration with Ricksher (1907–8) and Peterson (1907), used a string galvanometer and a pneumograph to record physical reactions exhibited by subjects undergoing word association tests. His other contribution to the subject was speculative: he postulated a "toxin" as the cause for the primary symptoms of schizophrenia. He was much criticize for this especially by psychoanalysts, and after some vacillations he ended up in favour of psychogenesis though a sort of translation of psyche into soma took place. The discovery of mescaline has done something to rehabilitate the idea of a chemical factor or "toxin".

Whether Jung thought of body and psyche as two distinct entities at the start is not known, but his adoption of instinct theory from psychoanalysis makes it clear that early on he thought of psyche as essentially related to soma; indeed, from time to time he makes it clear,

*Originally published as "Jungian views of the body–mind relationship" in *Spring* 1974.

with one or two striking contradictions, that psyche is rooted in the organic substrate. This idea is worked forward in his theory of archetypes as unconscious structures or forms that organize data and give rise both to mental images and to physical discharges called patterns of behaviour. At one time Jung conceived the archetype as the psychic representation of instinct only, but he often writes as if they were purely psychic forms. Later he developed a bipolar theory, which gives a better idea of the relation of psyche to soma. He conceived of the archetypal forms as being arranged on a scale which he compared to the spectrum in which the colours are arranged as a visible series; the different colours correspond to the archetypal images.

The archetypal forms shade off into two "psychoid" poles, one of which is formed of instinct (i.e. body processes), the other spirit (i.e. psychic forms). I want to insert here that, though the images appear to refer more directly to somatic or psychic structures and processes, all archetypes are affective whether they are spirit orientated or instinct orientated. Consequently they must be related in some way or other to physiological processes.

The analogy of the spectrum is also pertinent because at either end are the invisible infra-red and ultra-violet rays, which are to be compared with the unconscious itself. An additional aspect to this analogy is that a unitary integrated state is implied – the light from which the spectrum derives. This notion infers the unity of the person that can be deintegrated into its discrete entities, i.e. the different archetypal structures represented by a considerable variety of images.

Possibly on the basis that archetypal imagery at the red end of the spectrum may refer rather directly to physical changes, Jung (1931) published a case in which he concluded, from two dreams, that the imagery referred to an organic disease. He was presented with the dreams of a young girl in whom the differential diagnosis rested between hysteria and progressive muscular strophy. He pronounced that though there was evidence of hysteria, there was also a physical disease – he was proved correct.

In a second case (Jung, 1931) he was also successful. He was shown a dream from a patient with probable epilepsy and said that the dream showed evidence of a physical lesion, and even suggested a location for it in the medulla oblongata. Although he explained the reasons why he arrived at his conclusion in the first case, he never did so in the second. When challenged on this topic during the Tavistock Lectures given in 1935, he replied evasively that to show how he came to his conclusion would mean embarking on the description of a complex technique. Then he rambled around a lot of ideas and comparative studies including yoga, in which is found a system of symbolic arrangements referred to particular parts of the body, or rather the subtle body, as it is called in the Tantric system. He also touched on Eastern divination methods and on the concept of synchronicity. It was a sample of searching round various symbolic systems for ideas and hints on an obscure subject, a method he used to amplify a subject, and in which metaphors and analogy replace logical thinking. I think we can now understand why Jung did not publish in any detail (with one exception) his ideas on the diagnosis of physical disease from dreams: his investigations were in a preliminary state, and he had not discovered anything reliable that could be generalized. However, there is a short passage in Jung's Tavistock Lectures (1935b, p. 91) where he is quite emphatic; he asserts, with reference to the image of a "crab-lizard" in an archetypal dream: "I hold . . . that representations of psychic facts in images like the snake or the lizard or the crab or the mastodon or analogous animals also represent the organic facts." Jung published no more on these interesting data, but some analysts have been sufficiently interested to work his ideas further forward, and they will now be considered.

H. G. Heyer, who was close to Jung, researched in psychosomatic medicine and in 1933 published a book, *The Organism of the Mind*; so he was in the vanguard of the movement in which Wittkower and others participated. Heyer studied physiological changes that took place in patients under the influence of hypnotic suggestion: changes in the secretion of gastric juices, movements of the stomach, blood pressure etc. Also he set a definable aim couched in rather rich metaphor, for which I do not altogether understand the reason. He says: "We must discover the mental equivalent, the psychical method of expression, of each organic domain. Abstractions are accordant with the higher centres of the brain, with the cerebrum; imaginative ideas, metaphors, correspond to the lower, the unconscious, 'magical' domain" (Heyer, 1933, p. 86). Particular "magical" domains he called the "Vegetative vital cycle of nutrition" and the "Animal vital cycle of circulation". With reference to images he held ". . . the world of images is attuned to blind organic happenings . . . though these appear psychologically as images, they work physiologically" (ibid., p. 87). This verbiage may be handled by translating it to mean that imagery is related to affect and affect is as much physical as psychic, but he, like Jung, clearly believed that some kinds of psychic imagery are more related to the body than are others, and even to different parts of the body. However, he did not at any time provide convincing evidence in its support.

Heyer was very much interested in yoga and introduced into his practice a number of postural and breathing techniques. He attributed particular importance to a third intermediate domain which he called the "Pneumatic cycle of respiration", because breathing is at once controlled by rhythmic discharges, and also sufficiently subject to conscious control for effects on the total organism to be achieved: anybody who has watched yoga breathing techniques cannot fail to be intrigued by the degree of control over breathing and the states of body consciousness achieved in trance states. But Heyer never specified in any detail how body parts or systems expressed themselves psychically.

A few other Jungians have contributed to this study. Zeigler (1962) reported a case in which a dream occurred in a patient, who on the same night suffered from a coronary thrombosis. He thought that the dream could be synchronous (not synchronistic) with the physical state and that correlates could be found between the two. The dream contained archetypal images of the wind ushering in the appearance of a huge giant, massive like a rock, who tried to strangle him. Zeigler compares the dream with a number of experiences that patients generally report during and after such attacks. Unfortunately he did not attempt an analytical investigation of this patient, who, he thought, was not motivated for it.

The most elaborate study yet made of the correlation between imagery and a large spectrum of physical diseases has been made by Bach (1969). She found that by analysing in detail spontaneous pictures made by patients, she could detect those with organic disorders and differentiate them from those with mental disorders. She claims that her findings are valuable in both diagnosis and prognosis.

The nature of her correlations is obscure but she found it useful to divide the pictures into quadrants and to work on the assumption that the upper half represented psychic states and the lower half instinctual or somatic experience: the right side referred to the present or conscious states, the left to the shadow or unconscious – an arrangement which suggests that the body image is important. It would seem that this work could be subjected to statistical evaluation.

Using a different method and focusing on a single class of illnesses Elida Evans published (1926) a study of 100 cases of cancer who had been evaluated through intensive psychotherapy. Her viewpoint in therapy is essentially that of Jung. She found that her patients had lost a major cathexis before the tumour developed. The conclusion that affective states affect tumour growth was further investigated by Klopfer (personal communication). With the help of Rorschach profiles, he predicted with some success the rate of tumour growth in particular patients.

In 1963 C. A. Meier, another analyst close to Jung, published a paper: "A Jungian approach to pychosomatic medicine", in which he is keen to find a way out of the idea that there is causal relation between psyche and soma. Psychic manifestations, he maintains, are not the cause of physical states, or vice versa; psyche and soma are opposites, like spirit and instinct, and the conflict between them can only be resolved by discovering a symbol that unites them.

Since what might be called symbolic healing was a feature of Greek medicine, he invokes these procedures to expound his thesis. The sick man was first diagnosed and, if accepted for therapy, would have to undergo various rituals and sleep in an isolated place; if he dreamed the correct dream in which a divine image appeared, cure would take place. There does not then seem to have been much effort to separate physical from mental or psychic diseases, though there was quite careful screening of the patients.

This type of practice in the art of healing is quite widespread, and Meier takes this as support for his idea that it is desirable to look for a symbolic formula transcending the opposites of psyche and soma. As part of his historical approach, he considers as most valuable the "subtle body", an image which appears in Tantric yoga – also in late antiquity and early Christianity. He does not refer, as it seems to me he might have done, to the body schema nor the body image, contemporary concepts most related to the imagery he has in mind. Two Jungians, Scott (1956) and Redfearn (1966), have contributed to the very large literature on this topic. Scott in particular discusses the interrelation between body schema (as introduced by Head and used by Brain as an instrument to explain aphasia) and the body image. The two concepts Scott relates to the analytic ones of self and ego. He considers the schema disorganized in physical but not in mental disease. Redfearn took aspects of the body image as a point of departure and arrived at ideas about the physical location of psychic states. He summarizes that

> in the temporal lobes or centrencephalic system . . . there must be a topographically arranged system subserving the body image of affective experience, the "head" part of which corresponds with the "mind". When excitation reaches this part in sufficient quantities the centrencephalic system subserving self-awareness is excited to the point of functional disorganisation and this somehow liberates the sub-dominant regressive behaviour pattern (Redfearn, 1966, p. 16).

It is of course tempting to correlate psychic states with neurophysiology; I myself suggested that we might expect further enlightenment by relating archetypal patterns with those being investigated by ethologists. These investigators require the inheritance of organized neural systems analogous to archetypes in the unconscious. I also suggested (Fordham, 1957d) that the archetypes might be arranged in a hierarchical order analogous to the nervous system.

However, Meier has another suggestion which takes up what Jung was evidently playing with in his reply to questions put to him in his Tavistock Lectures, and which he had also referred to elsewhere, especially in his article on synchronicity. Meier puts forward the idea that the relation of psyche to soma may be wholly or in part synchronistic.

The idea of synchronicity was arrived at in an attempt to explain parapsychological data. Jung thought that they were not caused but were due to coincidences rendered meaningful by the activity of primitive archetypal forms. Thus a synchronistic phenomenon may be defined as:

> The coincidence of a psychic state in the observer with a simultaneous objective, external event that corresponds to the psychic state or content where there is no evidence of a causal connection between the psychic state and the external event and where such a connection is not even conceivable (Jung 1951a, p. 526).

To transfer this idea to psychosomatic processes as a whole would be to assume that the relation between body and mind is arbitrary but meaningful. Whilst there are psychic states in which a physical disease occurs which is not causally related to the psychic state (e.g. when a patient with a cancer phobia develops cancer), there is little to support an "acausal" relation between psyche and soma; it would run counter to the successful correlations between psychological and bodily events that have been made in recent decades.

Whatever its demerits, the thesis focuses attention on the meaning of symptoms whether they be what we term physical or psychological in origin. It is common to find that the discovery of meanings for reversible physical disorders, such as in hysteria, quite often helps and may remove symptoms in a variety of physical states: the physical expressions of anxiety in allergies, some forms of dermatitis, ulcerative colitis, infantile eczema and a good many infectious diseases of the respiratory tract, especially in children, are cases in point. I mention these because they are familiar from any analytical practice – many others could be added. That meanings can be discovered for organic diseases must also be familiar, though they do not often have evident effect on the physical disorder when it is "irreversible". So the discovery of a meaning seems most effective when the physical state is reversible – hence the idea of conversion introduced by Freud.

According to Jung, synchronicity is an alternative way of bringing order into disorder. It does not exclude causality, but complements it, and in this light the idea of meaningful coincidences gains value. However, a disadvantage of the synchronicity thesis is that it still treats the body as something "external" to or separate from the psyche. Something may be said for this idea, but only in states that we consider, such as unusual depersonalization syndromes or mystical states, from which it would not be justifiable to generalize.

Meier is correct in holding that we need a way of looking at the dichotomy psyche–soma that unites them – one might say, that reveals them as two ways of looking at the same thing. The emphasis on a meaningful connection is interesting, even though it is the psyche that gives meaning to events and not the physical events themselves, but here even this emphasis does not provide what is needed.

To summarize: The investigations of Jung, Heyer and Meier on symbolism still approach the subject of psyche and soma as if the two are separate systems obeying different rules that can be either interdigitated or else which correspond: and though Meier contests both views, he still continues along this line of thought for want of something better.

Another approach is possible if we start from self theory. We can hold to the idea of the psyche being at all points related to soma; we can then add a further dimension expressed in the challenging formulations of Leopold Stein (1967). He starts from the following proposition: "It is for epistemological reasons that I offer my first axiom: the body and mind are aspects of the same substance." He then develops his thesis by citing studies in immunology where the term "self" is used to indicate that the body is concerned to "maintain its organismic wholeness as distinct from other bodies". This means that there is a need for defensive organization – "defences against what is not-self are essential to health". He continues: "the self carries out defence actions on a much more basic level", in which destructive action features prominently and is directed against foreign bodies, i.e. those coming from sources external to the self and internally as auto-immune reactions.

The next significant passage in Stein's paper, the subtlety of which I shall not succeed in fully conveying, considers the elaboration of structures designed to receive and implement messages directed towards preservation of the identity of the self. The structures are archetypes which he holds "can equally be thought of as genes, enzymes, catalysts or pheromones ('social hormones': Wigglesworth 1964)". They are organized under the aegis of DNA. He states:

> The psychological message: 1. concerns a diversity of specific responses to stimuli from what is not-self; 2. must be all-pervasive so as to reach all defence outposts; 3. enables the individual to recognize what is imposed as not-self, even if the self shares with the not-self certain features; 4. must limit the power of each archetype within the structure of the self; 5. prohibits the wrecking of elements of the system as if they were extraneous [though it can attack elements of the self as if they were alien to it].
>
> It has in recent years become fairly evident how the defence system works in the tangible world of biology; it has been described as a somatic system with five analogous characteristics: 1. it shows a wide range of specificity; 2. its agents are ubiquitous; 3. it recognizes the not-self; 4. the distribution of the agents is ideally suited for maintaining the status quo among the tissues; 5. in predisposed persons the agents misguidedly attack self-tissues, which is presumed to be at the root of auto-immune disease (see Burch and Burwell, 1965, p. 254) (Stein, 1967, p. 104).
>
> [He concludes:] Neither the nervous nor the endocrine systems seem to be able to fulfil all these functions. This leads to the assumption that the biological

> analogon to the self would appear to be the vast realm of the lymphoid stem cells and/or the undifferentiated mesenchyme cells of the reticulo-endothelial system (ibid., p. 104).

Having overcome one's shock at this very unusual conclusion, one can proceed rather shaken to his list of "psychosomatic equivalents"; the archetypes are like the stem cells in their specificity; the reticulo-endothelial system is freed from the influence of, or control by, the nervous system, which is relegated to conscious systems and symbolization; the archetypes are analogous to antibodies; an element of disorderly function in the messages is found within the self and DNA itself.

Stein then turns to biochemistry for help in understanding how self is recognized and distinguished from not-self and chooses the theory of stereochemical fit, developed from the atoms in amino-acids by Libby, Burch and Burrell, which differentiates two kinds of fit: that of identity and that of complementarity.

In this part of his discussion, Stein uses some speculations of my own about early mother–infant relations. He finds useful the idea that the infant requires an absolute fit between his needs and his mother's fulfilment of them, and that, if his mother does not meet the needs, there is either no experience or his mother is treated as alien. In the first case, mother is treated as not-self; this is the equivalent of complementarity. On this basis there are two possibilities: either the infant becomes immune or disease results. Concerning this, Stein says:

> In view of the strong archetypal tendency to variation and disorder involved in the magnitude and subtlety of the 'message', it is not surprising if the steric, archetypal fit, necessary for genetic stability, can change from identity relationship to complementary relationship and thus go wrong, i.e., engender a pathological condition (ibid., p. 108).

It is indeed often recognized that inappropriate handling of infants leads to disease (psychic or physical or "psychosomatic"). It is also known that early in development disorders can apparently be generated by the infant himself.

Stein applies this part of his thesis to regional ileitis, which is an example of how the small intestine can be treated by the self as the not-self. This he thinks is related to the failure in maturation. Insufficient time has been allowed for the development of psychoimmunological tolerance since "the period of immaturity during which (introjected) not-self material can be accepted has been unduly shortened". In these cases, short breast-feeding (less than 1 month) was found to be twice as frequent as in a control group; further "in these cases high levels of antibodies in the constituents of milk, like casin and lacto-globulin, are seven times as frequent as in normal people" (ibid., p. 109).

I have detailed Stein's paper at some length because it is the only attempt by a Jungian to develop a radical psychosomatic theory of the self. Like any synthesis in a field where there is as yet little certainty, Stein's theories can be challenged. For instance, it may be said that he introduces a self theory that is not in line with what is known of the self empirically. The notion of the specificity of archetypes and their link with the hereditary DNA molecule has been postulated but not substantiated etc.

However, my object is not to present difficulties, but rather to show what a self theory of the mind–body relation looks like. I see no reason why Stein's procedure should not be valuable, even though it is somewhat startling to find him drawing together a psychological concept and a body system that is perhaps less psychological, if I may so put it, than any other body system, except the skeletal structures or connective tissues. We are used to thinking of central nervous system activity as correlated with mental states and also with other body systems. But if we can put these ideas aside and try to discern what is essential to body and psyche, I see no reason why we should pick out one system rather than another from which to start. If it so happens that work on immunology has led to ideas that are surprisingly like those developed by Jungian analysts, it may be that there is here a concept and language developing that can be applied to other systems and the organisms as a whole.

I cannot end without making some reference to the importance of infancy as a focus for study of states of the self. In infancy many of the observations which gave rise to the distinction between psyche and soma are absent, but we are faced with a person who is not basically different from an adult. Stein's thinking, shifting freely from psyche to soma on the basis of an abstract "quasi-mathematical form", can usefully be applied to the theory of the infant's early object relations. Terms like "unconscious" and "fantasy" can be replaced by *archetypal forms* no more psychic than somatic, which serve the preservation of identity. It is also useful to think of an infant as a unity, a self in, as it were, pure culture out of which psychic structures develop as part of physical ones. Quite small infants show the rudiments of mental activity that seems at all points united with bodily states and very dynamic activities.

The ideas which Stein develops can be translated to infancy to a greater extent than he did, and in an even more productive way. In particular, his ideas of aggression and the destructive action of the self gain meaning if we think of an infant as a person in whom identity is particularly linked with threats from alien intrusions by an actual mother (or as a bad object created by the infant) and who in reality cannot fit in with all the requirements of the infant self.

Thinking in this way, however, ignores the fact that in everyday practice it is essential to treat data as obeying the quite different rules which apply to psyche or soma. It is here that the concept of deintegration is useful. In the first place a deintegrate is psychosomatic in the sense that an infant cannot distinguish mental representations from bodily experience. But a deintegrate focuses infant activity in a specific direction, first of all on attachment behaviour and breast-feeding. In doing so, a field of perceptuo-motor activity is set up in which differentiation between mental and physical functioning can come about, and which has advantages in day to day living. The distinction between psyche and soma therefore acquires adaptive value. In treating these twin concepts, psyche and soma, as deintegrates, their origin in the self is not lost sight of, nor is their adaptive value left out of account.

Part Three

Religion, mysticism, alchemy

Part Three

What is below is like what is above
that the miracle of the one may be accomplished
Tabula smaragdina (Jung, 1942, p. 140)

Introduction

In this part I intend to discuss first the views of Freud and Jung on religion and follow this by a discussion of some mystical and alchemical data. I hope to leave the reader with an impression of how the self manifests in these fields. My choice of subject matter is also partly determined by a number of other considerations:

(1) I believe that the attempt to set up Freud as anti-religious in contrast to Jung, who has sometimes been acclaimed as a sort of saviour of religion, is in need of more careful consideration than has been or is usually given to it.
(2) I am impressed by the infrequency with which analytical psychologists give serious consideration to recognized saints of the Catholic Church.
(3) Although a large literature has grown up around Jung's monumental work on alchemy, there is little consideration given to the narrative descriptions that alchemists sometimes give of what takes place in alchemical work.

In my reflections I shall assume a theory of vertices, introduced by Bion, and apply it by asserting that the differences in the data are different by virtue of the vertices employed. I have preferred the idea of vertices to points of view because it covers a wider set of data than the one which the visual metaphor suggests. Thus a vertex includes such elements as hereditary endowment, the development of the individual from infancy onwards, the cultural setting and location in history.

I shall not define the term but instead shall specify its contents as occasion arises: three of them are employed: that of religion, alchemy and analytical psychology.

What I have to say must be classed as speculative imagination. By that I mean to assert my right to relate to the matter, religious, mystical and alchemical by making an imaginative leap into the writings of various authors. I can neither be religious, in the sense that ordinary people understand it, nor can I claim to be an alchemist. Therefore I must either decide that the work of each discipline produces something I cannot estimate or I can say: this is the way I relate to it from my vertex through speculative imagination.

All these developments have arisen because psychoanalysts have extended their investigations outside their traditional field (the psychoneuroses) and have studied border-line states, the psychoses, character disorders and the recently defined narcissistic neuroses. Much of their work is strangely familiar.

Chapter Thirteen

*Is God supernatural?**

I will introduce my subject by explaining that my vertex to religion is based on the assumption that analytical psychology, like psychoanalysis, is methodologically scientific. Some theories in each discipline have been submitted to experimental and statistical investigation under laboratory conditions; however, each science mainly relies on field work, in which observations are collected relevant to current theory. Analytical sessions themselves, however, provide evidence of both observational and experimental levels of sophistication. They provide information. When sufficient has been collected, it becomes possible to initiate experiments. The experimental instrument is the interpretation of data provided by the patient and the validity of the interpretation is tested by its effect on the patient. It is these tested interpretations and the collected information which form the basis on which generalizations, commonly found in analytic literature, rest.

The generalizations have been applied in a variety of continguous fields of study one of which is religion, since that is a manifestation of the psyche. It can be assumed that the arguments of analysts when applied to religion can have the same validity as the theories they evolve and data they discover in the clinical field; I do not hold this view. I trust that my position will be apparent in the rest of the argument, but I will note here that, since clinical data are collected on the assumption that whatever the patient says is an expression of part of the total personality, they cannot refer directly to the transcendent religious field. Therefore, whatever analysts have to say about religion is essentially conjectural and less reliable than conclusions referable to their psychological vertex.

It was the researches of Freud which, in modern times, inaugurated a new version of the old conundrum: is God or are the gods manifestations

*Originally published in *Theology* vol. 62, no. 555, September, 1966.

of human imagination, or do they exist in their own right? Freud was an atheist, but he could accept religious men as collaborators, Pastor Pfister being the best known example. So it cannot be that he thought his position was inimical to religion. Freud was uncompromising when it came to scientific issues which he considered important, so he cannot have thought that his views on religion were central to his thesis and he did indeed think that they were influenced by or even originated in his personal attitude or in the tradition of scientific rationalism to which he belonged. In short, he must have believed that his views belonged to the conjectural order of validity.

At the same time there is no doubt that Freud thought that the next step in man's evolution would be to increase the effectiveness of his rational scientific mind, but he had little hope that mankind as a whole would use what rational gifts were available to him. He further thought that the main bulk of human beings have little enough sense anyway and that the destructive and sexual drives in them are far too powerful to be regulated by such a recently acquired and precariously organized mental activity as thought.

The value of the rational ideal, which he maintained throughout his life, was supported by the gains of biological science. Starting with the theory of evolution, there had followed researches which showed that commonly held religious beliefs were untenable. In the aggregate they led many thoughtful people to agnosticism, atheism or indifference. Freud belonged to this tradition and he took to atheism with a frankness and commitment which was characteristic of him.

The most criticized and misunderstood publication is his rather short volume *The Future of an Illusion* (Freud, 1927). In it is found his definition which links illusion with belief as follows: "We call a belief an illusion when a wish fulfilment is a prominent factor in its motivation and in doing so we disregard its relations to reality, just as the illusion itself sets no store by verification" (ibid., p. 31). The phrase "sets no store" means that the wish fulfilment becomes strong enough for the believer not to mind whether his belief can be verified or not. In amplification Freud states: "Illusions need not necessarily be false – that is to say unrealizable or in contradiction to reality" (ibid.). Thus the illusion that God exists can neither be proved nor disproved: it is not in contradiction to reality, by which is meant a mental construct based on perceptual data derived from the external world. It is only when the illusion collides drastically with reality, that an illusion becomes a delusion. It may be noted here that Freud sometimes oversteps his brief and calls religion a delusional system – but though he may believe this to be true, he is not justified in extending his argument thus far.

These ideas on the relation between illusion, belief and reality are crucial to understanding Freud's work. It may be added that he studies only the parts of religion which involve illusions that lead to beliefs. In his view there is no point in trying to verify the belief – only the illusion is worthy of consideration. It follows that religious people operate essentially with illusions and beliefs that are powerful enough not to call for verification. The accumulation of such delusions and beliefs need not be encoded in dogmatic formulations that demand the assent, faith or belief of such people, but later that may occur.

The widespread prejudice that illusions are essentially bad has led many to conclude that this part of what Freud said is a more destructive attack on religion than is warranted. This can be seen if we remember that illusions can be good and valuable and lead on to discovery. This is quite a tenable position; indeed, some psychoanalysts so argue and the negative interpretation of Freud's work is apparently reversed. It cannot be too strongly underlined that Freud himself understood the place illusions could take in the development of the individual and of society. He especially valued their use by arists whom he greatly venerated. He objected to their use in religion only because their nature is frequently denied and made into supposed objective truths which are then used to resist or destroy evidence that contradicts them. Freud further thought that illusions were only *now* disadvantageous and not before the present era. They are now redundant because, in the light of psychoanalytic understanding, means have been made available to submit them to understanding and so discover their origin and functional importance in man. His procedure was strictly in line with scientific method and so need not be used to destroy religious experience any more than a knowledge of biochemistry destroys trees or other living structures. Mistakenly the reduction of religious belief in God to the childhood of the individual and of the race has been used to obscure what is more important, namely, Freud's conversion of metaphysical reality into a psychological proposition which could be tested by using well-defined criteria. In doing so he opened up the study of religious experience to the psychoanalyst.

There have of course been others that thought about religion as an illusion; the *credo quia absurdum* attributed to Tertullian is a case in point. Freud's merit was not to promulgate the idea itself, but to be the first to use psychoanalytic method to investigate systematically the psychological roots of religious experience in man's affective (emotional) life.

To the essential definitions Freud added a more general theory, based as we have seen on analogy with the individual, of how religion began. He linked religion and civilization: ". . . religious ideas have arisen from the same need as have all the other achievements of civilization: from the necessity of defending oneself against the crushingly superior force of nature" (ibid). The gods were created by man from a store of ideas that had two sources: in the childhood of the individual and in his ancestors who refined developed and transformed (sublimated) a child's mode of thought, adapting it to the needs of the masses of mankind. Thus it is quite wrong to make Freud say that religion was *only* an infantile activity, though he drew an analogy between the belief in God and the infant's wish for his father to be God-like. If he had said this, he would not have included the ancestors in his argument nor linked religion with the growth of civilization.

There is a highly characteristic feature of Freud's concept of mankind's cultural achievement: it was created and developed by a minority. The masses (the majority) were lazy, unintelligent or lacked the ability to renounce instinctual satisfaction; in a word, they are "natural" and they are hostile to civilization because it does not bring them sufficient immediate rewards. Religion – and he says that only a religion that appeals to the masses is worthy of that name – holds out the hope of illusory rewards and establishes laws to control three basic natural drives, cannibalism, incest and the lust for killing. Only the first has been sufficiently mastered for no laws against it to be necessary, while killing is still allowed under controlled conditions, i.e. warfare.

Freud thus regarded religion as a method of controlling "nature" as expressed in the masses, and, in so far as it succeeds, it is in one rather crude sense supernatural, i.e. above nature. In this it has the characteristics of civilization as a whole.

It is thus wrong to say that Freud thought religion was valueless even though he derived it from the real murder of the primal father. He can say, for instance, that

> the primal father was the original image of God, the model on which later generations have shaped the figure of God. Hence the religious explanation is right [he ought surely to have said here historically right]. God actually played a part in the genesis of that prohibition; it was his influence, not any insight into social necessity, which created it. And the displacement of man's will on to God is fully justified. For men knew that they had disposed of their father by violence, and in their reaction to this impious deed, they determined to respect his will henceforward. Thus religious doctrine tells us the historical truth – though subject, it is true, to some modification and disguise – whereas our rational account (which gives the reasons for making rules against murder) disavows it. (ibid., p. 42)

The word disguised involves a deception and it thus leads moralists to suppose that should not be. Nevertheless, Freud does open himself to the reproach that he thinks religion is nothing but disguised infantile wishes. Nonetheless, I would like to draw particular attention to the historical dimension to which Freud repeatedly refers and he does so because he relies on the theory of evolution.

He clearly thought that religion had historical importance. Just as magical thinking has importance in child development, religion has done much, but not enough, and he calls for "a fundamental revision" of the "relationship between religion and civilization". He states that, if what he says is correct, as a beginning, "it would be an undoubted advantage if we were to leave God out altogether and honestly admit the purely human origin of all the regulations and precepts of civilization". Religion is thus a method which was devised to control man's affect so as to make tolerable the burden of civilization, which was essentially contrary to "nature". It had served us well but could now be superseded. The essence of this statement is also found in Jung's conceptions, but with a different emphasis whose source we shall consider later.

It is common to set up Jung as an opponent of Freud with respect to religion, though like Freud – and this is most relevant to our thesis – he has treated religious experiences and practices as a branch of psychology. He was much more meticulous than Freud in following up his study into all branches of religion, Oriental or Occidental, and he caused much less offence to the "vulgar" because his general attitude was different and his theories were reduced to a bare minimum. He did not push his study systematically back into infancy; instead he applied historical and comparative methods with great vigour. He did not open the door to the reproach, which ought not really to be attributed to Freud, that religion is made into *nothing but* an infantile wish fulfilment having no significance to adult man. He gave even more emphasis than Freud to the historical and, in a qualified sense, the contemporary scene and he did not mention the word illusion, a highly pejorative one anyway, nor did he specifically tie down belief to the theory of unconscious wishes. He thus left more space for manoeuvre and could claim that his patient's conflicts were basically religious in nature without making it seem that he was denigrating religion.

However, his definition of religion is not at all usual. It runs as follows: "Religion . . . is a careful and scrupulous observation . . . of a dynamic agency or affect that seizes and controls the . . . subject who is always rather its victim than its creator" (Jung, 1940a, p. 7). It is a short step to say that religion consists in the careful and scrupulous observation of the usually unconscious data perceivable as archetypal images. These were indissolubly linked to the neurophysiological substrate, and so not at all supernatural in the sense of originating in a single or in a hierarchy of divine transcendent beings.

Yet a wish in Freud's sense corresponds rather closely to the "dynamic agency" in Jung's definition. Of wishes Freud says: "They share the character of indestructibility with all other psychic acts . . . [whose] paths [of discharge] have been opened once and for all; they never fall into disuse. . . . To speak metaphorically, they suffer no other form of annihilation than did the shades of the lower regions in the Odyssey, who awoke to new life the moment they drank blood.''

In this passage I can see some but no essential difference between the indestructible agencies, called wishes by Freud, and the archetypes in Jung's writing; their form of expression is characteristic of religious experience. It is surely significant that Freud takes his analogy from a religious theme.

Thus we can claim that Freud paved the way for transforming God from a metaphysical and supernatural to a psychological datum. Jung did this also, particularly in his book *Psychology and Religion*. There he heads a chapter 'The history and psychology of a natural symbol', and by doing so changes the frame of reference in which supposedly supernatural experiences had been set in the past. The data he records are natural in the sense that what was the province of theology becomes that of psychology. It is an example of the way science takes over a segment of religion. However, for Jung, I think it would be fair to say that the mysteries of religion, and the supernatural attributes of God, had become converted, through psychology, into the ''super-naturalness'' of man.

One difference stands out, however: Jung gives much more value to mysticism than Freud; indeed he revels in it, while Freud's experience, and his whole method of conceptualizing, is hostile to the mystical meaning of supernatural data, which he conceives to be a turning away from reality as the source of discomfort and pain. Jung attacks those who wanted to make it seem that he was converting religion into *nothing but* psychology – clearly a snipe at Freud – by claiming that all he could know is that psychology could explain much of religion and denying that psychology could be used as an instrument to tell whether God really existed apart from man. This is not a psychological issue at all and could only be tackled by philosophy.

When thinking about this chapter I decided to re-read Freud's *Future of an Illusion* (Freud, 1927) and I was startled again and again at the amount of common ground he shared with Jung. We know that each had influenced the other, but it seems to me that they were both compelled to think the same way by a common *Zeitgeist*.

Each of them is quite ready to jump from their knowledge of individuals to far-reaching conclusions about groups; each of them has a poor regard for the masses; each of them regards religion as a means of controlling drives (instincts); each of them emphasizes the importance of the incestuous and destructive potentialities in man. Though Jung did not believe that religion can be displaced by reason, or even that this is desirable, he certainly called for a ''fundamental revision'' in the ''relation of religion to civilization''. He poured out book after book with this aim in view.

A reference must now be made to the subject of symbolism.

Both men held that there was evidence for a hereditary basis of psychic life. Since it is often overlooked that Freud thought so, we may quote him rather than Jung, whose theory of archetypes is so well known. Freud writes:

> . . . dreams bring to light material which cannot have originated either from the dreamer's adult life or from his forgotten childhood. We are obliged to regard it as part of the *archaic heritage* which a child brings with him into the world. . . . We find the counterpart of this phylogenetic material in the earliest human legends and in surviving customs (Freud, 1940, p. 167).

This might quite easily have been written by Jung; for him, as for Freud, symbols represent man's archaic heritage.

Here we may leave the matter, only observing that the conscious attitudes lead to differing evaluations of the material and so to different treatments of it. While Freud mainly confined himself to noting that symbols regularly referred to bodily functions, Jung, without denying this, took the view that symbols had enough in them to treat them as entities in their own right having important synthetic and redeeming functions in the psyche. Freud did not put it this way.

To summarize: the main difference seems to be one of an individual value judgement, for Freud could say that religion was a transitory phase in the development of man – it was thus demoted – but Jung could say that religion was an ongoing process, meaning thereby that it was especially valuable. Jung clearly held that most if not all of religion could become primarily the subject matter of psychology but particularly that of the individual in whom the values could alone reside – thus he recognized it often explicitly as an expression of the self. In saying so he placed the individual high in his estimation because of his contention that psychological thinking individualized religion, which reveals itself as an evolving system and part of man's evolution. It is easy to see from this that he did not think of religion being superseded but of evolving, though he never said so explicitly, into a careful and essentially individual study of unconscious processes.

Much has been made of Freud's pessimism, but he was optimistic in being convinced that reason and psychoanalysis were in the position to inaugurate a new age in civilization. Jung did not believe reason could do it, but be believed that human affects could evolve so that religion could become an inner individual representation of the self.

It may be held that the different attitudes towards religion in these two men may be accounted for on the basis of different philosophic assumptions. However, this is not a line which I will take, because the psychological structure of the two personalities is so glaringly different that it is not necessary to embark on philosophy to account for the issues.

Freud claims that he never had religious experiences of the kind people wrote to him about, he never felt the need to belong formally to a religious organization and he had never experienced any of the benefits of redemption. He never felt the presence of God and he often did not seem to think much of those who did have such an experience.

Whatever may have been religious about him took on quite a different form from any of these experiences. Freud was a Jew and a number of people built on this to try to show that psychoanalysis is the outcome of a logical development in Jewish religion. For instance, David Bakan (1958) argues that Freud's method and discoveries derived from the Sabbatian tradition, and others have tried to establish that Freud's general attitude was like that of the Jewish prophets – in particular Moses – that Freud had a Messianic mission or that his doctrine of sexuality was an essentially religious principle. But supposing all this was true – which, so stated, I do not believe for a moment – Freud's main and most important identifications and ideals were in line with science and all the consequences that result from identifying with the search for scientific truth and the power that comes from it.

Jung also identified himself with the scientific attitude: the basic idea of searching for truth through the application of intelligence and experiment was inviolate to him. But Jung, in absolute contra-distinction to Freud, owed a great deal to religious experiences of his own and he described them in *Memories, Dreams, Reflections*, published posthumously in 1963. They were not orthodox but they are manifestly religious in the ordinary sense. No doubt much in them was conditioned by his father's being a Swiss pastor; indeed, his whole family background was saturated with religion. Much was also due to his early infantile experience, but it takes a very special combination of circumstances and a very unusual person to go through what Jung did and remain sane. He could not possibly identify himself with aspects of Freud's attitude because he was a different kind of person. Jung had felt the redeeming effect of the presence of God, i.e. the self; Freud had not, never did and probably never needed to.

I think I have said enough to show how personal experience and cultural influences can be decisive in determining general attitudes. Freud's lack of mystical experience had led him to direct his main energies to explaining the psychic structures out of which religion was built. Jung's mystical trends made him take religious experience as basic; he observed what happened if it were given free reign and even fostered. Only after this had occurred did he think about it and try to understand its significance, not so much in terms of causes as in terms of meaning. He was bound to be far more sympathetic to the religious life and much more interested in mysticism than Freud.

His most personal book before *Memories, Dreams, Reflections* was *Answer to Job* (1952b). It is imaginative and open to subjective appraisal, but in it Jung, the creative visionary, stands openly before us. He makes it clear that he thinks of God as the more primitive aspect of human nature and insists, in no uncertain terms, that in Job, man could be superior to God and so unwittingly compel God to develop. This, he held, was the dynamic origin of God becoming man in Christ. He pushes the consequence of this idea to its logical conclusion as follows: we are now witnessing the next step, man becoming more and more god-like through an advance in man's awareness of himself. This is as much a social as an individual necessity and the development of psychological science is a manifestation of its actualization.

It would appear that Jung also thought of the religion we know, or have known, as historical and so it must be superseded by a thorough revision, which meant that religion was to be recognized as originating in man. But whereas Freud thought the best hope was the dominance of the intellect, Jung thought the best hope lay in Man's greater realization of his nature as a whole, i.e. of the self. It is this which made him value the archaic archetypal inheritance so highly. Symbols and his idea of them lie at the root of self-realization.

Let us turn to how these two men conducted their treatment of patients. Since each claimed that his conclusions about religion were derived from his study of human beings in distress, we must know what they did. It is quite clear that in practice there are many differences. In his analytic work Jung paid little attention to the reductive process to which Freud gave so much importance. Jung largely ceased to trace the patient's experiences to their origins in infancy; because of his interest in the emergent, developing, ongoing trends in the psyche. He looked mainly to the present and the future to help his patients to find solutions to their conflicts.

We will now examine how a theologian uses psychoanalysis. This will show up a basic difference in vertices and, I hope, justify the emphasis on similarities between the work of Freud and Jung. In view of the more positive attitude to religion taken by Jung, it is surprising to find that Freud's ideas have been taken up by just as many theologians – possibly by even more than have made use of Jung's researches. For instance, H. A. Williams (1962, 1963) estimates Freud highly and even agrees that he initiated a revolution comparable to those brought about by Copernicus and Darwin. He considers that theologians must realize this and incorporate the teachings of analytic disciplines into their formulations. His position as a theologian is that scholarly criticism has gone a long way and given room for manoeuvre, but it has got as far as possible and more attention needs to be paid to the way people live and how they implement God's will in their lives. William's ideas are most ingenious and penetrating, but they are not, I think, what Freud himself would have accepted as a true representation of what he meant. The difference appears to stem from the different vertices, for Williams refers his examples to the sayings of Jesus. He also uses psychological ideas to interpret passages in them, but there is no doubt that the Gospels represent his frame of reference.

He contends that there is a true or real self to which man should seek to conform if he is to fulfil the Divine Will. God made man in his own image and he loves the man who fulfils this image of himself. Just as God is true to himself so should man be also. God himself is ultimately loving and his anger or wrath, being actuated by love, is directed to helping man to realize his true self.

Now, for an unspecified number of reasons, man does not fulfil his true self but develops a false self which can equally be pious and religious or patently disgraceful and irreligious. It is usual to bring in Freud at about this point to provide a way of showing where man has gone wrong and is false to his whole or true self to whose realization of God's love is continuously directed. Williams is more radical than this. He recognizes that analysis challenges religion as a whole and not just its supposedly pathological application by complex-ridden persons. However, his thesis is far more like Jung's, whom he does not mention, for Freud does not use the concept of true and false self which is used freely by Jung if we translate false self as *persona*. But this is in passing; the point I want to emphasize is that Williams uses the New Testament as his frame of reference and I do not see how any Christian can do otherwise.

Examination of his illustrative examples is significant. For instance, there is the case of a young and pious theologian who finds himself drunk in a brothel in Algiers. Williams suggests that because Jesus thinks better of prostitutes than of well-behaved hypocrites, the behaviour is in some sense in order; indeed, Williams is led to think that the theologian's behaviour could be following God's will. This conclusion is irrelevant to an analyst, who might think as follows: it might be well to bear in mind that if the man whom Williams cites had been going to an analyst and he had started behaving in the way described, the following considerations would have become important: (*a*) is not the analyst making rather serious mistakes in his treatment of his patient or (*b*) has his diagnosis been correct and is he not trying to treat a case who is beyond analytic help? But supposing the case turned out all right, in the end there would be no reference to Jesus or the New Testament as authoritative and the behaviour would never be accepted as such, i.e. as the will of God, but submitted to analysis, so as to find the infantile origin of the motives which led him to behave as he did.

In spite of all this, if the findings of psychology are going to be assimilated into religious thought, Williams is surely going about it in the right way. He does not abandon religious ideas nor the Christian belief, but builds the findings of psychology into the theological vertex in which he is skilled. Jung tried to do just this, but in reverse. His sympathy with religion led him to try to find out whether its formulations would shed light on human psychology, of which they are conceived to be a reflection. He found that they did so and showed that psychology can benefit from the study of religion. Therefore, there is no doubt that communication has been and can continue to be mutually productive.

In conclusion, to an analyst who does his work on the assumption that the human psyche exists as a natural datum, related to the body, the psychological vertex, God as a supernatural transcendent being, is redundant. All that any analyst can and ought to do is to study man's experience of himself in his social setting. He will take note of experiences of God, but must consider them as representing psychic activity. A theologian starts from a vertex which may be stated as follows. What to a psychologist is a special kind of illusion, is to him no illusion but a perception of transcendent Being. He does not need to explain it in psychological terms nor to consider the role it plays in the system made up of psychic structures, but if his discipline is not to become unbearably abstract, he must use all that psychology can provide in understanding human nature. If man is made in God's image, he has nothing to lose and everything to gain, for the study of man must reveal the nature of God as far as it can be understood by man.

Chapter Fourteen

*Notes on the mysticism of Saint John of the Cross**

Introduction

My choice of subject matter is inspired by Jung. He investigated mysticism but especially the Eastern variety. My effort is to supplement his, especially because though he refers to Saint John from time to time, he only does so in passing.

Saint John of the Cross was a great Spanish mystic who lived in the sixteenth century. He also wrote beautiful poetry and thus possessed unrivalled capacity to express the mystical experience. He did that not only poetically but also in long and clear commentaries which I shall consider.

Before developing my thesis I will outline the vertex of Saint John and then elaborate some essentials of my own.

Vertices

Saint John of the Cross

Central features

(1) The Christian belief in the transcendent reality of God, the Virgin, angels, the devil and the life after death.
(2) Emphasis on the spiritual inner life and its three enemies the world, the flesh and the devil.

*This chapter is much revised and altered from its previous versions, "An analytical approach to mysticism" in *Revue Suisse de Psychologie et de Psychologie Appliqué* vol. 4, no. 3-4 and "The dark night of the soul" in *The Objective Psyche*, London, Routledge, 1958.

(3) Knowledge that God can be related to directly and eventually united with through the mystical experience.

Conditions for the mystical experience to take place

If the mystic lives in a monastery, his life is austere and there is much mortification of the flesh and strict obedience to the rules of monastic life is demanded. Obedience to superiors in the hierarchy is required. A particular feature of the discalced Carmelite order was its extreme austerity and the cultivation of contemplation.

Factors contributing to establishing the vertex

(1) Childhood: a life of poverty intensified after his father's death when young – between two and six years old, the exact date is variously given. Whether his father was alive or dead, the family seem to have lived on the bread-line. A devoted mother who cared for his mental and spiritual life, for she sent him to school where he received religious instruction by the Jesuits. The importance of his real mother can be inferred from his vision of her beatified in heaven after her death.
(2) When a child he was saved from drowning by a visionary woman (probably the Virgin). He recurrently received visions of her often in periods of crisis.
(3) He became proficient in theological knowledge. Besides the Bible his main authorities were: Dionisius the Areopagite, Saints Augustine, Gregory, Thomas and Bohmhard, Boethius, Boscan and Madre Teresa. Probably many others since he used the monastery library intensively. Suggested by Crisogono (1958): John Baconthorp, Tauler, Buysenbroek and "the popular *cancioneros* – collections of songs and poems"; some of the phrases in these are repeated in his writings almost verbatim.
(4) The starting of the discalced Carmelite order by Saint Theresa and her perception of Saint John's spiritual capacities.
(5) The state of life of a "religious" at the time. The discalced order may have been a reaction against the exploitation of monasteries as a relatively pleasant retreat from the rigours of life outside them.

Manifestations of the religious vertex

(1) The mystical experience.
(2) The life of the mystic imbued with meaning: God's divine presence was everywhere – so also was the devil's.

(3) Miracles indicating divine intervention in the order of nature.
(4) The holiness of the mystic, his goodness, his lovableness and his capacity to transmit spiritual wisdom to others.
(5) In the case of Saint John must be added a great creative literary capacity.

My Own Vertex

This is expressed by this book, but it is nowhere summarized, so I will attempt to do that now; I will consider it under the same headings as I have used in outlining Saint John's.

Central features

Belief in the search for truth through the acquisition of knowledge.

Conditions for inner experience to take place

(1) Living an ordinary life in the world, i.e. working, marrying, procreating a child, writing and believing that what I do is in the ultimate interest of those close to me and of humanity as a whole.
(2) Recognizing that all these activities could not be rendered meaningful without rather intense study of my own inner life in personal analytic experience and the motivation that proceeds from it.

Factors contributing to establishment of the vertex

(1) A financially secure childhood with parents that I mainly loved and admired enough to go through the hating inevitable to maturation. Both parents cared for my mental life in the sense that they provided me with the education that first they found desirable and later I wanted.
(2) I became reasonably proficient in scientific studies (biology, physiology, medicine and surgery).
(3) I pursued my inner needs by undergoing analyses and continued them with the help of patients over most of my adult life.
(4) Personal contact with Jung and the various identifications that I formed with him and my analysts.
(5) The fact that, when I started on my career as an analyst, the Jungian movement in Great Britain wanted somebody like me to further their interests. I preferred to do that, in the belief that basically it furthered my own, rather than becoming what is commonly called a member of the establishment.

In viewing Saint John's mysticism from my vertex I shall lay emphasis on its infantile roots, but I do not identify mysticism with infancy: no baby could survive the rigours of the mystical life.

If it is thought that what I say provokes the ghost of reductionism, i.e. that a mystic is nothing but a baby in disguise, it could also be said that it is a divine miracle that a baby is born with mystical characteristics which are then submitted to the depredations of the world, the flesh and the devil. The rigours of mysticism are designed to relieve the essential nature of the infant united with God. Neither of these propositions appeal to me – they appear to be statements designed to make believe that we understand more than is possible in a highly complex field.

The Dark Night of the Soul

The writings of Saint John of the Cross reveal a spectrum of mystical experiences with extensive interpretations and commentaries. *The Dark Night of the Soul* lays great emphasis on the torments of the soul in mortifying its sensual and spiritual functions so that it may be freed from its natural state and attain the ultimate of union in love with God. In so doing the soul itself becomes relatively divine: only after death is its complete divinity attained – a theme that runs through all Saint John's writings.

Though following through the same theme, the other books differ in important respects: *The Ascent of Mount Carmel* was written as a guide to those concerned with the care of souls and gives in much detail the experiences of souls and the behaviour of spiritual directors. Whereas in *The Dark Night of the Soul* the ruthlessness of God is emphasized, in *The Ascent of Mount Carmel* we find numerous instances of God giving loving revelations ("touches") to the soul at the level at which they can be appreciated. There is a more poetic element in it and that is greatly increased in *The Living Flame of Love* and *The Spiritual Canticle*, both of which are full of beautiful passages about the experiences of the soul.

Each volume is based upon a poem the stanzas of which are analysed in detail. One line or part of a line in the poem is interpreted and discussed at length and related to passages in the Bible which either are used to support what Saint John says or are given a mystical interpretation. The format gives space for detailed description of experiences of the soul, they are then given meanings and from time to time desirable or undesirable attitudes to them are defined.

I am very much aware that my outline account of Saint John's labours do not express the great wealth of experience that his writings contain. To get an impression of that, there is nothing for it but to study the original text. What I shall do is to select passages which make sense experientially from my own vertex. Others with different vertices would inevitably extract different passages.

The Dark Night of the Soul is an account of the soul's journey in search of God. Starting on a relatively human plane, it gradually becomes more and more remote from earthly life, until it reaches the final union with God on the tenth step of the *scala mystica*. Though the complete union only takes place after death, yet the soul is able in this life to come into an intense and intimate relation with God, through which many sublime results accrue.

The main bulk of the book is made up of a commentary on the "Stanzas of the soul" who "is now in a state of perfection".

Stanzas of the Soul

(1) On a dark night, Kindled in love with yearnings – oh, happy chance! –
I went forth without being observed, My house being now at rest.
(2) In darkness and secure, By the secret ladder, disguised – oh, happy chance! –
In darkness and in concealment, My house being now at rest.
(3) In the happy night, In secret, when none saw me,
Nor I beheld aught, Without light or guide, save that which burned in my heart.
(4) This light guided me More surely than the light of noonday
To the place where he (well I knew who) was awaiting me – A place where none appeared.
(5) Oh, night that guided me, Oh, night more lovely than the dawn,
Oh, night that joined Beloved with lover, Lover transformed in the Beloved!
(6) Upon my flowery breast, Kept wholly for himself alone,
There he stayed sleeping, and I caressed him, And the fanning of the cedars made a breeze.
(7) The breeze blew from the turret As I parted his locks;
With his gentle hand he wounded my neck And caused all my senses to be suspended.
(8) I remained, lost in oblivion; My face I reclined on the Beloved.
All ceased and I abandoned myself, Leaving my cares forgotten among the lilies.
(transl. E. A. Peers, 1953, vol. I, p. 326)

The commentary applies only to the first two stanzas; it is these that are concerned with the Dark Nights. The last six stanzas depict the benefits which come to the soul after sufficient purgation has taken place. The house refers to the faculties of the soul, which have to be dealt with before it is able to realize the benefits that result from the dark experiences of God. It will be noted that the house is stated to be *now* at rest; it had not been and might not be again.

The secret ladder refers to the *scala mystica*. Of the darkness and safety Saint John says:

> The darkness of which the soul here speaks relates, as I have said, to the desires and powers of the sense, interior and spiritual, all of which are deprived of their

natural light in this night, that, being purified as to this, they may be supernaturally enlightened. . . . This is the darkness in which the soul says that it travels in safety . . . 3. It follows from this, that the greater the darkness and emptiness of its natural operations in which the soul travels the greater is its security (*Dark Night*, transl. Zimmerman, 1935, p. 146).

The disguise indicates the necessity for protection against the three enemies of the soul – the world, the flesh and the devil, whose main function is to prevent the soul's mystic quest coming to fruition.

Thus the livery which it [the soul] wears is of three chief colours – white, green and purple – denoting the three theological virtues, faith, hope, and charity. By these the soul will not only gain the grace and good will of its Beloved, but it will travel in security and complete protection from its three enemies (ibid., p. 422, par. 3).

All the three phases in the mystical experience are initiated by the action of God on the soul. Throughout the whole process, God is the prime mover. The first phase is preparatory and those in this period are called beginners. The next is concerned with the first Dark Night in which the senses of the soul and its activities of meditation and discoursive reflection are thoroughly purged. The second Dark Night purges the soul of its spiritual activities, so that the pure light of God's spiritual love may guide the soul up the ten steps of the *scala mystica*, through stages of more and more burning the lofty love of God, to the final union, in which the whole soul conforms itself to God to become divine itself in a loving embrace referred to in the last three stanzas. Those in the last two stages are termed "proficients". Between each stage there is a period of spiritual quiescence and it seems that the phrase "my house being now at rest" refers to that. The calm may be of longer or shorter duration, but as progress takes place, fewer and fewer souls succeed in passing the severe tests to which they will be subjected.

The first stirrings of the spirit in beginners derive from God, who tempts the soul to taste of spiritual pleasures by offering his breast of tender love (the loving mother – the grace of God):

We are to keep in mind that a soul, when seriously converted to the service of God, is, in general, spiritually nursed and caressed as an infant by its loving mother, who warms it in her bosom, nourishes it with her own sweet milk, feeds it with tender and delicate food, and carries it in her arms and fondles it (Zimmerman 1935, p. 6)

Paradoxically the very pleasure which God provides is a major source of error: the beginners will not submit to their spiritual advisors ". . . they either change or vary or add to that which is commanded of them, as any obedience in this respect is so bitter to them" (ibid., p. 330, par. 2);

or ". . . they become as peevish as children and go about in great displeasure, thinking that they are not serving God when they are not allowed to do that which they would" (ibid., pp. 344–5, par. 2); and "They are, in fact, as we have said, like children who are not influenced, neither act by reason, but from pleasure" (ibid., p. 346, par. 6 (literal translation)) "having no regard to that mortification, and perfection of interior poverty of spirit to which they ought to apply themselves" (ibid., chapter 3).

The first section of the book, dealing with the conflicts of beginners, is an exceedingly human document, and contains a description of imperfections caused by beginners departing from the prescribed way owing to the pleasure of spiritual communication. The imperfections are the seven deadly sins: spiritual pride, avarice, voluptuousness, anger, gluttony, envy and sluggishness.

Next God starts to withdraw the breast:

> . . . as the child grows bigger, the mother gradually ceases caressing it, and, hiding her tender love, puts bitter aloes upon her sweet breast, sets down the child from her arms and makes it walk upon its feet, so that it may lose the habits of a child and betake itself to more important and substantial occupations (ibid., p. 330, par. 2).

It is when the breast has been sufficiently withdrawn that the first Dark Night of the senses begins.

The soul, presumably for purposes of description, is divided into two parts which are really two aspects of the whole soul. These two aspects are the sensual or sensitive aspect and the spiritual. In the first dark night which results from God's action on the sensual elements sinful manifestations arise with great insistence and obstinacy. There can be little doubt that these arise from the soul's sexual needs: "there arise and assert themselves in the sensual part of the soul impure acts and motions" during prayer or even when taking part in the sacred rites such as the sacrament of Penance or the Eucharist. That is hardly surprising, since the whole of the mystic's reproductive life is renounced and it would be very unlikely if all the drives and fantasies of it could be transformed without great difficulty. That God does purify these primitive elements and that they become transformed is shown in the often beautiful erotism of the *unio mystica*, which is full of sexual symbolism and metaphor.

The Dark Night is also called the purgative night and is divided into two parts: the first purges the soul of its senses and the second of its spiritual activities. In consequence, attachment to material objects on one hand or objects of imagination, visions and dreams on the other, all the functions of relation to the outer world and all those of the inner world are systematically purged by the divine action. Only the blinding image of God remains. It is for this reason that the mystic experience is called the Dark Night of the soul.

The features of entry into it are described clearly and systematically. The soul finds no pleasure in anything, its attention becomes fixed on God; a sense of dryness (aridity) and displeasure arises. We learn that the soul sinks into a state of silence and solitude; she does nothing but allows herself "... to be led by God, to receive and to listen with loving interior attentiveness ...", and "... if it desires to work with its faculties, it hinders the work which God is doing in it rather than aids it".

In the place of mental activity, in the place of prayer and the "breast" of reflection and meditation arises the process of contemplation which consists in leaving

> ... the soul free and disencumbered and at rest from all knowledge and thought, troubling not themselves, in that state, about what they shall think or meditate upon, but contenting themselves with merely a peaceful and loving attentiveness toward God, and in being without anxiety, without the ability and without the desire to have experience of Him or to perceive Him. For all these yearnings disquiet and distract the soul from the peaceful quiet and sweet ease of contemplation which is here granted to it (ibid., p. 357, par. 4).

Then God will work upon the soul:

> He binds its interior faculties, and allows it not to cling to the understanding, nor to have delight in the will, nor to reason with the memory (ibid., p. 354, par. 7).

The binding is terrible for if

> The first purgation is bitter and terrible to sense ... The second bears no comparison with it, for it is horrible and awful to the spirit ... (ibid., pp. 349–50, par. 2).

The Communication of God with the Soul

After this it is with some relief that we learn how there are intermissions and relief, during which, by the dispensation of God, the dim contemplation, divested of its purgative form and character, assumes that of the illuminative and of love. Under this form of it, the soul, like one that has escaped from the dungeons of its prison into the space of freedom, enjoys the sweetness of peace and the loving tenderness of God in the flowing abundance of spiritual communications. This to the soul is the sign of spiritual health which is being wrought within by this purgation, and a foretaste of the abundance for which it hopes (ibid., p. 98, par. 6).

Experiences of this kind are given prominence in Saint John's other books but especially in *The Spiritual Canticle*. He is sceptical as to their value and so they should not be sought after, for some souls seek these supernatural divine communications believing erroneously that they are advancing so to speak directly towards the love of God. Furthermore, the communications are not always reliable and it is often difficult to know whether they come from God or the Devil; in addition they are difficult to interpret and so God's meaning, which is always the truth, may be grossly, sometimes disastrously misunderstood.

Therefore, the communications should not be sought after or induced. Nevertheless they happen even when the soul has not sought them, and Saint John gives quite specific instructions as to how they should be taken: they should be assessed according to the law, reason and the ecclesiastical doctrine and their effects. No special account should be taken of them – that the communication is through a vision is not in itself a special event. As to the soul which seeks direct communication with God, even though God may reply, it can be displeasing to Him so that His reply may be obscure or even, it sometimes seems, deliberately misleading.

Saint John has an ingenious reason for that: God might think that He has finally delivered the truth by giving His only Son to men. All the soul need do is to study His life and follow in His footsteps. What need can there therefore be for further divine revelations. However, the visions and insights can be rewarding, for they give understanding on all levels, but most of all they can be direct communications as to the nature of God and have long-lasting effects on the soul. Nevertheless they are diversions from pursuing the way of faith which leads through the Dark Night to the final union with God besides which all else should be rendered relatively insignificant. Why then does God dispense these relatively minor revelations? It is because of His understanding of the soul's need at any particular stage in its development.

It is of interest to compare these "touches" of God and other communications from the supernatural world, with active imagination. It is quite clear that spontaneous visions and other communications from the "persons" of the inner world are frequent and of the kind met in both disciplines. But the passivity of the soul, in relation to the visitations and the instructions to remain detached from them lest they interfere with the soul's entry into the Dark Night of unknowing, could not be thought of as active imagination in which active interchanges are fostered.

Saint John evidently has a distaste for visions, mental communications, prophesies etc., so he refers his readers to Saint Theresa who evidently does not. It is only amongst beginners that we learn from him much about conversations with God. They occur, as we have seen, later on but it is only as union with God approaches that the soul becomes passionately active.

Activity and Passivity

In the main, then the soul is passive; lovingly attentive to the actions of God. He is active in three forms: there is His hand that leads, there is the touch of the Son and the phallic burning, penetrating powers of the Holy Ghost:

> Beneath the apple-tree
> You came to swear your troth and to be mated,
> Gave there your hand to me,
> And have been new created
> There where your mother first was violated.
>
> (*Poems*, transl. Campbell, 1951, p. 25)

The soul is not entirely passive as we have seen amongst beginners, though many of its activities are undesirable. In addition to these, however, the soul will make efforts to eradicate imperfections through mortifications but these, we are told can only be partly successful: "It is only when God does it for it" that an effective purgation can take place. Besides its efforts the soul cultivates, as far as it can, a meek, quiet, humble and attentive love towards God.

Another aspect of passivity is the required obedience in spiritual directors and so the rules of the Carmelite order as well. They apply until a particular state of the soul is reached: it is when the soul is in a quiet passive state being led by God into the Dark Night, so that the soul may despair at nothing happening and feeling that it has been abandoned and does not serve God; it cannot pray or meditate or pursue those other religious practices to which it has become accustomed. The change here seems to be that obedience has been internalized so that the soul is obeying God alone. Therefore spiritual directors should only go along with the action of God in the soul. It becomes a grave fault if they seek to intervene: should they do so, "They will not be forgiven". The state is a preparation for the final transformation of the soul on the seventh step of the *scala mystica* when she becomes vehemently bold, inspired by her burning love of God.

> 2. On the seventh step the soul becomes vehemently bold, in this intense and loving exaltation, no prudence can withhold it, no shame restrain it, no council control it: for the favour which God hath shown it has made it vehemently bold . . .
> 3. From this boldness and courage which God grants to the soul on the seventh step, that it may be bold with him in the vehemence of its love, the soul ascends to the eighth, where it lays hold of the Beloved and is united with Him (*Dark Night*, transl. Zimmerman, 1935, p. 174).

The benefits are mutual, for God as well as the soul, for God is loved "as he should be loved, for himself as he is":

> The soul now being one with God is itself God by participation, and though not so perfectly as it will be in the world to come, is still, as I have said, as God in a shadow. Thus, then, the soul, by reason of its transformation, being a shadow of God, effects through God in God what he effects within it Himself by Himself, because the will of both is one. And as God is giving Himself with a free and gracious will, so the soul also with a will, the more free and the more generous the more it is united with God in God, is, as it were, giving back to God – in that loving complacency with which it regards the divine essence and perfections – God himself (*Living Flame*, transl. Lewis, 1934, pp. 113ff.).

The relationship is exclusive and full of comfort so great

> . . . that it seems as if there were no other soul in the world for Him to comfort, no other object of his care, but that everything was done for this one soul alone.

The Self, Deintegration and Splitting

Based on Jung's work, I translate God as the self, and from that vertex many features of the mystic's life can be understood as manifestations of its deintegrated forms. At first sight, the experiences of God look as if they were derived from the Christian dogma to which they are conformed, and they are indeed interpreted in the light of it. But throughout Saint John's writings, the experiences of the soul are so convincingly described that they could not possibly be thought of as the expression of abstract theological principles. To put it somewhat differently, the experience may be given form by Christian myth, ritual and dogma, but the essential element is the archetype within the form of expression (Fordham, 1957a).

The three persons of the Trinity – Father, Son and Holy Ghost – can therefore be understood as experiential data. When he indicates that the Holy Ghost is the Flame of God, that was the experience of souls, likewise the hand of the Father and the touch of the Son were moving experiences.

In Saint John's mystical life, there were other elements – the Virgin and God's angels. All these may be taken as deintegrates out of the godhead. The devil and his angels, all opposed to God, are only completely split off in the final union. There is for instance a passage in which God's angel stands aside whilst the devil's angel tempts the soul and this is said, as elsewhere, to be needed so that the soul may learn to resist evil; and thus it would seem that the devil is needed to further God's purpose.

The Opposites: Reflections on God and the Devil

It might be supposed that the relation between good and evil, God and the devil, would be clearly distinguished, but when we learn that the devil can produce visions to proficients which deceive them because their guise is angelic, and when we learn that the angel of God will allow the soul to be tempted without intervening, as a test of the soul's capacity to resist evil, it almost seems that God and the devil were a pair working together, reminding one of the devil who could not succeed in his evil intentions because they always produced a good ending. It is an idea which shows the tendency of God and His opposite to merge. Saint John, however, attributes it all to the subtlety and cunning of the devil. Whichever view is taken, it is apparent that a communication by either supernatural power to the soul is often difficult for the soul to estimate. Furthermore, spiritual directors also have difficulty, differing amongst themselves. The wiser ones apparently will defer their conclusion and wait to observe the consequent effects on the soul. However, the difficulties do leave open the other possibility that the separation postulated by the dogma is not altogether satisfactory and the relation between the two is more like that of the Book of Job, which is quoted quite frequently by Saint John. There the devil still has access to God and is one of the sons of God. There can be no doubt that he is allowed access to the soul, which seems inconsiderate of God to say the least of it. However, at the eighth step of the *scala mystica* the persecutions cease; the soul is immune to the assaults of its enemy. That may be understood in two ways: either a final split has taken place, in which case the devil will continue to exist and practise his arts on other souls, which is in accordance with ecclesiastical witness, or an individual solution has been found by the soul becoming whole in God. Faith is the most powerful influence in bringing that about.

There is something to be said for the second solution, for in *The Spiritual Canticle* Saint John writes:

> . . . for being transformed in God, they will live the life of God, and not their own life, and yet it will be their own life, for the life of God will be their own life. . . . This may come about in this life . . . – not however in a complete and perfect way, although the soul may reach such a transformation of love as the spiritual marriage, which is the highest estate than can be attained in this life (transl. Peers, 1978, p. 68, par. 7).

That solution would presumably not be acceptable formally speaking, since it involves going beyond good and evil. It does depict the shift from the ego to the self which is a characteristic of individuation.

Transformation

I believe that it may be helpful if I introduce the subject of transformation. It is a term that Saint John uses and it seems to depict the same processes as those known to analysts. It is my intention to relate mystical processes to their infantile roots and that may easily be cast aside as ridiculous unless the fact of transformation is grasped. Nor can what I shall say about infancy be fully illuminating without that idea. As in mysticism, many transformations take place between the real relationship of an infant with his parents and later life.

The no longer purely infantile characteristics of an ordinary adult are expressed in a spectrum of behaviours. Nevertheless, the past never disappears it is transformed. Saint John understood that very well within the mystical vertex. He frequently refers to transformations of the soul in God, for instance when "the eye of the sense is enlightened and rendered pleasing" (*Living Flame*, transl. Lewis, 1934, p. 109, par. 82). That could only take place after the senses had been purged of their capacity to estrange the soul from God.

We can also recognize the result of transformation in the contrast between the natural will which is an imperfection and different to the will of God with which the soul makes contact and then wills to unite with Him. Again,

> The spirituality of the object is to little purpose, if the desire of it proceed from itself, having its root and strength in nature . . . but only then when the motive is supernatural, and when the strength of the desire proceeds from God; that is a very different thing (ibid., p. 111, par. 85.)

Having in mind that it is the aim of the soul to unite with God, its desires can become divine by transformation.

Previously when I wrote on this subject, I considered the part that repression took in the mystical development so as to account for its one-sidedness. I instanced the case of a nun with whom Saint John was exceedingly severe (Fordham, 1978, pp. 149ff). It would be surprising if repression did not take place and there is further evidence for it in trance states and fits; we learn that amongst those who are insufficiently spiritual "raptures, and trances and dislocation of the bones" (Lewis, 1934, p. 375, par. 2) can take place. Now, however, I conceive that the transformation processes require more primitive and radical operations. I do not think that the supposed eventual exclusion of the devil is dealt with adequately by evoking such a sophisticated operation of the psyche as repression. Splitting is far more appropriate.

The Breast

It will have been noticed that the mystic development is initiated by God's breast which is given by God to beginners. Everything follows from that. The development of the Dark Nights proceeds from the breast being taken away and the drive to eradicate all its derivatives becomes paramount or so it seems at first.

I now want to consider the descriptions of Saint John with current analytical thinking and observations. In analytic work a concept is needed to describe an infant's experience for he makes a relation to his mother not only through the nourishing aspect of the physical organ.

It is evident that the mother performs a sequence of actions besides conveying her breast to her infant's mouth: there is the holding containment of him and the caressing; she exchanges looks and she talks to him in a way that the infant appreciates. In the interchange there seem to be mental as well as physical activities on the part of both members of the couple, in which there is more or less projective and introjective identification. If all these activities function well then there is a good feed and the infant forms an image of a good breast.

But that is not the whole picture: there is an intimate relation between the mother with her breast and the father with his penis. Just as the breast becomes a focus for a set of experiences, so the father's penis also represents, in fantasy as well as reality, a comparable spectrum of imagery. An infant experiences the breast as comforting and feeding or penetrating and potent. The latter experience becomes transferred to the real father, but the emphasis changes: the phallic power of the father and his penis becomes central. As development proceeds, the characteristics of mother and father are differentiated, so that the father becomes more related to the child's activities and especially his mental life. That is the basis for his coming to represent the *logos* or spirit, whilst mother becomes *eros* and the representative of bodily sensual existence. In other words, their archetypal aspects are capable of extended development. At the start, however, the two elements are not readily distinguished. From this vertex the female elements in God become understandable as a transformed state reflecting the earliest state of infancy in which father and mother are not differentiated, which means that they are one. That state is nearest to the whole self.

Saint John observed that the beginners acted like children – he might more accurately have said like children who have regressed in some respects to infancy. In numerous passages Saint John uses the language of the breast. Sometimes it is quite direct, when he refers to the breast of meditation and reflection, other times it is indirect, when we learn that God feeds the soul or "the desire, which previously longed for creative food, now tastes and relishes the food that is divine, influenced by another more efficacious principle, the sweetness of God (*Living Flame*, transl. Lewis, 1934, p. 53, par. 39.). And "Finally all the motions and acts of the soul, proceeding from the principle of its natural and imperfect life, are now changed in this union with God into motions divine" (ibid., p. 53, par. 40).

If we put together the food of God, the breast of God, His touch (through Christ), His unguents, there emerges a pattern that is a transformation of the relation first predominantly between a mother and her baby and second between father and his child. Furthermore, the loving destructiveness of God and the pain at the recurrent loss of natural love can be included. Finally the exclusiveness and intimacy of the union in which the interchanges between the soul and God occur show clear evidence of projective and introjective identification.

The No-breast

I am adopting this formulation from Bion without claiming that I am representing him correctly. The idea is as follows: the absence of the breast is equated by an infant with a bad internal breast, which the infant deals with in the various ways available to him and dependent upon the operation of beta elements: he can evacuate it (purge) or vomit it in each case using his digestive system, alternatively his respiratory system can be brought into action and so he can cry or scream and this may be related to muscular vigour of a discharging kind. There is one other and more important result: through the action of alpha function, the beta elements may be converted into a primitive thought process via alpha elements.

It is thought that an infant may get the experience of no-breast through his having destroyed it – that is not expressed in Saint John's account, but the ideal blissful states of the beginner suggest a defence against it displaced on to the spiritual directors. However, the analogy is cogent if we consider the suffering which results from loss of the breast and the entry into the first Dark Night, in that the pain is transformed into mental life – the "breast of reflection and meditation".

The predominant feature of the first night is God's loving destruction: it is the type of experience an infant can have when he knows that the breast, whether good or bad, is one and the same breast. His imagined destruction of it can lead to the depressive position in which the good breast is restored internally.

Experience of the no-breast occurs in an infant periodically and must not be too frequent. Sufficient good breast experience, both in relation to his mother and internally, is essential – the infant's capacity to tolerate and manage his pain is variable, depending on the amount of good breast he internalizes. In all this a mother's holding function is essential.

The parallel in the Dark Nights, when the painful loss is emphasized so much, is the holding function of the spiritual adviser using his superior knowledge and the touches of God.

Reflections on Saint John's Personality and History

Very little information is available about Saint John's early life, but what there is is indicative; indeed, if anybody was going to develop into a saint, one might say that St John's development strongly predisposed it.

He was born in 1542, the son of an aristocrat and a poor but beautiful and loving woman. As the result of the marriage his father was disinherited and the family lived a life of poverty. His father died when Saint John was six (?) years old. The poverty increased and it seems clear that from time to time there was hardly enough to keep the family alive. Saint John's mother struggled on earning money as a weaver, moving from one place to another in order to find a means of livelihood.

Eventually in despair she decided to approach her husband's family, and one uncle, a doctor, agreed to take responsibility for the eldest son. It did not turn out well: not receiving any news about her son she journeyed to her brother-in-law to find that his wife had been exploiting the child and that he was not getting any of the care and education that had been promised. In spite of the uncle's protestations that there would be a change now that he knew what was going on, the child was removed and his mother shouldered the extra burden that he must have been.

The mother cared not only for her children's emotional well-being but also for their mental life and Saint John was educated at the College of the Society of Jesus, subsequently going to the Jesuit college in Salamanca where he studied theology and became a monk. A measure of his devotion to her may be instanced in the vision of a woman (sometimes presumed to be the Virgin) who saved him from drowning. Such visions were repeated and finally, after her death, he saw his mother beatified in heaven.

The strong feminine influence in his life was reinforced by his meeting with Saint Theresa. She had initiated a new discalced order of Carmelites which was struggling for survival. The order was devoted to the inner life with emphasis on the life of contemplation; it was exceedingly austere. Even the solicitation of alms was not allowed and in consequence the nuns were sometimes near to starvation. Here was a woman close enough to his life-style for him to give her his allegiance. Saint Theresa was impressed by Saint John's spiritual capacities and he joined her at a time when she was wanting to extend her order to monks as well as nuns – he became the "father" of the order.

However, there were enemies in the "calced" friars of the mitigated rule and at one time Saint John was captured by them, submitted to an inquisition, regular flagellations and nearly starved to death. He submitted to all this until he realized that his life was in danger. He then succeeded, with the tacit help of his gaoler, in escaping. It was whilst in prison that he wrote the "Stanzas of the Soul". As Saint John was only thirty-six years old at the time, it may be asked how it could have been that his soul was "in a state of perfection".

After he had recovered from that traumatic experience, Saint John returned to an active life: for a time he was prior of the monastery of El Cavano, travelled between and founded monasteries, acted as spiritual director of souls, attended Chapters, wrote poems, commentaries, instructions and precautions to spiritual advisers and the spiritual maxima. There was, it is true, one period, "rather prolonged", when he was at the convent of Los Matieres, during which time he had continuous peace of mind.

Shortly before his death he attended the Chapter General in Madrid. The order had by this time grown and there was a movement to increase rules and regulations. Saint John was vehemently against their needless multiplication and was deemed a dangerous person – it was even thought that his habit might be removed and attempts were made to send him abroad as a missionary. After all this he became seriously ill and died in 1591 at the age of forty-nine.

It is apparent that Saint John, like other mystics, led an active life and was not exclusively devoted to contemplation as his writings might suggest. Besides he had a great love of nature. At first sight that would seem a contradiction, since it had been God's intention to deprive the soul of natural desires. Saint John liked to pray in natural surroundings, especially in caves, and would "lead his fellow Monks to 'some delightful stream or pleasing crag' and thence send them into the hills to pray". Furthermore, there is no lack of beautiful images of nature in his poems and commentaries, so how are we to understand the discrepancy?

It would appear that the journeys of the soul are autonomous though the human being participates in them. In that transformations are continually taking place, different attitudes emerge. Whereas at first the search is for God in nature, where he will not be found, secondly nature becomes God Himself and so He does not need finding.

It would follow that the mystical journey increasingly informs the natural desires with divine love. Nevertheless, in Saint John's case, although it is clear that for him the soul, which aims to unite with God and so become divine, wishes to eschew the world altogether, it does not seem that he actually did that.

It is, however, quite possible, indeed it is inevitable to suppose that all his activities could go on whilst the soul was coming increasingly into direct relation with God. Thus Saint John's life would be increasingly informed by directions from God. Saint John does not write about that but we know that Saint Theresa did sometimes act on such instructions. It is of course inevitable that Saint John should remain human and, as a human being, suffer the imperfections of the soul: it was he who submitted in obedience, it was he who enacted penances and suffered flagellations. There were basically three entities interacting: the human being, the soul and God corresponding to the ego, the anima (or animus) and the self.

Conclusion

Analytical psychology has often been called mystical. The mystics by contrast, or at least some like Saint John of the Cross, thought of themselves as scientists of Christianity. Within the confines of Christian tradition and doctrine they described in great detail the experiences that a mystic could have and also the means for dealing with such experiences. Moreover, within the confines of the knowledge at that time he was thought of as a consummate psychologist: in his introduction to the *Ascent of Mount Carmel*, Allison Peers asserts that "He may well be termed the greatest psychologist in the history of mysticism" (Peers, 1953, p. xi).

His psychology is not ours but his descriptive work has sufficient objective characteristics to be termed scientific. So it does appear that just as some alchemists were recognizing the psychological ("philosophic") nature of their work, Saint John was going in the same direction, but using Catholic dogma and theology as his frame of reference. One might say that he was a mediaeval prototype of an analytical psychologist.

Chapter Fifteen

*Alchemy**

Saint John's works exemplify the aspiring aims of Christian mysticism. There are some trends in alchemy which are similar. The alchemists also worked to detach the soul from the body which ascended to arrive at a spiritual unity, the *Unio mentalis* in the upper reaches of the universe called the *caelum*. They also thought that there were sensual and spiritual aspects of the soul, but there was much more emphasis on an often obscure and also grotesque imagery, presumably of the kind that Saint John disliked so much. However, they were religious-minded men and extolled the Christian virtues that were needed to develop the right attitude to the work. In contrast to Saint John, they gave great importance to dreams and visions which took on peculiar turns by reason of their chemical operations. These were not the refined chemistry of modern science but a combination of dreams and visions with physical changes that they observed in their retorts and other apparatuses; indeed, they often seemed to have related to their operations with hallucination. There is no need for me to go into the psychological understanding of the symbolism in this subject, since Jung has dealt with that at such length, drawing analogies between the alchemist's work and individuation. It may be remarked that they were subject to persecution largely because some of them claimed to make gold and that excited the avarice of men in influential positions.

Besides this, they believed that they were possessed of a secret; however, unlike Saint John, it was not an essential inexpressible mystery but a secret of the art which must not be divulged. Various reasons for that were given: they centre around the idea that it would be misused; for instance, the more materialistic alchemists would say that they knew how to make gold and, if that knowledge were misused, what would

*A much altered version of "The relevance of analytical theory to alchemy, mysticism and theology", *The Journal of Analytical Psychology* vol. 5, no. 2, 1960.

happen to the economy? Less materialistic alchemists apparently felt they had a "philosophical secret" which could be misused in a comparable way. Whichever view is taken, it is clear that they would suffer greatly not to divulge the "secret" (I leave aside the possibility that the whole thing was a fraud and that just as they never discovered how to make gold, so there was no "philosophical gold" to be revealed and there was no "philosophical" secret either).

If we follow their writings it seems that they were in a quandary: they knew how to detach the soul from the body, which was usually reduced to ashes (cf. Saint John's burning of the sensual part of the soul by the fire of the Holy Ghost) but they could not reunite the spirit elevated to the caelum, an analogue of heaven, with the purified body which concurrently became ashes.

It is clear that they knew how to renew the pulverized body: there is for instance a description of the renewal of the ageing king in the *Mysterium Coniunctionis* (Jung, 1955–6, p. 274) but the result is not transformation; the king is renewed after the fashion of the phoenix; he becomes a more vigorous version of the old king.

One is inclined to think that the alchemists were in difficulties partly because they were working on paradoxical subject matter and partly because of Christian dogma; the flesh is the play-ground of the devil and if the alchemists reinvested the body with spirit, the consequences might be awkward: the descent of the spirit might only too easily be interpreted as an act of the devil and so the door would now be opened once again to his predatory acts, from which so much effort had been exercised to make it invulnerable. The alchemists never became arraigned as heretics, but it may be that much of their obscurity was designed to avoid that very disagreeable possibility. Jung considered that subject with care and concluded that the alchemists were in fact heretics but not recognized as such. From his vertex, however, the alchemists' work compensated the aspiring spiritual aims of Christianity rather than opposing them. Jung considered that their work had a progressive content which led, on one hand, to modern chemistry and was, on the other hand, the prototype of individuation. In what follows, I have selected material which illustrates how the alchemists viewed their work. The descriptions record the failures of two alchemists (real or imagined).

It will be remembered that Saint John tells us that some souls had a greater capacity to progress than others. Saint John does not tell us what took place to disrupt or bring to a limit the mystical development. The alchemical accounts leave us in no doubt and it is open to the reader to infer the kind of difficulties which arose in the mystical process. He can then consider whether my belief that they are similar is of any use to him.

Some Alchemical Texts

Passages from *The Hermetic Museum* published in 1678 and translated by Waite in 1953 will now be selected for study. Nearly all of what I shall relate has already been said by Jung, and what is elaborated here must be taken mostly as an introduction to, but in some parts amplification of, what he has already stated.

One of the features of the alchemical treatises in this volume is that the authors spend a considerable time asserting that they deliberately conceal the truth so that the uninitiated shall not debase their art which is at the same time a ''science''. They say that if you read widely and meditate on the books for a long time, everything will become clear. Alongside this, they often give evidence of persecutory ideas, combined with a rather ostentatious show of virtue; they either conceived themselves to be, or else actually were subjected to persecution. ''Do not wonder that I conceal my name and refuse to appear to you face to face'', says the anonymous author of *The Golden Tract* (transl. Waite, 1953, I, p. 8). ''I have come forward, not for the sake of any paltry glory, or of worldly praise, but to do you good.'' It is not only unethical, however, but also dangerous to seek worldly fame, for ''Experience teaches that many philosophers who gave no thought to their personal safety, have been killed and deprived of their tincture . . .; and it stands to reason that any one going about with a great treasure in his hand, must fall a prey to brigands'' (ibid., p. 8).

The material benefits which alchemy was said to bring about are clearly stated; they did indeed make the alchemists the victims of greed and avarice. For instance, Alexander Sethon (died 1604) was imprisoned by the Duke of Basil, who proceeded from persuasion to all species of torture without, however, inducing him to divulge the secret of how to make the philosopher's stone. Neither, incidentally, would he divulge it to his liberator, Sendivogious, another alchemist to whom he replied, ''I have suffered; my nerves are shrunk, my limbs dislocated, emaciated almost to an extremity, and my body almost corrupted; even to avoid this, I did not disclose the secret of philosophy'' (p. 67). It seems likely, therefore, that the deliberate concealment which they often claimed to practise, was supported by real danger to their persons.

They sought to mitigate that this was necessary in self-defence, but qualified this by saying that diligent study of numerous books which amplify each other would reveal the truth. In this way serious students could get to the heart of the matter, whilst superficial and greedy persons would only get in a muddle and so be put off. Nevertheless there is a great deal of confusion combined with a persecuted attitude and display of virtue.

In the texts under consideration, the alchemists were at great pains to state their Christian faith and they say that the truth can be arrived at only by prayer, right living and the grace of God. This they could formulate clearly.

"In the first place", says the anonymous author of *The Sophic Hydrolith* (Waite, 1953, I, p. 74) "let every devout and God-fearing chemist and student of this Art consider that this arcanum should be regarded, not only as a truly great, but as a most holy Art (seeing that it typifies and shadows out the highest heavenly good)." The author then goes on to specify, at some length, virtues which need to be cultivated by the adept, who "must remember that it is obtained not by the might of man, but by the grace of God . . .".

A main feature of the art is its revealed nature. There are a number of indications in this in *The Hermetic Museum*, and the following account shows how it leads to the activation of images when the coherence of the ego becomes weakened and when it, or part of it, fragments. The description comes from *The New Chemical Light* by Michael Sendivogius, who lived between 1562 and 1646. First there is a meeting of Sages; they consulted about the best substance from which to prepare the philosopher's stone, but before their discussion is ended they are dispersed, rather disconcertingly, by "a wind". There follows accounts of how two of them fare: one had contended that mercury was the best *prima materia*, the other sulphur; both, as we shall see, start from the substance itself operating chemically along prescribed lines. The advocate of mercury proceeded as follows: "Then he [the sage] took (common) Mercury, and began to work with it" (ibid., II, p. 116). He placed it in a glass vessel over the fire and after an initial disaster he kept a close watch until "The Mercury rose to the top of the vessel in vaporous steam" (ibid., p. 117). Full of joy the alchemist then ". . . began to subject the Mercury to all sorts of chemical processes, to sublime it, and to calcine it with all manner of things, with salts, sulphur, metals, minerals, blood, hair, aqua fortis, herbs, urine and vinegar. All these substances were tried in succession; everything that he could think of was tried"; until in the end ". . . he fell into a deep sleep, and there appeared to him an old man, who elicited from him the cause of his sadness, and bade him use the pure Mercury of the Sages."

From now on we can see how the activities of a different kind take place and archetypal imagery takes over. In the alchemist's imagination, Mercury as a "person" appears and the alchemist discourses with him as in active imagination. The alchemist is very arrogant and Mercury complains to Nature. She becomes angry with the alchemist and eventually reduces him to humility. He then asks Nature who Mercury is, and she replies: "Know that I have only one such son; he is one of seven, and the first among them; and though he is now all things, he was at first only one. In him are the four elements, yet he is not an element. He is a spirit, yet he has a body; a man, yet he performs a woman's part; a boy, yet he bears a man's weapons; a beast, and yet he has the wings of a bird. He is poison, yet he cures leprosy; life, yet he kills all things; a King, but another occupies his throne; he flees from the fire, yet fire is taken from him; he is water, but does not wet the hands; he is earth, and yet he is sown; he is air, and lives by water" (ibid., pp. 124–5). The philosopher is much taken aback, but dares not accept the "truth" because he would "lose the good opinion of my neighbours, and they would no longer entrust me with money for my experiments". This *dénouement* provokes a sharp retort from Nature: "Such philosophers are only fit for the gallows. Be off, and take with you my most grievous curse."

The second philosopher, who advocated the use of sulphur to produce the stone, also starts with elaborate chemical operations culled from the books. However, he is more humble and so gets further. He has a vision of how the stone is made; we read: "Then Saturn took two kinds of quicksilver [i.e. Mercury] of different substance but one root, washed them with his urine, and called them the sulphurs of sulphurs; then he mixed the fixed with the volatile, after which he placed them in a proper vessel, and set a watch to prevent the sulphur from escaping; afterwards he placed them in a bath of very gentle heat – and thus they made the Philospher's Stone, which must always follow as the outcome of the right substance" (ibid., p. 155). But alas it was all brought to nothing, for "Then the Alchemist took it in his hand, admired its beautiful purple colour, and danced about with it, shouting aloud with joy and delight. Suddenly the glass slipped out of his hand and broke into a thousand pieces; the stone vanished; and the Alchemist awoke with nothing in his hand but some pieces of sulphurous tow."

It will have been noticed that both alchemists start off with chemical operations: they end up with dreams or visions which contain archetypal imagery. In both cases it is clear how understanding comes from revelation and not from the alchemical operations, though it would appear that the conscious operations are a necessary preliminary. This can only be interpreted as the necessity for the coherence of the ego to be relaxed, exhausted, before the unconscious can become manifest, but using deintegrates which contain in experience the form of the conscious alchemical philosophy and practice.

Both enterprises come to grief through failings of the philosophers; one lacks courage to act on what he learns, the other gets too excited (manic defence) at success and the stone is lost. Both examples reinforce the frequent admonitions to cultivate the Christian virtue of humility.

The chemical operations and the preliminary discourses belong to the sphere of the ego; the dreams and visions pertain to the archetypal level in which processes get what appears to be confused, i.e. the boundaries between images are fluid. Mercury, for instance, is so many things that we cannot say precisely what he is; moreover, almost everything he is said to be is compounded with its opposite; this kind of language is necessary if archetypal processes are to be placed on record and they can be amplified by comparative study. The way in which the comparative method is useful can be illustrated by building on the alchemist's admonition to read carefully and compare the texts. Thus, in the light of Nature's discourse on Mercury in the first part of the text, it becomes clearer why Saturn, in the second part, takes "two kinds of quicksilver of different substances but one root"; it means that Mercury is of this double nature, yet *au fond* a single element.

The naming of the two kinds of quicksilver, washed in urine, suggests a transformation; they are called the "sulphurs of sulphurs". The naming of people and objects often signifies a change in them, and this interpretation is confirmed by the now apparent existence of two classes of substance, the "fixed and the volatile", separate and no longer having one root. They are then put together and subjected to a heat which takes part in uniting them and changing them into a single object, the philosopher's stone. This leads to a central feature of alchemy, the uniting of opposites or conjunction; it is sometimes expressed in terms of a parable which is evidently based on visionary experiences. In *The Golden Tract* there is a very elaborate account of how an alchemist was set to warm a bride and bridegroom; they go through a sequence of transformations until the resplendent king with his queen emerge. They take the alchemist to their kingdom in which is to be found gold and precious carbuncles without end: "There was also to be found renewal and restoration of youth, and of the natural faculties, and recovery of lost youth, with a never failing panacea for all diseases" (ibid., I, p. 50). There are the visionary consequences of finding the philosopher's stone which arises from the familiar and widespread theme of rebirth, preceded by a union of opposites, the conjunction, expressed in the union of the sulphurs, or the union of the king and queen, or the embrace of the sun and moon, a dog and a bitch etc. In Christianity it is found in the union of Christ with His bride the Church, the *unio mystica* between soul and God. In each the form which the union takes on fits the vertex in which it appears.

Discussion

Jung recognized that the alchemists' work, or much of it was dependent upon projections and that in studying them he could discern a prototype of individuation. He showed that the alchemists were on the way to symbolize the whole man. Their vertex prevented that development, though some of the more philosophical alchemists got very near it – Dorn was the example Jung took to illustrate that state of affairs. Jung worked on the symbolism using the theory of archetypes and that led him to conclude that the philosopher's stone was the self.

He did little or no work on the genesis of these symbols, because he thought they represented primary entities. However, he did give recognition to Silberer's (1904) essay early on, but it proved inadequate for his purpose; for him it looked too much for the infantile roots of the process and especially the primal scene or conjunction. Jung recognized, however, the incestuous nature of the process and that sexuality and birth and rebirth were powerful influences.

It is my object to show that, in infancy, processes take place which develop and transform into the activities, mental and physical, of later life. Thus I aim to establish that there are basic patterns that run right through life: in short, that infancy is not so much a state of being that has to be given up as that its patterns of behaviour, whether mental or physical, need rather to become readapted to the requirements of differing environments whether they be inner or outer. What is often called infantile is the failure of that readaptation. In this I expand the theory of archetypes.

It is quite evident that alchemists operated in terms of part objects called chemical substances which were associated with imagined "persons" and bizarre objects and that these "persons" and substances were related with the cosmos through astrology. Thus they developed a sophisticated system. But all the same they experienced great difficulty in distinguishing their objects from their mental life – their dreams and visions – and that is why Jung evokes the theory of projection.

What are the sources of the difficulty? A powerful factor is the alchemical tradition, the lack of chemical science as we know it now, and the cultural idiom and religious vertex which held sway when they were operating. But let us look more carefully. They laid great emphasis on containment: the alchemical vessel in which their substances were heated must be firmly closed so that nothing shall escape from it. In the relation between a mother and her baby the mother's containing function is essential; first she contains her child physically in her womb, then she holds him in her arms and also contains him in her mind and her emotions. Periodically, in an emotional crisis, all she is required to do is to hold her baby whilst he works through an emotional conflict. Then all interference from other persons or such-like distractions are contra-indicated: that applies especially to what Klein has called the depressive position. But the containment is not only physical. In the first place her maternal reverie reflects and digests her infant's state of mind and she can feed back to her baby the result of her mental but non-verbal activity through action and talk.

In inspecting the part objects with which the alchemists operate there are a number which are striking. Most of them derive from alchemical "science" but what about their inclusions of parts of the body: urine, faeces, semen and we may include here small animals. These are the preoccupations of infants which need to be transferred into mental operations with the help of their mothers.

As an infant grows, the containing functions of his mother become taken over, through introjection, by the infant and so his inner world begins to develop – he adopts her containing functions. Furthermore, as he grows, he creates images, imagination and dreams (it is very uncertain when dreaming begins, but it is possible *in utero*).

I would now like to consider the projective element in alchemy to which Jung paid so much attention. It is striking how difficult it was for alchemists to disentangle the chemical operation from its mental content, so that some of them never did so and claimed to have produced real gold; indeed there were certificates produced from time to time by presumably disinterested persons to say that it had been done. It seems therefore that something more than projection is required. Such alchemists were identified with their projection. The formulation of projective-identification was introduced by Jung in another context without giving it that title (Jung, 1921, especially para 491) but he never applied it to alchemy.

I want to consider somewhat further concepts that have proved useful in understanding infancy and the infant in adult persons; they derive from the concept of psychoid elements in the archetype. Bion's notion of beta elements which could develop, through the action of alpha function, into alpha elements which are the raw material of thought, appears to develop Jung's idea. That is why I use his notation: in addition it is more elegant.

I postulate that the alchemists often operated with beta elements. Indeed the second alchemist appears to be an example of doing so. The "stone" was so much an object that it could be played with and get broken. Perhaps it was in reality a glass vessel, but whatever it was, he becomes exultant and triumphant and so departs from the religious virtues extolled in the art. It can be translated into the theme of a manic defence against disillusionment: he broke it but it *had* "really" existed.

The first alchemist had, according to my postulate, developed further. He had succeeded in detaching from the object and developed a vision, i.e. the beta elements had been transformed. His fault is therefore different. Mother Nature develops a paradoxical form of expression and so introduces him to the inner world. That frightens the alchemist who wants to revert to beta element functioning, and so he does not recognize the true nature of the alchemical opus.

In infancy beta elements are acted on partly by the infant's own alpha function. Its development is greatly facilitated by his mother's reverie. Mother Nature's communications were certainly not a reverie and seem to have been much too forceful for the alchemist.

Returning to projective identification, we may believe that it is at the level of beta elements that projective identification is most prominent. If not excessive, it can lead to information about the object; that is when alpha function is brought into operation satisfactorily. If that is not the case, projective identification can lead to annihilation of the real object and the result is delusion formation – some alchemists seem to have operated in that way.

We can now elucidate the nature of the two kinds of alchemists: those who believed that they could or had really produced gold (excessive projective identification) and those who believed their operations were essentially "philosophic" (alpha function had led to the formation of alpha elements and so on into mental life).

A concluding note: it may be speculated that it was the untransformed patterns of infancy and the infant in the adult that led to each of the alchemists we have considered failing in their separate ways to work out the implications of their respective discoveries.

Chapter Sixteen

Concluding reflections

This last chapter is an attempt to present background information about the other contents of this book. None has more than a tenuous logical framework; indeed, each is more an outline of my various interests over the years.

It is fundamental to analytic practice for an analyst to recognize the basic forms which determine human behaviour and give rise to experience. We search for these patterns and seek to transform their infantile and archaic characteristics into an equivalent suitable for differing cultural conditions and personal relationships.

The patterns are in part useful in immediate relationships with the environment. Those that can not be so employed can hopefully give rise to transformations of mental and spiritual life. Alternatively they may be directed to bring about changes of the environment, in either in the short or the long term, through the physical sciences and technology.

The development of these two lines of thought and imagination is a subject of great interest. It lead me to study the assimilation into Western culture during the Middle Ages and the Renaissance of the thinking of Greek and Arabic scientists and philosophers. That reveals the process of discovering and sorting out of theology and philosophy on one hand and the rudiments of the sophisticated scientific and psychological sciences of the present day on the other. It was during that time that the truth, as established by reason and revelation, was gradually being replaced by the supposedly less reliable scientific method. However, that method turned on the philosophers to show the error of their conclusions about the nature of motion and the place of the earth in the cosmos (see Crombie, 1961). We ordinarily date the change by thinking about the great scientists Galileo, Copernicus, Harvey, but in each case their work was built on that of their precursors of great learning and perspicacity. The Arabic influence was considerable, not only because of the discoveries they had made, but also because many of the Greek texts were brought to Europe by them. That is of particular interest to us here because of Jung's work on alchemy – the Arabs were great alchemists.

Since the scientific revolution, which showed that so many beliefs about the material world were false, the sorting out of the theological, philosophical and scientific methods and their discoveries has promoted much heated conflict and often violent controversy. The arrival of psychoanalysis initiated the latest revolution in the series, especially with its discovery of the psychological origins of many religious beliefs, dogmas and revelations. The theory of archetypes on which much of this book is based was Jung's great contribution.

A special element in my essay is the conviction that the basic, archetypal patterns needs to be understood from two vertices: that of maturation in the individual starting from conception, and that of the culture patterns and their history. If I have seemed to give less importance to the historical dimension, that is not out of indifference to it but because others have done so much about it. It is nonetheless my contention that in their historical and cultural researches they have lost sight of the often over-riding importance of maturation in the individual.

Central in this volume has been the exploration of the self. That investigation started in about 1940 and followed discovery of self symbols in childhood. That was contrary to the accepted studies and so it led to a need to assess Jung's pioneering studies and see how far my own and later formulations related to his. That meant investigating psychoanalysis and Part 2 of this book shows how my investigation developed. I was immediately plunged into a complex situation, for just as Jung and his followers had produced a great wealth of knowledge on religious and mythological symbolism, once again there was a wealth of sophisticated study on development in childhood.

My study of psychoanalysis was facilitated by the very alive collection of Kleinians assembled in London after World War II. It was possible to meet them and discuss with them at the Medical Section of the British Psychological Society. From these meetings and also private conversations, I learned of the rapid developments in which they were taking part and I could consider these in relation to my own work. That became no longer simply a matter of an active dialectic in which members of the denominations could present and discuss their views and findings; it appeared that there was good agreement on a number of topics – the relation between archetypes and internal objects, for instance, whilst there seemed little difference between how we looked at transference and countertransference.

The dialectic has gone on since then between Jungian, Kleinian and other psychoanalysts working together in clinics and other professional activities, not to mention in one or two small groups where both the principles and the techniques used are considered in the context of clinical work.

The situation at that time differed from that in other centres where Jungians had tended to become embattled in their own institutes, with the exception of San Francisco, and had lost contact with psychoanalysts who had taken up entrenched positions *vis-à-vis* Jung and who had rejected Klein. It was not surprising, therefore, that there was considerable bewilderment at International Congresses of Analytical Psychology when analysts from London presented their views and they were defensively stigmatized under various categories: "Non-Jungian", or "Freudian" etc. These mostly indicated confusion, especially the category "Freudian", for it was no longer with Freud that we were discussing but with Klein and her followers about whom most of my erstwhile colleagues from other countries knew literally nothing. Later some members of the London Society became disturbed and eventually a minority group formed a Society of their own, in which these ongoing discussions could be more successfully resisted and the "true blue" Jungians could more happily meet. In my view, these members tend to worship Jung and are far away from the spirit of Jung that I knew. His mind was open-ended and, as far as my own work was concerned, he never once expressed objections and sometimes was openly and warmly appreciative. That was so in his "Foreword" to *New Developments in Analytical Psychology*.

The work of most psychoanalysts on the self was helpful in clarifying the relation between the ego and the self. Only a few laid emphasis on the self as I conceived it in infancy and none of the dynamic sequences of integration and deintegration. Something like it appeared in Mrs Klein's development of the idea of splitting, but it was the ego that split and, even though the depressive position included a reminiscent sequence including quite a radical transformation and integration, that was not what I really meant since the self did not feature prominently or explicitly. It is not my intention to claim in this book that I have a deep understanding of Klein, so I have paid most attention to clinical data and formulations that I found illuminating in my analytic practice with children and adults.

Concurrently with my interest in psychoanalysis, I continued my study of Jung's works – it was greatly facilitated by my co-editorship of the *Collected Works*. His emphasis on alchemy and religious experience is well known, but that much of it derives from transformed infant experience is only hinted at in a number of places – perhaps his essay on "The child archetype" is the most indicative. However, he could not do more than touch on the psychology of actual children because he had not the apparatus for penetrating the mind of a child let alone an infant.

It will be remembered, however, that by 1912 Jung had reformulated the battle of the hero with various monsters in pre-oedipal terms so that the monster could be understood as the mother whom the hero dismembers or enters into and destroys from within. He also collected material to show the two aspects of the mother: her feeding, nurturing, protecting nature and her terrible, destructive, devouring attributes. In reality, mothers are only marginally like that, so that he believed that the myths were reflecting inner archaic processes.

In the early 1930s, I became convinced that Klein was looking into the inner world from a different vertex from myself, and that there she was discovering archetypal fantasies. Klein uncovered them in small children and then extended her findings to infancy: the dual mother in myths corresponds to the two breasts, good and bad, and this distinction was then extended to his mother's body as a whole through the operation of his epistomophylic instinct. The consequent ravages of envy and jealousy motivate him to destroy, in fantasy, the very object of his love and interest – only his concurrent gratitude to her for all the good things he has received from her mitigates the pain of that situation.

By 1912 Jung had also developed the concept of transformation in contrast to repression – that Klein also introduced. It has been further developed by Bion.

In her metapsychology Klein accepted Susan Isaac's definition of unconscious fantasy – I can see no difference between that and Jung's definition of archetypes.

Another concept of Klein's may be said to help in drawing together a number of features in Jung's description. Gianna Henry (1969) pointed out that Jung gave a clear description of projective identification but under the heading of "Empathy" and that was in 1921 (p. 286). In addition the primitive notion of loss of and invasion by a soul is better understood if we combine the word identification with projection or introjection.

I have I think said enough to indicate why I think that Klein went far to add the dimension to Jung's labours which I was seeking to elucidate. That she did not develop a theory of the self does not alter the fact that she opened up the way to it by uncovering "unconscious fantasy" in an infant's and a child's mental life. That she also provided an interpretative instrument made it possible for me to make contact with children in a way that had not been possible before.

I have so far listed the similarities between these two great innovators, I must now mention a significant difference. Klein gave much more importance to guilt in its persecutory and depressive forms than Jung. That is not found in his formulations: guilt does not seem to have interested him much; indeed, he only wrote one essay on the subject and said little or nothing about it in childhood.

I have found it necessary to make this all too brief statement about Klein because I have not mentioned her enough in this volume, though much of its structure derived from my developing interest in her researches. I have mentioned mostly pupils, Winnicott, Bion and Scott in particular, who all derived their work from her, but she was the real innovator.

It might be thought that my interest would have led me to undertake a Kleinian psychoanalysis and so gain inside information. I never did so for various reasons, amongst which was my love for and loyalty to Jung himself. However, I have worked quite closely with Kleinian analysts and they have deepened my understanding of her work, thus enabling me to incorporate many of her ideas and practices into my own analytic endeavours.

Though a large part of my essay is engaged in assessing or analysing, sometimes critically, Jung's propositions, I have included three chapters in Part 2 which deal with clinical problems and analytic method. That is demanded because of Jung's insistence that clinical experience lay at the root of his opening up the inner world and also to his abstract generalizations. The vital instrument that he used in this revolution was the interpretation on the subjective plane.

The subject of technique and management in the analytic dialectic focuses nowadays on transference and countertransference and also the ethics of analytic practice. In this context I would like to mention a consequence of self theory and experience which needs underlining.

Jung maintained that the self combined opposites and so transcended them. It follows that a "good" analyst cannot be only good in the ordinary infantile or social senses of the word. An instance of the dilemma may be given as follows: it is sometimes maintained that a patient is healed by the analyst's love, and that in being a "good parent", he can redress the faults of his patient's upbringing or heal the patient's self image. It is an idea of the infant self representation that has become damaged by his mother's treatment of him. That, though it can happen, implies far too innocent an understanding of mother–infant interaction; it leaves out the infant's part in creating a good enough mother. The study of mothers and infants demonstrates clearly that a mother can be a good enough mother with one child and not with another of the same family or that an infant can virtually create a good enough mother by the precision of his signals and the apparent knowledge of what his mother can tolerate and what she cannot.

Whilst something can be done to heal the self image with warmth and kindness, that is not enough. Suppose a patient evokes warmth and compassion in the analyst; that needs scrutinizing, because it may be a grave mistake to provide it. That is so because the supposed feeling in the analyst can be a response to his patient's projective identification, and then it is the analyst's job to feed it back to the patient so that he or she becomes capable of such feelings as well. Furthermore, if an analyst becomes identified with such experiences and believes that he can sustain them all the time, he has been caught by a defensive illusion. He has lost his shadow and can even overlook the shadow of analytic work: not only the destructive acts done when by taking mental structures to pieces but also his hate of the patient may be wrongly evaluated. During the analysis he invades his patient mentally, just as a surgeon cuts into the body and disrupts its functioning to reveal the pathological organ. That analogy, and it is only that, is useful in understanding the need for recovery after the analysis is ended – in discussion with colleagues they put this time at between two and three years.

Such features of analysis raise moral and ethical questions and in that context the study of religion is valuable. In the Christian mediaeval dogma, there could be no doubt about the difference between God and His divine goodness and the devil's equally supernatural badness or evil. That dichotomy is found in experiences of the archetypal forms, but the movement of individuation can, to a large extent, transcend it. That is brought about by the transcendent function of the self which Jung noticed and which I have inferred is implicit in the mystical experiences of Saint John of the Cross.

It is sometimes thought that analytical psychology with its intensive study of symbolic life, is a thinly veiled religious movement with a tendency to cult formation. It is, I think, true that analysts are concerned with ethics and are also interested in religious experience but in a different way from formal religion: the analytic ethic is to facilitate the person's self realizations and, with that in mind, to release and scrutinize previously unconscious mental, spiritual and instinctive capacities so that they can be included in the self representations of the individual in relation to his environment.

The history and development of a moral sense are a parallel to their growth in infancy and childhood. One, probably the first, clear distinction is that between good and bad objects; it is arrived at in the first weeks of extrauterine life. An infant's reactions are often total, extreme and expressed physically. Therefore, his parents, mostly the mother, are compelled to exercise physical control combined with thought (maternal reverie), thus helping the infant's innate capacity for mental operations. Through them the violence becomes converted into rudimentary moral feelings used at first in the infant's self interest.

The further development of moral and ethical feelings and behaviour determined by them is increased first by fostering a child's inner capacities for them and secondly by introducing him to the customs, morals and ethics of the community into which he has been born.

So as to increase the patient's inner capacity for responsibility towards the community and himself, analysts use their analytic attitude, which requires, within limits, moral and ethical neutrality. Since parts of some patients are insufficiently developed, however, it may be necessary for him to exercise controls as well and that means taking responsibility for his patient – a feature more prominent in the case of child treatment when parents are more or less irresponsible. That is a severe test of his ethical responsibilities for he needs to be sure that his containing and controlling functions do not interfere with his patient's growing capacity to know himself.

The quandary is beautifully expressed by Saint John of the Cross and his instructions to his spiritual advisors. There comes a time when, because of the soul's closeness to God, the soul is in utter despair and aridity. The spiritual advisor must not interfere, even though the soul ceases to follow the rules of the community. Those who do try to draw the soul back from its experience, he says, "will not be forgiven".

Such comparisons highlight human dilemmas. Analysts do not institute anything like the rigorous disciplines of the Catholic Church of the Middle Ages, so their work is far from identical. However, the capacity for moral neutrality is only possible within the analytic frame (Fordham, 1978, pp. 65, 70ff.) which contains the two members in their analytic endeavours. Rules are minimized but not excluded.

Before closing I wish to make a final comment on the importance given to mother–infant studies. These were almost demanded by my early speculations about the primal self in infancy, but I had neither the time nor a method of so doing. It was therefore with excitement that I learned of the research being done, initiated by Esther Bick, at the Tavistock Clinic. It was being continued by Martha Harris and I made contact with her. She deputed Gianna Henry to lead seminars on studies made by the students of the Society of Analytical Psychology. I attended these seminars and they opened up vistas of knowledge which replaced the plethora of speculation about the first two years of extrauterine life.

Bibliography

Adler, G. (1961). "The Living Symbol", London, Routledge and Kegan Paul.

Algrisse, G. (1962). Character re-education and professional re-adaptation of a man aged forty-five. *J. analyt. Psychol.* **7**, 2.

Bach, S. (1969). Spontaneous paintings of seriously ill patients. *Documents Geigy: Acta Psychosomatica.*

Bakan, D. (1958). "Sigmund Freud and the Jewish Mystical Tradition", Boston, Beacon Press.

Balint, M. (1968). "The Basic Fault", London, Tavistock.

Balint, M. (1955). Notes on para-psychology and para-psychological healing. *Int. J. Psycho-anal.* **36**, 1.

Baynes, H. G. (1955). "The Mythology of the Soul", London, Routledge and Kegan Paul.

Bennet, E. A. (1961). "C. G. Jung", London, Barrie and Rockcliff.

Bion, W. R. (1967). "Second Thoughts", London, Heinemann.

Bion, W. R. (1977). "Seven Servants", New York, Aronson.

Bowlby, J. (1969). "Attachment and Loss" Vol. I: Attachment. London, Hogarth.

Bronowski, J. (1960). The Commonsense of Science", London, Pelican.

Campbell, R. (transl.) (1951). "The Poems of Saint John of the Cross", London, Longman.

Coppolillo, H. P. (1967). Maturational aspects of the transitional phenomena. *Int. J. Psycho-anal.* **48**, 2.

Cresogoño de Jesus (1958). "The Life of Saint John of the Cross', London, Longman.

Crombie, A. C. (1961). "Augustine to Galileo", London, Mercury Books.

Davidson, D. (1966). Transference as a form of active imagination. *In* "Technique in Jungian Analysis", L.A.P. Vol. 2, London, Heinemann.

Edinger, E. F. (1960). The ego self paradox. *J. analyt. Psychol.* **5**, 1.

Ehrenzweig, A. (1957). Creative surrender. *Amer. Imago.* **14**, 3.

Evans, E. (1926). "A Psychological Study of Cancer", New York, Dodd, Mead.

Federn, P. (1953). "Ego Psychology and the Psychoses", London, Imago.

Fintzey, R. T. (1971). Vicissitudes of the transitional object in a borderline child. *Int. J. Psycho-anal.* **52**, 2.

Fordham, F. (1964). The care of regressed patients and the child archetype. *J. analyt. Psychol.* **9**, 1.

Fordham, M. (1944). "The Life of Childhood", London, Routledge and Kegan Paul.

Fordham, M. (1947). Integration and deintegration and early ego development. *The Nervous Child* **6**, 3.

Fordham, M. (1955). The origins of the ego in childhood. *In* "New Developments in Analytical Psychology", London, Routledge and Kegan Paul.
Fordham, M. (1956). Active imagination and imaginative activity. *J. analyt. Psychol.* **1**, 2.
Fordham, M. (1957). "New Development in Analytical Psychology", London, Routledge and Kegan Paul.
Fordham, M. (1957b). Reflections on images and symbolism. *J. analyt. Psychol.* **2**, 1.
Fordham, M. (1957c). Some observations on the self and ego in childhood. *In* "New Developments in Analytical Psychology", London, Routledge and Kegan Paul.
Fordham, M. (1957d). Reflections on archetypes and synchronicity. *In* "New Developments in Analytical Psychology", London, Routledge and Kegan Paul.
Fordham, M. (1957e). Notes on the transference. *In* later edition: "Technique in Jungian Analysis", L.A.P. Vol. 2, London, Heinemann. 1974.
Fordham, M. (1957f). Biological theory and the concept of archetypes. *In* "New Developments in Analytical Psychology", London Routledge and Kegan Paul.
Fordham, M. (1958a). "The Objective Psyche", London, Routledge and Kegan Paul.
Fordham, M. (1958b). Repression in Christian practices. *In* "The Objective Psyche", London, Routledge and Kegan Paul.
Fordham, M. (1958c). Problems of active imagination. *In* "The Objective Psyche", London, Routledge and Kegan Paul.
Fordham, M. (1958d). The development and status of Jung's researches. *In* "The Objective Psyche", London, Routledge and Kegan Paul.
Fordham, M. (1960a). Counter-transference. *Brit. J. med. Psychol.* **33**, 1.
Fordham, M. (1960b). The relevance of analytical theory to alchemy, mysticism and theology. *J. analyt. Psychol.* **6**, 1.
Fordham, M. (1967a). Active imagination: deintegration or disintegration. *J. analyt. Psychol.* **12**, 1.
Fordham, M. (1967b). Technique and counter-transference. *In* later edition:"Technique in Jungian Analysis", London, Heinemann. 1974.
Fordham, M. (1968). Individuation in childhood. *In* "The Reality of the Psyche" (ed. Wheelwright, J. B.), New York, Putnam.
Fordham, M. (1969). "Children as Individuals", London, Hodder and Stoughton.
Fordham, M. (1971). Primary self, primary narcissism and related concepts. *In* "The Self and Autism", L.A.P. Vol. 3, London, Heinemann.
Fordham, M. (1974a). Jung's conception of transference. *J. analyt. Psychol.* **19**, 1.
Fordham, M. (1974b). Defences of the self. *J. analyt. Psychol.* **19**, 2.
Fordham, M. (1975). On interpretation. *Z. anal. Psychol.* **6**, 3.
Fordham, M. (1976). "The Self and Autism", L.A.P. Vol. 3, revised edition, London, Heinemann.
Fordham, M. (1978). "Jungian Psychotherapy", Chichester, John Wiley.
Freud, S. (1900–1). "The interpretation of dreams". *Std. edn* **4** and **5**.
Freud, S. (1910). The future prospects of psycho-analytic therapy. *Std. edn* **11**.
Freud, S. (1911). Psycho-analytic notes on an autobiographical account of a case of paranoia. *Std. edn* **12**.
Freud, S. (1927). The future of an illusion. *Std. edn* **21**.
Freud, S. (1939). Moses and monotheism. *Std. edn* **23**.
Freud, S. (1940). An outline of psycho-analysis. *Std. edn* **23**.
Freud, S. and Pfister, O. (1963). "Psycho-Analysis of Faith" (ed Meng, H. and Freud, E. L.), London, Hogarth.
Giovacchini, P. L. (1977). The impact of delusion and the delusion of impact. *Contemp. Psychoanal.* **13**, 429–441.
Goodheart, W. B. (1984). C. G. Jung's "patient". On the seminal emergence of Jung's thought. *J. analyt. Psychol.* **29**, 1.
Gordon, R. (1961). The death instinct and its relation to the self. *J. analyt. Psychol.* **3**, 2.

Gordon, R. (1963). Gods and deintegrates. *J. analyt. Psychol.* **8**, 1.
Greenacre, P. (1960). Further notes on fetishism. *In* "The Psychoanalytic Study of the Child", New York, International University Press.
Harding, E. (1947). "Psychic Energy", New York, Pantheon.
Hartmann, H. (1950). Comments on the psychoanalytic theory of the ego. *In* "Psychoanalytic Study of the Child" Vol. 5, London, Imago.
Henderson, J. (1975). C. G. Jung: a reminiscent picture of his method. *J. analyt. Psychol.* **20**, 2.
Henry, G. (1969). Some aspects of projective mechanisms in Jungian theory. *J. Child Psychother.* **2**, 3.
Heyer, H. G. (1933). "The Organism of the Mind", London, Routledge and Kegan Paul.
Hoffer, W. (1949). Mouth, hand and ego integration. *In* "The Psychoanalytic Study of the Child" Vols. 3–4, London, Imago.
Hoxeter, S. (1977). Play and communication. *In* "The Child psychotherapist" (ed. Boston, M. and Daws, D.), London, Wildwood House.
Hubback, J. (1966). VII sermones ad mortuos. *J. analyt. Psychol.* **11**, 2.
I Ching or *Book of Changes* (1950). Translated by Baynes, C. F. from the German translation of Wilhelm, R. 1950. New York and London, Routledge and Kegan Paul.
Jackson, H. and Plaut, A. (1955). Psychological aspects of ulcerative colitis in childhood. *Archives of the Middlesex Hospital.*
Jacobi, J. (1967). "The Way of Individuation", London, Hodder and Stoughton.
Jacoby, M. (1981). "Reflections on Kohut's concept of narcissism." *J. analyt. Psychol.* **26**, 1.
James, W. (1950). "The Principles of Psychology" Vol. I, London, Constable.
Jung, C. G. (1902). On the psychology and pathology of so-called occult phenomena. *Coll. Wks* **1**.
Jung, C. G. (1906–9). Experimental Researches. *Coll. Wks* **1**.
Jung, C. G. (1909). The significance of the father in the destiny of the individual. *Coll. Wks* **4**.
Jung, C. G. (1911). On the significance of number-dreams. *Coll. Wks* **4**.
Jung, C. G. (1912). "Psychology of the Unconscious", New York, Moffat Yard.
Jung, C. G. (1913). A contribution to the study of psychological types. *Coll. Wks* **6**.
Jung, C. G. (1914a). Some crucial points in psychoanalysis. *Coll. Wks* **4**.
Jung, C. G. (1914b). The content of the psychoses. *Coll. Wks* **3**.
Jung, C. G. (1917). Author's preface to the second edition of "Collected papers on analytical psychology". *Coll. Wks* **4**.
Jung, C. G. (1921). "Psychological types". *Coll. Wks* **6**.
Jung, C. G. (1926). "Two essays on analytical psychology". *Coll. Wks* **7**.
Jung, C. G. (1928a). On psychic energy. *Coll. Wks* **8**.
Jung, C. G. (1928b). The relations between the ego and the unconscious. *Coll. Wks* **7**.
Jung, C. G. (1929). Commentary on "The secret of the golden flower". *Coll. Wks* **13**.
Jung, C. G. (1930a). Some aspects of modern psychotherapy. *Coll. Wks* **16**.
Jung, C. G. (1930b). Richard Wilhelm: in memoriam. *Coll. Wks* **15**.
Jung, C. G. (1930–1). The stages of life. *Coll. Wks* **8**.
Jung, C. G. (1931). The practical use of dream analysis. *Coll. Wks* **16**.
Jung, C. G. (1934). The development of the personality. *Coll. Wks* **17**.
Jung, C. G. (1935). Principles of practical psychotherapy. *Coll. Wks* **16**.
Jung, C. G. (1935b). The Tavistock Lectures. *Coll. Wks* **18**.
Jung, C. G. (1937a). The idea of redemption in alchemy. *In* "The Integration of the Personality", New York and London, Routledge and Kegan Paul. (Revised in Jung *Coll. Wks* **12**.)
Jung, C. G. (1937b). Appendix. *Coll. Wks* **16** (2nd Bollingen edn).

Jung, C. G. (1939a). Foreword to Suzuki's "Introduction to Zen Buddhism". *Coll. Wks* **11**.
Jung, C. G. (1939b). Conscious, unconscious and individuation. *Coll. Wks* **9**, 1.
Jung, C. G. (1940a). Psychology and religion. *Coll. Wks* **11**.
Jung, C. G. (1940b). The meaning of individuation. *In* "The Integration of the Personality", London, Routledge and Kegan Paul.
Jung, C. G. (1942). Paracelsus as a spiritual phenomenon. *Coll. Wks* **13**.
Jung, C. G. (1943). The psychology of the unconscious. *Coll. Wks* **7**.
Jung, C. G. (1944a). " Psychology and Alchemy". *Coll. Wks* **12**.
Jung, C. G. (1944b). The Holy men of India: introduction to Zimmer's "Der Weg zum Selbat". *Coll. Wks* **11**.
Jung, C. G. (1946). The psychology of the transference. *Coll. Wks* **16**.
Jung, C. G. (1948a). A psychological approach to the dogma of the trinity. *Coll. Wks* **11**.
Jung, C. G. (1948b). The psychological foundations of belief in spirits. *Coll. Wks* **8**.
Jung, C. G. (1950a). A study in the process of individuation. *Coll. Wks* **9**, 1.
Jung, C. G. (1950b). Concerning mandala symbolism. *Coll. Wks* **9**, 1.
Jung, C. G. (1950c). Foreword to the *I. Ching*. *Coll. Wks* **11**.
Jung, C. G. (1951a). "Aion: researches into the phenomenology of the self". *Coll. Wks* **9**, 2.
Jung, C. G. (1951b). Fundamental questions of psychotherapy. *Coll. Wks* **16**.
Jung, C. G. (1951c). On synchronicity. *Coll. Wks* **8**.
Jung, C. G. (1952a). Symbols of transformation. *Coll. Wks* **5**.
Jung, C. G. (1952b). Answer to Job. *Coll. Wks* **11**.
Jung, C. G. (1952c). Synchronicity: an acausal connecting principle. *Coll. Wks* **8**.
Jung, C. G. (1953). Psychological commentary on "The Tibetan Book of the Dead". *Coll. Wks* **11**.
Jung, C. G. (1954a). Transformation symbolism in the mass. *Coll. Wks* **11**.
Jung, C. G. (1954b). The psychology of the child-archetype. *Coll. Wks* **9**, 1.
Jung, C. G. (1954c). On the nature of the psyche. *Coll. Wks* **9**, 1.
Jung, C. G. (1955–6). "Mysterium Coniunctionis". *Coll. Wks* **14**.
Jung, C. G. (1957). The undiscovered self. *Coll. Wks* **10**.
Jung, C. G. (1958a). Flying saucers: a modern myth of things seen in the sky. *Coll. Wks* **10**.
Jung, C. G. (1958b). Schizophrenia. *Coll. Wks* **3**.
Jung, C. G. (1958c). The transcendent function. *Coll. Wks* **8**.
Jung, C. G. (1959). A study in the process of individuation. *Coll. Wks* **9**, 1.
Jung, C. G. (1963). "Memories, Dreams, Reflections". London, Routledge and Kegan Paul.
Kahn, M. J. (1967). The persistence of transitional phenomena into adult life. *Int. J. Psycho-anal.* **48**, 2.
Kernberg, O. F. (1975). "Borderline Conditions and Pathological Narcissism", New York, Aronson.
Klein, M. (1955). On identification. *In* later edition "Envy and Gratitude", London, Hogarth, 1980.
Klein, M. (1957). "Envy and gratitude". In later edition "Envy and Gratitude", London, Hogarth, 1980.
Klein, M. (1975a). "Love, Guilt and Reparation", London, Hogarth.
Klein, M. (1975b). "The Psycho-analysis of children", London, Hogarth.
Kohut, H. (1971). "The Analysis of the Self", New York, International Universities Press.
Kraemer, W. (1958). The dangers of unrecognized counter-transference. *In* later edition, "Technique in Analytical Psychology", L.A.P. Vol. 2. London, Heinemann, 1974.

Kris, E. (1956). On self observation. *Int. J. Psycho-anal.* **37**, 6.
Lambert, K. (1977). Analytical psychology and the historical development of western consciousness. *J. analyt. Psychol.* **22**, 2.
Lambert, K. (1981). "Analysis Repair and Individuation", L.A.P. Vol. 5. London, Academic Press.
Langs, R. (1976). "The Therapeutic Interaction", 2 Vols, New York, Aronson.
Layard, J. (1959). Home-erotism in primitive society as a function of the self. *J. analyt. Psychol.* **4**, 2.
Leshan, L. L. and Worthington, R. E. (1956). Personality as a factor in the pathogenesis of cancer. *Brit. J. med. Psychol.* **29**, 1.
Lewis, D. (transl.) (1906). "The Ascent of Mount Carmel" by Saint John of the Cross, London, Baker.
Lewis, D. (transl.) (1934). "The Living Flame of Love" by Saint John of the Cross, London, Baker.
Little, M. (1957). "R" – The analyst's total response to his patient's needs. *In* "Transference Neurosis and Transference Psychosis", York, Aronson, 1981.
Little, M. (1960). On basic unity. *In* "Transference Neurosis and Transference Psychosis", New York, Aronson, 1981.
Little, M. I. (1981). "Transference Neurosis and Transference Psychosis, New York, Aronson.
MacDougal, J. and Lebovici, S. (1969). "Dialogue with Sammy", London, Hogarth.
Maduro, R. (1980). Symbolic equations in creative process. *J. analyt. Psychol.* **25**, 1.
Meier, C. A. (1963). A Jungian approach to psychosomatic medicine. *J. analyt. Psychol.* **8**, 2.
Meltzer, D. (1973). "Sexual States of Mind", Ballinluig, Clunie Press.
Milner, M. (1957). "On Not Being Able to Paint", London, Heinemann.
Money-Kyrie, R. E. (1956). Normal countertransference and some of its deviations. *Int. J. Psychol-anal.* **41**, 4–5.
Moody, R. L. (1955). On the function of countertransference. *J. analyt. Psychol.* **1**, 1.
Nacht, S. and Vidermann, S. (1960). The pre-object universe in the transference situation. *Int. J. Psycho-anal.* **41**, 4–5.
Neumann, E. (1955). Narzisismus, Automorphismus and Urbeziehung. *In* "Studien zur analitischen Psychologie C. G. Jungs", Vol. 1, Zurich, Rascher.
Neumann, E. (1959). The significance of the genetic aspect for analytical psychology. *J. analyt. Psychol.* **4**, 2.
Neumann, E. (1973). "The Child", London, Hodder and Stoughton.
Pauli, W. (1952). The influence of archetypal ideas on the scientific theories of Kepler. *In* "The Interpretation of Nature and Psyche", (Jung, C. G. and Pauli, W.)., London, Routledge and Kegan Paul.
Peers, E. A. (1953). "Complete Works of Saint John of the Cross", vol. I. Burns Oates.
Peers, E. A. (undated). "Saint John of the Cross", London, Faber and Faber.
Peers, E. A. (1954). "Handbook to the Life and Times of Saint Theresa and Saint John of the Cross", London, Burns Oates.
Peers, E. A. (transl.) (1978). "The Spiritual Canticle of Saint John of the Cross", London, Burns Oates.
Perry, J. W. (1953). "The Self in Psychotic Process", Berkley, University of California Press.
Perry, J. W. (1957). Acute catatonic schizophrenia. *J. analyt. Psychol.* **2**, 2.
Perry, J. W. (1962). Reconstitutive processes in the psycho-pathology of the self. *Ann. N.Y. Acad. Sci.*
Peterson, F. and Jung, C. G. (1907). Psychophysical investigations with the galvanometer and pneumograph in normal and insane individuals. *Coll. Wks* **2**.
Plaut, A. (1959). A case of tricksterism illustrating ego defences. *J. analyt. Psychol.* **4**, 1.

Plaut, A. (1956). The transference in analytical psychology. *In* "Technique in Jungian Analysis", L.A.P. Vol. 2, London, Heinemann.
Plaut, A. (1966). Reflection on not being able to imagine. *J. analyt. Psychol.* **11**, 2.
Redfearn, J. W. T. (1966). The patient's experience of his mind. *J. analyt. Psychol.* **11**, 2.
Redfearn, J. W. T. (1985). "My Self, My Many Selves", London, Academic Press.
Ricksher, C. and Jung, C. G. (1907–8). Further investigations on the galvanic phenomenon and respiration in normal and insane individuals. *Coll. Wks* **2**.
Rosenfeld, R. (1965). "Psychotic States – a Psychoanalytical Approach", London, Hogarth.
Racker, H. (1968). "Transference and Countertransference", London, Hogarth.
Rhine, J. B. (1948). "The reach of the mind", New York, Morrow.
Saint John of the Cross. "The Dark Night of the Soul", see Zimmerman (1935) and Peers (1953).
Saint John of the Cross. "The Living Flame of Love", see Lewis (1934).
Saint John of the Cross. "The Ascent of Mount Carmel", see Lewis (1906).
Saint John of the Cross. "The Spiritual Canticle", see Peers (1978).
Sandler, J. (1962). Psychology and psychoanalysis. *Brit. J. med. Psychol.* **35**, 2.
Schafer, R. (1976). "A New Language for Psycho-analysis", New Haven, Yale University Press.
Schwartz-Salant, N. (1982). Narcissism and Character Transformation. Toronto, Inner City Books.
Scott, R. D. (1956). Notes on the body image and schema. *J. analyt. Psychol.* **1**, 2.
Scott, W. (1924). "Hermetica", Oxford, Clarendon Press.
Scott, W. C. (1948). Some embryological, neurological, psychiatric and psycho-analytic implications of the body schema. *Int. J. Psycho-anal.* **19**, 3.
Scott, W. C. (1949). The body schema in psychotherapy. *Brit. J. med. Psychol.* **22**, 3–4.
Searles, H. F. (1965). "Collected Papers on Schizophrenia and Related Subjects", London, Hogarth.
Segal, H. (1957). Notes on symbol formation. *Int. J. Psycho-anal.* **38**, 6.
Servadio, E. (1955). A presumptively telepathic-precognitive dream during analysis. *Int. J. Psycho-anal.* **36**, 1.
Sethon, A. An undated chapter, without title, in "Lives of the Philosophers", Watkins, 1955.
Silberer, H. (1904). "Probleme der Mystik und ihre Symbolic", Vienna, Leipzig. (translated by Jedliffe, S. E. (1907). "Problems of Mysticism and its Symbolism", New York, Moffat Yard.
Spiegel, L. A. (1959). The self perception. *In* "The Psychoanalytic Study of the Child", Vol. 14, London, Imago.
Sprott, W. J. H. (1947). "General Psychology", London, Longman.
Stein, L. (1966). In persuit of first principles. *J. analyt. Psychol.* **11**, 1.
Stein, L. (1967). Introducing not-self. *J. analyt. Psychol.* **12**, 2.
Storr, A. (1935). A note on cybernetics and analytical psychology. *J. analyt. Psychol.* **1**, 1.
Waite, A. E. (ed.) (1953). "The Hermetic Museum Enlarged and Restored", London, Watkins. The translated texts referred to are: 1. Anon. *The Golden tract*. 2. Anon. *The Sophic hydrolith*. 3. Sendivogius, M. The new chemical light.
Weaver, R. (1964). "The Old Wise Woman", London, Vincent Stuart.
Wickes, F. G. (1927). "The Inner World of Childhood" (2nd edn), New York, Appleton-Century. 1966.
Wickes, F. G. (1938). "The Inner World of Man", New York, Farrar and Rheinhart.
Wilkinson, A. (1972). Assessment of symptoms. *Brit. J. med. Psychol.* **45**, 3.
Williams, H. A. (1962). Theology and self-awareness. *In* "Soundings" (ed. Vidler, A. R.), Cambridge, Cambridge University Press.

Williams, H. A. (1963). Psychological objections. *In* "Objections to Christian Belief" (ed. Vidler, A. R.), Cambridge, Cambridge University Press.
Wilhelm, R. and Jung, C. G. (1929). "The Secret of the Golden Flower", London, Routledge and Kegan Paul.
Williams, M. (1963a). The indivisibility of the personal and collective unconscious. *In* "Analytical Psychology: a Modern Science", L.A.P. Vol. 1, London, Heinemann.
Williams, M. (1963b). The poltergeist man. *J. analyt. Psychol.* **8**, 2.
Winnitcott, D. W. (1958a). The capacity to be alone. *In* "Maturational Processes and the Facilitating Environment", London, Hogarth.
Winnicott, D. W. (1958b). "Collected Papers", London, Tavistock.
Winnicott, D. W. (1971). "Playing and Reality", London, Tavistock.
Wisdom, J. O. (1967). Testing an interpretation within a session. *Int. J. Psychol-anal.* **48**, 1.
Zeigler, A. (1962). A cardiac infarction and a dream as synchronous events. *J. analyt. Psychol.* **7**, 2.
Zimmermann, B. (Ed.) (1935). "The Dark Night of the Soul", by Saint John of the Cross, London, Baker.

Index

*n indicates the index entry will be found in the footnote.

For Product Safety Concerns and Information please contact our EU representative GPSR@taylorandfrancis.com
Taylor & Francis Verlag GmbH, Kaufingerstraße 24, 80331 München, Germany

www.ingramcontent.com/pod-product-compliance
Ingram Content Group UK Ltd.
Pitfield, Milton Keynes, MK11 3LW, UK
UKHW022203190926
475702UK00003B/181

* 9 7 8 0 3 6 7 1 0 7 4 1 3 *